THE ABORTION CONTROVERSY

THE ABORTION CONTROVERSY

BETTY SARVIS
and
HYMAN RODMAN

COLUMBIA UNIVERSITY PRESS
NEW YORK AND LONDON 1973

LIBRARY OF CONGRESS CATALOGING IN PUBLICATION DATA

Sarvis, Betty, 1943–
The abortion controversy.

Bibliography: p. 201
1. Abortion—United States. I. Rodman, Hyman, joint author. II. Title. [DNLM: 1. Abortion, Induced. HQ 767 S251a 1973]
HQ767.5.U5S25 301 72-12534
ISBN 0-231-03656-6

Printed in the United States of America

FOR MY MOTHER AND FATHER
Jane and Joe Sarvis

TO THE MEMORY OF MY PARENTS
Wolfe and Bertha Rodman

PREFACE

This book is uneven and inconsistent, passionate or radical on some issues, conservative on others, with a fair mixture of the noncommittal. Some people have told us that it is scandalous to have such an untidy position, but abortion is not a tidy thing. That is part of the abortion issue for us and, we think, for many other people.

The abortion situation in the United States is itself disorderly, with several different kinds of laws and a multitude of practices. From 1967 to 1972 the legal situation in some states was completely transformed from highly restrictive to highly liberal, and the proponents of abortion need to stay active to retain the liberal legislation. Opponents of abortion fought successful battles in other states to keep the restrictive laws, and they must remain organized to retain their victory. Court challenges, legislative battles, public hearings, demonstrations, state referenda, and the mass media continue to stir the abortion pot, and changes in either a liberal or conservative direction often bubble to the surface.

In spite of continual changes, some general issues in the abortion controversy remain fairly constant through time and across national and group boundaries. We have presented these general issues in a way that should illuminate the abortion controversies as they rage in different parts of the world. These general issues are illustrated by specific occurrences, but it is not possible to keep the particulars involved in the medical, legal, political, moral, or social issues in Bulgaria, California, India, New York, or Japan up to date.

Chapter 1 briefly discusses the general issues of the abortion controversy that continually appear throughout the book. The particulars of chapter 1 deal with events in the United States that turned abortion into a political issue.

The moral issues of the abortion controversy as they apply especially to Western nations are presented in chapter 2. This chapter also deals with the extent to which moral beliefs are, or should be, reflected in the law.

Chapter 3 deals with the several ways in which abortion is regulated in the United States and with the discrepancies between abortion laws and medical practices.

Societies usually have specific ways of inducing abortion and certain circumstances under which abortion is acceptable or expected. Chapter 4 discusses these issues as they apply particularly in the United States, and it points out the unique role that the medical profession has played in deciding what is an acceptable "indication" for abortion.

Viewing abortion as a medical procedure which may result in complex psychological and physical aftereffects is the product of a society with a relatively specialized medical profession and technology that permits looking for aftereffects. Chapter 5 on the psychological aftereffects and chapter 6 on the physical aftereffects deal with the findings and feelings of the medical profession. Although sometimes difficult to separate, these findings and feelings contain a peculiar mixture of, first, belief that women violate taboos by having an abortion and therefore should suffer some aftereffects and, second, evidence on the nature and extent of the psychological and physical aftereffects.

People in most societies have used some technique to control their reproduction. In the early twentieth century the family planning or birth control movement in the Western world set out to gain acceptance for contraception, and they have been so successful that contraception has now become the most desired form of birth control. Chapter 7 discusses the place of abortion as a method of birth control.

Within any society, attitudes and practices regarding abortion vary among groups. Chapter 8 deals with class and race differences and similarities in attitudes to, access to, and use of abortion in the United States.

Chapter 9 addresses itself to the way birth control and abortion efforts throughout the world, and especially in the United States, are sometimes viewed as a boon to the poor and the black, and sometimes seen as a form of black genocide.

Postscript to Preface, January 26, 1973. The problem of keeping up to date with specific changes on the abortion scene was dramatized by the United States Supreme Court decision of January 22, 1973. That ruling drastically altered the legal situation in the United States, and for the most part turned the abortion decision over to the woman and her physician. Since we anticipated the decision we were able to rewrite the final three paragraphs of chapter 3 (pp. 68–69) to take it into account. But the rest of the book was completed before the Court's decision, and several comments in the book unavoidably refer to the legal situation in mid-1972 as though it still applies.

Despite this extremely important legal change in the United States, the general issues that fuel the abortion controversy remain the same. Whether in the United States or elsewhere, the moral questions pitting the woman's rights against the fetus' rights remain significant. For many, indeed, the moral questions became more poignant because the Court's decision will lead to a very substantial increase in the number of abortions in the United States. Patrick Cardinal O'Boyle called the decision "a catastrophe for America" and emphasized that the Court's ruling that abortion is legal "does not make it morally permissible." Abortion, in fact, "remains a hideous and heinous crime" (Washington *Star-News,* January 23, 1973, p. 1-B). Cardinal Cooke pointed out that "judicial decisions are not necessarily sound moral decisions" and said: "I hope and pray that our citizens will do all in their power to reverse this injustice to the rights of the unborn." Cardinal Kroll called the Court's action "a monstrous injustice" and added, "One trusts in the decency and good sense of the American people not to let an illogical court decision dictate to them on the subject of morality and human life" (New York *Times,* January 23, 1973, p. 20). The Vatican referred to the Court's action as "morally monstrous" (Washington *Post,* January 24, 1973, p. 14-A). Pro-abortionists, with equal fervor, praised the decision of the Court as a wise one that places the decision about whether or not to get an abortion where it belongs—in the hands of the pregnant woman consulting with her physician.

Other issues besides the moral ones become more intense, too. The liberalization of the laws, by sharply increasing the number of abortions, will give further importance to the questions raised about the physical and psychological aftereffects of abortion. The especially sharp increase in abortions expected for black women will exacerbate the black genocide arguments that revolve around abortion, sterilization, and family planning generally. While it is impossible to predict the specific forms that abortion controversies will take in the future, we can say with confidence that the substance of these controversies will be found in the basic issues that we discuss in this book.

ACKNOWLEDGMENTS

Many thanks for their helpfulness to Helene Barnes, Sheila Blanchard, Katheryn Bullard, Estelle G. Burke, George Daniels, Henry P. David, Joyce Gartrell, B. James George, Alan F. Guttmacher, Bernice Howell, John D. Moore, J. William Rioux, Keith P. Russell, Marian Samuels, Jane Brackett Simon, Anntarie Singleton, Christopher Tietze, Lawrence P. Tourkow, and Diane Wilkins. We appreciate the superb service given to us by the Association for the Study of Abortion, the Merrill-Palmer Institute, and the libraries of Wayne State University. Harper & Row kindly gave permission for the various quotations from Calderone, *Abortion in the United States*.

CONTENTS

THE ABORTION CONTROVERSY

1958, with Paul Gebhard and his colleagues finishing the volume after Kinsey's death. This book presented some of the first "hard data" on abortion in the United States and like many of the Kinsey studies has taken its place as a classic.

Two other important books appeared before the Gebhard and Calderone volumes were published. Harold Rosen, a psychiatrist, edited an anthology of articles on many aspects of abortion written by lawyers, obstetricians and gynecologists, psychiatrists, and clergymen. It was originally published in 1954 as *Therapeutic Abortion* and reissued in paperback in 1967 as *Abortion in America*. One of the participants in the Arden House conference commented on the public reaction to the topic of abortion: "Dr. Rosen told me that many bookstores refused to stock his book, . . . many newspapers refused to review it, and I suppose the same thing will happen to the proceedings of this conference" (Senior, 1958:146).

The second book of significance, Glanville Williams' *The Sanctity of Life and the Criminal Law* (1957), was based upon lectures given at Columbia University in 1956. Williams, a lawyer, addressed the book to the general reader on the question of "the extent to which human life, actual or potential, is or ought to be protected under the criminal law of the English-speaking peoples" (Williams, 1957:ix).

Until 1960, this group of books formed the core of the United States literature on abortion. Most of the writers and conferees were interested in alerting the professional community to the abortion problem, and they were only secondarily interested in communicating to the general public. They frequently called for action, but their recommendations for legal change were restrained. In any event, their pleas went largely unheeded until the 1960s.

THALIDOMIDE AND GERMAN MEASLES

In 1960 professional and public concern about the abortion problem was limited. Two events of the early 1960s, however, received international publicity and brought abortion and related social problems to the attention of a mass audience. Between 1961 and 1963 there was much furor over the new drug, thalidomide. Widely used in European sedatives and sleeping pills, physicians discovered that this drug could cause fetal abnormalities (Taussig, 1962).

The abortion-related aspects of this issue received the most publicity in the United States in 1962 because of the experiences of an Arizona couple. Mrs. Sherri Finkbine learned, when she was two months pregnant, that she might bear a deformed child because she had taken a thalidomide-containing tranquilizer which her husband had obtained in Europe. Although the Arizona law permitted abortion only to save the life of the woman, her doctor recommended an abortion. Hospital approval was given, and arrangements made for the operation. In an effort to warn others of the dangers of the drug, Mrs. Finkbine phoned a local newspaper and talked with the medical reporter, who agreed not to use her name in the article. Mrs. Finkbine recalls that, rather than merely being an article warning of the drug, "the front-page, black-bordered story screamed in bold print: 'Baby-deforming drug may cost woman her child here.' That did it. The story went out on the wire, and before the day was two hours along the way it stirred international interest" (Finkbine, 1967:18).

The publicity led to the cancellation of Mrs. Finkbine's abortion through fear that the doctor, hospital, or Mrs. Finkbine could be criminally prosecuted. The hospital unsuccessfully petitioned the State Supreme Court of Arizona in the hope of obtaining judicial clarity of what it considered vague laws. At this point the names of the Finkbines became a matter of public record, and they subsequently received thousands of letters filled with advice and hate. After numerous inquiries and much anxiety, the couple went to Sweden and waited a week for a decision from a Swedish medical board —the abortion was approved and done (Finkbine, 1967:15–24).

The same question of performing abortions in cases of possible fetal deformity came up in 1964 when a German measles epidemic hit the United States. This event once again provided an excellent opportunity to focus the attention of a mass audience upon the abortion problem. It again raised questions that the Finkbine case had forcefully brought to public attention—medical, social, and legal questions: 1) Why were hospital practices not strictly in compliance with the law? 2) What should be done about socioeconomic inequalities in access to abortions (the Finkbines could afford to go out of the country to obtain an abortion, but others could not)? 3) And what could be said about the purpose and effectiveness of the abortion laws?

Under the dramatic impact of the German measles and thalidomide problems, the arguments of the abortion controversy gained wide currency. Many advocated liberalized laws, while many others resisted any change in the laws. Those who wanted to change the laws found that the American Law Institute's 1962 revision of the Model Penal Code contained a ready-made proposal for abortion reform. The prestige of the organization and the timeliness of their publication gave the Model Penal Code an important role in the reform movement of the 1960s, and this Code became the model for many proposed and passed abortion bills.

PUBLICATIONS OF THE 1960s

During the 1960s the country was flooded with information on abortion. Writings directed to a primarily professional audience continued to multiply, and at the same time the mass media spread the controversial issues to a much wider public. This was especially marked after 1966, when abortion reform became a political issue in many states, and when the rounds of public hearings and legislative debates began.

New data and new evaluations of earlier data appeared in the professional literature. Heightened public interest stimulated professional concern, and the abortion controversy engaged the attention of many physicians and lawyers, as well as some specialists in other fields—such as sociologists, public health workers, demographers, child welfare workers, clergymen, family life educators, and marriage counselors.

The mass communications of the 1960s reached a far greater number of people than ever before. It was (and is) not uncommon to see an item a week about abortion in many major newspapers, the television networks aired several programs on abortion, and from 1966 to 1970 articles on abortion appeared in such widely read and diverse magazines as *America, Atlantic, Christian Century, Commonweal, Cosmopolitan, Life, Look, Mademoiselle, The Nation, Newsweek, Parents' Magazine, Playboy, Reader's Digest, Redbook, Saturday Evening Post, Saturday Review, Science,* and *Time*. Prior to 1930 only a single article is indexed in the *Reader's Guide to Periodical Literature;* during the 1930s there were 25 articles; in the 1940s, 26 articles; in the 1950s 42 articles; and the flood of interest during the 1960s deposited 180 articles (Plant, 1971). By 1967, when Rosen's once-shunned anthology was reissued, he could comment in the Preface that "this book, in its 1954 hardback edition, has been used in a number of states as a reference work by various legislators" (Rosen, 1967a:xix).

Several books directed toward the general reader as well as a professional audience also came out in the 1960s—Dr. X's *The Abortionist* (1962), Lader's *Abortion* (1966), Guttmacher's anthology, *The Case for Legalized Abortion Now* (1967), Shaw's *Abortion on Trial* (1968), and Granfield's *The Abortion Decision* (1969). Trends that were apparent in the books published earlier became intensified in the publications of the 1960s. As already noted, the pre-1960 books frequently called for action from the professional community, and they sometimes included recommendations on legal or social measures to alleviate the problem of abortion. Although these publications were partisan, they were much more centered upon explaining and exploring the problem than pushing for particular legal changes. In contrast, the books and other communications of the 1960s more typically marshalled the accumulated information on abortion to a position for or against particular legal changes. With few exceptions, magazine and newspaper articles, television programs, and popular or professional books showed considerable bias in their presentation and use of information in order to justify a particular moral or legal position.

As Taussig said in 1936, "abortion has become a world problem." Trying to alleviate the problem, many countries adopted liberal abortion legislation before any of the states of the United States. As a result, much of the research on abortion comes from these countries—particularly the Scandinavian and Eastern European countries, Japan, and the USSR. The experiences of these countries became important in the United States when states began to investigate various legal models and to speculate on "what will happen if" the laws are like those of Denmark or Japan. It became quite common in the United States publications of the 1960s to include information from other countries, and many countries were represented in some U.S. conferences.

The final trend that became more pronounced during the 1960s and that reflects the widening interest in abortion is the tendency to view abortion in connection with other issues. For example, a list of books which contain a section on abortion includes: Schur's *Crimes Without Victims* (1965), Trainer's *Physiologic Foundations for Marriage Counseling* (1965), Slovenko's anthology *Sexual Behavior and the Law* (1965), the Proceedings of the International Conference on Family Planning published as *Family Planning and Population Programs* (1966), Labby's anthology *Life or Death: Ethics and Options* (1968), Guttmacher's *Birth Control and Love* (1969), Cutler's anthology *Updating Life and Death* (1969), and Rice's *The Vanishing Right to Live* (1969).

ORGANIZATIONS INTERESTED IN THE ABORTION ISSUE

Many organizations have also influenced the reform movement. National and local groups sprang up in the 1960s, especially after 1967 when the first major abortion reform legislation passed. The Association for the Study of Abortion (ASA), established in 1965, was one of the first national organizations committed solely to the issue of abortion. The ASA, along with its affiliated state groups and other similar organizations, provide valuable services. They conduct research, circulate newsletters of current happenings, offer inexpensive reprints of articles from popular as well as relatively inaccessible professional periodicals, and answer a variety of questions on abortion.

Other organizations, established mainly during and after 1967, offer consultation services and work for reform. The Clergyman's Consultation Service on Problem Pregnancies started in 1967 in New York City, and aimed to "include referral to the best available medical advice and aid to women in need" and to work for a liberalized abortion law (*New York Times,* May 22, 1967). The National Association for Repeal of Abortion Laws (NARAL), established in 1969, offers services but is especially interested in political action: "The group will attempt to unify local and state groups opposed to abortion laws by recruiting members and forming citizens' committees in all 50 states" (*Detroit News,* Feb. 17, 1969, p. 4-A). Groups at the state and local levels also carry out the major activities of the national organizations in research, education, organization, service, and political action. For instance, in Michigan in 1970 state groups included the Michigan Organization for Repeal of Abortion Laws (MORAL), the Michigan Women for Medical Control of Abortion, and a local branch of the Clergymen's Consultation Service.

In addition to groups concerned entirely with abortion, established organizations with broader interests have joined the fight for reform, and some of them have issued position statements. The American Civil Liberties Union (ACLU) and its local affiliates have been active in challenging state abortion laws, lobbying in state legislatures, and drafting new state laws. The ACLU has also issued a position paper advocating a change in abortion laws, as have the following influential organizations, among others: American College of Obstetricians and Gynecologists, American Medical Association, American Medical Women's Association, American Public Health Association, Group for the Advancement of Psychiatry, National Council of Women of the United States, and Planned Parenthood-World Population.

The contribution of women's liberation groups to the reform movement should not be underestimated, although their influence is not always obvious. Testimonials about abortion, where women tell of their experiences, have moved many people. Women discovered that they shared many experiences and feelings, and their humiliation and anger about their abortion experiences led them to push for legal changes. Court suits have been filed by women demanding a right to abortion, and women's groups have put pressure on legislators and organizations to declare themselves on the abortion issue.

Alongside the organizations that work to change the laws, other groups oppose change. The Catholic church is most often associated with an anti-abortion position, though Catholic groups favoring changes in the abortion laws have also formed. Anti-abortion organizations at the national level are: Alliance Against Abortion; the National Commission on Life, Reproduction, and Rhythm; The Human Life Foundation; and the National Right to Life Committee. Such diverse groups as the Salvation Army, the Mormons, Black Muslims, and Protestant fundamentalists are also among the anti-abortion forces. Many local Right to Life Committees work to retain or return to restrictive laws, and Birthright groups have formed to counsel against abortion as a solution to unwanted pregnancies and to provide other alternatives. In comparison to the reformers, the anti-abortionists have conducted an equally energetic campaign, but they have generally not received as much favorable publicity from the mass media.

ATTITUDES TOWARD ABORTION

Part of the research of organizations and individuals committed to reform involves opinion surveys. A crucial question in reform movements becomes: Does a majority of the public favor reform? Surveys documented public support for liberalized laws, and combined with the support of physicians and prestigious organizations, they bolstered the reform movement. The results of these polls have been published in professional journals as well as newspapers and popular magazines. These survey results, as well as endorsements by physicians and other professional groups, have been widely quoted by reformers to argue that a majority desires a change in the laws.

A brief review of some newspaper articles illustrates how a picture of broad support for reform was created by reference to public opinion and other endorsements. Three articles in Detroit newspapers in 1967 suggest growing support among physicians and the public. "The majority of American physicians believe abortion laws should be liberalized according to a recent survey of over 40,000 doctors. Almost 87 percent of the doctors answered "yes" to the question: Are you in favor of liberalizing the existing laws on therapeutic abortion?" (*Detroit Free Press,* May 20, 1967, p. 8-C)

Shortly after these results were quoted, an article headed "AMA Eases Stand on Abortion" reported: "The AMA action came after 18 months of study by a committee which queried state medical societies, nationwide medical and legal organizations and every major faith for their views on the matter" (*Detroit News,* June 22, 1967, p. 11-D).

These two articles established that an important and influential group—physicians—and their most prestigious association—the American Medical Association—favored a change in the laws. This support by the medical profession was used in an article several weeks later by a Michigan state senator who was sponsoring a reform bill; he stated that the AMA, Michigan State Medical Society, and "95% of all professional groups" supported the bill. The article headline read "Public Favors Abortion Bill, Says Legislator," and the senator was quoted as saying, "support for the bill is growing . . . hundreds of letters to me are about 5 to 1 in favor of it" (*Detroit News,* August 6, 1967, p. 15-B).

By the end of 1967 the pattern of quoting opinion surveys, endorsements by groups, and support by physicians was an established practice in many newspaper articles on abortion, and many newspapers ran editorials in favor of legal change. The January 8, 1968 *New York Times* (p. 28-C) ran almost a full-page story on abortion clearly favoring change. Physicians and clergymen favoring change were quoted and two opinion polls and the AMA policy statement were also mentioned. Referring to a 1965 survey, the article commented:

> While this survey is comparatively recent, many observers believe that the climate of public opinion is changing so fast that a survey today would show considerably higher percentages favoring the provisions of the model abortion law [i.e., American Law Institute's Model Penal Code].
>
> Some observers . . . think that a majority of adults would now sanction social indications for abortion as well. This would make abortion essentially a matter of personal choice.

At least seven national surveys were conducted between 1962 and 1969 on attitudes toward abortion, and public opinion shifted only a little during these years (Blake, 1971). This is in sharp contrast to the interpretations of abortion reformers and newspaper stories that were reporting dramatic changes in public opinion favoring a liberalization of the laws. It took until 1971 for public opinion to catch up to the optimistic prophets. One survey carried out in 1971, and another in 1972, finally did show much more favorable public attitudes toward abortion (Lipson and Wolman, 1972).*

* For other results of surveys of the general population see Rossi (1966); Kantner et al. (1968); and Ryder and Westoff (1971). For surveys of physicians see Hall (1965a); Crowley and Laidlaw (1967); and *Modern Medicine,* November 3, 1969. For an excellent account of how the Abortion Law Reform Association in Britain used opinion surveys to establish that the public and physicians supported reform, see Hindell and Simms (1968).

THE SITUATION IN THE 1970s

By 1970 one-third of the states had new abortion laws, almost all states had considered new bills during the 1960s, several court cases had been heard, and the experiences of women who had abortions were out in the open. Many individuals and organizations involved in legislative and court actions and in helping women get abortions were experienced in the politics of abortion. Several books published in the early 1970s reflect the experience gained by a decade of struggle.

In 1971 two lawyers, Diane Schulder and Florynce Kennedy, published *Abortion Rap* which consists mainly of material from a 1969 case to declare the New York law unconstitutional. Far from being a collection of legal documents, this book dramatically presents "testimony by women who have suffered the consequences of restrictive abortion laws." The authors compiled a book that "is not to be regarded as a dispassionate travelogue through the topography of New York abortion law repeal and reform. It is in no sense an effort to extend the myth of 'objectivity.' It should rather be viewed as a brief to be presented to a people's tribunal. We were and are advocates of the women's case" (Schulder and Kennedy, 1971:xv).

Hendin in *Everything You Need to Know About Abortion* and Ebon in *Everywoman's Guide to Abortion* also act as advocates of the woman's case. Ebon (1971:14) wants to "wipe out ignorance and to replace it with the truth about abortion" and "to help every woman who wants to avoid 'compulsory motherhood.' " These books show very clearly how really open the abortion topic has become, how strong the advocacy for women is, and how much information is available on getting an abortion.

Two other books published in 1970 reflect a different kind of approach and can be characterized as a "summing up" of the accumulated knowledge and experience of past years. Daniel Callahan wrote a long summary volume called *Abortion: Law, Choice and Morality*. As the title suggests, he intended "to discuss how a moral policy and legal policy on abortion might judiciously be formulated" and finally to present his own solutions of what seemed "wise moral and legal policies" (Callahan, 1970:20). Callahan (1970:12) approaches his task by discussing moral, medical, social, and legal questions and considering "an array of theories" and a "mass of data." Indeed no other single volume presents and evaluates as wide a range of theory and data as this one does before setting forth policy recommendations.

Another summing up publication of 1970, *Abortion in a Changing World,* edited by Robert Hall, presents the proceedings of an international conference held in 1968 and convened by the Association for the Study of Abortion. Rather than debate legal reform, Hall (1970:iii) states that the conferees wished "to explore the field of abortion, to exchange knowledge about abortion, and to expose this knowledge to public view." Knowledge about abortion was clearly exchanged during this conference. The roster of participants and observers reads like a Who's Who of the abortion world—all the U.S. veterans of the abortion controversy and most of the international ones were present, along with representatives from a wide range of specialties. The formal papers and panel discussions placed the abortion problem in every conceivable context. Several of the participants stated their position on abortion law reform, and this led to some sharp exchanges of opinion. No matter how "objective" the intention, it seems that most evaluations of the data on abortion eventually lead to some partisan conclusion about how the laws should or should not be formulated.

Two final examples of a summation are Germain Grisez's *Abortion: The Myths, the Realities, and the Arguments* and John Noonan's anthology, *The Morality of Abortion: Legal and Historical Perspectives.* These books give a comprehensive and excellent summary of the anti-abortion arguments. Noonan (1970:viii) writes of the purpose of his anthology: "At a time when abortion is the cry, when the orthodoxies of the hour make questioning of the postulates underlying its imminent acceptance impertinent, when the well-informed managers of the media know that abortion will sweep all before it, it is not too late to face the central issues." For Noonan, as well as many others, the central issues in the abortion controversy are moral issues.

punishment. He informs us further that "as society has developed, this right to take guilty life has been more and more dispensed with, until today in many nations of the West the state has given up its right to take the lives of its citizens, or else restricted it to very narrow circumstances."

THE ORIGINAL INTENT: PROTECTION OF THE WOMAN

Until 1971 pro- and anti-abortionists agreed that at common law abortion was not a crime before quickening and was a misdemeanor after quickening. But in 1971 Cyril Means published an article which examined the common law in detail and which was the first to conclude that a common law right to abortion existed at *every* stage of gestation. To explain why statute law abolished this right, pro-abortionists focus upon the medical conditions of the 1800s. At that time, when the original laws were passed, any surgical procedure was very risky and often fatal. The abortion statutes were therefore intended to protect the woman from the medical dangers of abortion. Now, the argument continues, childbirth is more dangerous than early abortion, and the laws are no longer necessary. Means (1968:513–14; 1971:392–96) refers to this as the "relative safety test" since the legislature intended abortion to be unlawful where it was more dangerous than childbirth so that the woman was "forced" to take the least dangerous course. Means (1971:388) describes the "unbelievable historical irony" of the present situation: "A statute was passed more than a century ago for the purpose of imposing on women the duty of protecting their lives from destruction through wanted but dangerous abortional surgery. Now that the danger has all but disappeared, the State's obstinate persistence in enforcing the law's letter, but not its purpose, denies its intended beneficiaries (pregnant women) the very right to protect their lives from death which the law originally imposed on them as a duty."

A logical reply to this position is: Were there laws passed at the same time imposing upon other people the duty of protecting their lives from all kinds of surgical procedures? Means answers this question by looking at the history of the United States statutes and concluding that the original intent of the legislation *was* to protect people from surgical procedures. The English abortion statutes of 1803

CHAPTER TWO

THE MORAL ARGUMENTS AND LEGAL IMPLICATIONS

One approach to the central issues in the abortion controversy is to ask: 1) When does human life begin? 2) What role should the law play in answering the first question? On one side are those who claim the abortion laws should protect the rights of the fetus, while on the other side are those who claim the laws should protect the rights of the woman. This argument over what the law should do reflects different beliefs about when a fetus becomes a human being or person and is entitled to all the rights of those already born. That time can be set at conception, or implantation, or quickening, or viability, or birth. One's position on this issue would then color one's view of the intent of the original laws and of the relative weighting the present laws should give to the rights of the fetus and the woman.

THE ORIGINAL INTENT: PROTECTION OF FETAL LIFE

In the United States the original abortion laws became part of statute law during the nineteenth century and were based upon English abortion laws. Few dispute the origin of the state laws, but opinions vary as to the intent of the original abortion statutes. Most anti-abortionists agree that at English common law abortion was not a crime before quickening and was a "misprision" or misdemeanor after quickening. Quickening, the first feelings of fetal movement, usually takes place between the sixteenth and eighteenth week of pregnancy, although its occurrence varies for different women and in the same woman for different pregnancies. When the state abortion statutes in the United States were passed, this common law distinction disappeared.

Anti-abortionists argue that clearly the abortion, or rather anti-abortion, statutes were designed to protect the fetus. David Louisell and John Noonan (1970:226) state that "English and American criminal law in the nineteenth century moved to a protection of the fetus throughout his life in the womb. . . . The purpose of the change was not to protect the life of the mother but the life of the fetus. The response of the legislators and then of the courts to the new medical data was a response to data which showed the unreality of distinctions based on differences in the stage of fetal development." The anti-abortionists contend that these abortion laws embody the Judeo-Christian prohibition against the destruction of innocent human life. Thomas O'Donnell (1970:38) expresses this position as follows:

> Since a new and distinct human life may very likely be present from that moment [conception], directly to destroy the products of human conception, even at a very early stage of development, is at least very likely the destruction of an innocent human life.
>
> One who does even this has already discarded from his moral code the inviolability of human life and the human person and falls far short of that regard for the dignity and rights of the individual which is basic to the entire Judeo-Christian theology and tradition. Such an action is identified with the moral malice of murder since it implies a willingness to take a human life.

Lest this be labeled a religious dogma, Norman St. John-Stevas (1964:117) reminds us that "the concept of the right to life has profoundly influenced men throughout the Western world and is accepted by many who would reject the Christian doctrine on which it is based."

Three points need to be made in order to straighten out some common misunderstandings. First is the distinction between direct and indirect abortion. Only the former is prohibited, and O'Donnell expresses his abhorrence about "directly" destroying the products of human conception. Abortion is permitted, however, "where the operation could in some way be justified independent of the concept of abortion—e.g., where the uterus is dangerously diseased" (Williams, 1957:201; cf. Ramsey, 1968).

The second point is the distinction between murder and kill. O'Donnell uses the word murder, but at least he does not make the mistake of describing abortion as the "murder of innocent human lives." Rather, he identifies the act of abortion as possessing "the *moral* malice of murder." The emotional appeal of the phrase "murder of innocent human life" is obvious, but the laws of English-speaking peoples traditionally distinguish between killing and murdering. To "kill" means to destroy life (animal or plant as well as human) while the term "murder" is reserved for what society defines as *unlawful* killing of human life with malice aforethought. The destruction of the fetus has usually not been defined legally as murder nor, until recently, has it ever been viewed as just another electiv surgical procedure. O'Donnell preserves the distinction between mu der and a lesser wrong by identifying abortion with murder ir moral sense only. He does not imply that abortion is or has been gally defined as murder. Abortion, where it is a crime, is most c classified legally as a lesser crime than murder, with less severe alities. At the same time, however, it is frequently viewed mor murder.

Finally we must clarify the distinction between taking inn guilty human life. Many argue that the state should not have to take human life regardless of whether this life is judged or guilty. But the emotional appeal of the word "innocent' and O'Donnell, like many others, uses this word when the life of the fetus. As St. John-Stevas (1964:115–1 however, moral beliefs and legal practices can eliminat tion between innocent and guilty, as in the prohibit

and the Connecticut law of 1821 were the first abortion statutes and made abortion of a willing woman before quickening a crime; neither of these statutes contained the therapeutic exception for abortion "necessary to preserve the life of the woman." The New York Revised Statutes of 1829, which went into effect January 1, 1830, contained the first abortion statute in the United States which included the therapeutic exception. Most other state legislatures followed the New York example of including this therapeutic exception, and "in the few cases where the legislatures neglected to do this, the courts have read such an exception into the statutes" (Means, 1968:450). This early New York statute is therefore highly significant, and an examination of the meaning of the therapeutic exception hints at the reason for the abortion statutes.

Means (1968:451) quotes a section of the law that was proposed in 1828 but which the legislature did not pass:

> Every person who shall perform any surgical operation, by which human life shall be destroyed or endangered, such as the amputation of a limb, or of the breast, trepanning, cutting for the stone, or for hernia, unless it appear that the same was necessary for the preservation of life, or was advised by at least two physicians, shall be adjudged guilty of a misdemeanor.

Further clarification of the intent of this proposal is provided by the commissioners who formulated the revised statutes for the New York legislature of 1828 and included the following note in their report:

> The rashness of many young practitioners in performing the most important surgical operations for the mere purposes of distinguishing themselves, has been a subject of much complaint, and we are advised by old and experienced surgeons, that the loss of life occasioned by the practice, is alarming. (quoted in Means, 1968:451)

Means argues that the purpose of the original abortion statutes, as exemplified by detailed information about the actions of the New York legislature of 1828, was to protect the health and life of the woman against the dangers of abortional surgery. He explains that the legislature rejected the sections forbidding the performance of other operations because "only in the case of abortion were both patient and surgeon under strong extramedical pressures to undergo the risks of the operation. In other types of surgery, professional conscience and patients' caution could be relied upon to prevent unnecessary operations without the aid of a new penal law. It can scarcely be said that such a legislative differentiation between abortion and other equally dangerous types of surgery was, in 1828, unreasonable" (Means, 1971:389).

THE ORIGINAL INTENT: KEEPING WOMEN IN THEIR PLACE

Another view holds that the intent of the original laws, consciously or unconsciously, was to confirm the woman's role as childbearer and childrearer and thus to maintain male control over women. The resurgence of the women's liberation movement in the late 1960s and 1970s in the United States has given added emphasis to the issue of male chauvinism in the abortion controversy. The importance of liberty with respect to one's own body led Williams (1957:223) to write about European developments in recent decades: "It is under this banner of personal liberty that a feminist movement has arisen throughout Europe, maintaining that a woman has exclusive right in respect of the functioning of her own body, including the freedom to decide whether she shall continue a pregnancy. All abortion laws have been made by males."

Lana Phelan and Patricia Maginnis (1969:9; cf. Fletcher, 1970:26–27) give a strong case for how and why abortion laws were intended to keep women in their place:

> Abortion laws are woman-control laws, or chattel laws, if you prefer. Enacted a century ago, before women could vote, they form the dubious cornerstone of the double-standard in sexual attitudes which has resulted in widespread social and psychological disorganization in the U.S. They are largely responsible for keeping American women firmly second-class citizens. Because their physical bodies remained in custody of the state under penal law, American women could never attain the full human rights extended to them under the Bill of Rights.
>
> Forced by law into unending pregnancies and child care and rearing, most women had absolutely no opportunity to free their energies or money for other occupations.

The proponents of legal change are quick to point out that, except for the undesirable intent of reinforcing the inferior social status of women, the restrictive laws do not fulfill the other possible original intents. Fetal life is not effectively protected because of the widespread evasion of the law, and the pregnant woman is not protected because abortions done in the first trimester are now less risky than childbirth.

BUT WHAT IS A FETUS?

The anti-abortionists insist upon the similarities between the stages of human development: a zygote, embryo, fetus, infant, or senior citizen is a human being, and it is wrong to destroy any one of them. All are weak and must be protected by law. The pro-abortionists emphasize the differences between the stages of prenatal development. A fetus is a fetus, not a human being. In a superbly clearheaded discussion of the abortion argument, Roger Wertheimer (1971:85) writes the following:

> The liberal asks, "What has a zygote got that is valuable?" and the conservative answers, "Nothing, but it's a human being, so it is wrong to abort it." Then the conservative asks, "What does a fetus lack that an infant has that is so valuable?" and the liberal answers, "Nothing, but it's a fetus, not a human being, so it is all right to abort it." The arguments are equally strong and equally weak, for they are the *same* argument, an argument that can be pointed in either of two directions. The argument does not itself point in either direction: it is *we* who must point it, and *we* who are led by it. If you are led in one direction rather than the other, that is not because of logic, but because you respond in a certain way to certain facts.

These different perceptions of a fetus are irreconcilable, as many confrontations have shown. A *Time* magazine article (Mar. 29, 1971, pp. 70, 73) reports that "when 400 abortion foes demonstrated oustide a California Medical Association meeting in Anaheim, some carried bags of aborted fetuses. On another occasion, a Right-to-Life spokesman turned up at an abortion discussion in San Fernando, Calif., with a fetus in a bottle. Commented one member of the pro-abortion group: 'If I had known props were in order, I would have brought a casket with a dead mother in it.' " Or the cover of the March 1971 issue of *Social Action* pictures two abortion demonstrators. One holds a sign saying "Thanks Mom, you didn't flush me down a toilet," and the other demonstrator's sign reads "Abortion is a woman's right."

But what is a fetus? There are answers, not one answer. Does this mean that a fetus is whatever a person believes it is? Wertheimer (1971:88–89) answers no and replies rather that "whatever you believe, it's not true—but neither is it false" for *"we seem to be stuck with the indeterminateness of the fetus' humanity"* (emphasis added). This indeterminateness makes most people take a middle position. The fetus is not a human being but neither does a woman always have a right to do whatever she wishes to the fetus. A *human* fetus has a special status, and according to this middle position, abortion is permissible under certain circumstances and up to a certain period of gestation. The American Law Institute's Model Penal Code proposed that these circumstances be cases of rape, incest, fetal deformity, and threats to the physical or mental health of the woman.

The pro- and anti-abortion forces often agree that legalizing abortion under certain circumstances is an entirely unsatisfactory solution. Robert Drinan (1970:16) explains the anti-abortionist objection to this kind of law.

> [The] major premise assumes that the state should grant to parents the right to terminate a pregnancy when these parents consider a temporal good to themselves of more value than the very existence of the life of the fetus. The Model Penal Code puts into operation for the first time in American law the concept that the state may grant to individuals the right to terminate a life which is inconvenient for these particular individuals.
>
> The law under this so-called model abortion legislation allows mothers to prefer their own mental health to the very existence of a forthcoming child, and tells married people that they may not terminate the life of a healthy fetus (unless it results from rape or incest) but may snuff out the entire future of a child whose physical or intellectual qualities might not be perfect. Such a provision in the law is primarily social or non-medical and, at least to me, appears to have ominous overtones.

The pro-abortionist objects to the restrictions that are placed upon having an abortion which should be legally available at the woman's request. Neither the pro- nor anti-abortionist finds it morally or legally possible to accept the idea that abortions are available for certain justifiable indications. The pro-abortionist believes that abortions should be readily available without requiring special justification; the anti-abortionist is not prepared to accept any justification for abortion.

The idea of using a time limit to define the special status of the fetus has gained great popularity. Drinan (1970:16) says that the "withdrawal of criminal sanctions from the protection of all 'nonviable' life (the first twenty weeks of fetal existence) might be preferable to the only other alternative—the Model Penal Code." This approach tries to solve the problem by saying that the fetus becomes a human being when it is sufficiently developed to be capable of living outside the uterus. The importance of the stage of gestation in deciding what a fetus is, how one should respond to it, and what role the law should play is emphasized by Wertheimer (1971:89) who believes that "ultimately, most liberals and conservatives are in a sense, only extreme moderates." He gives some vivid examples to illustrate this point:

> Few liberals really regard abortion, at least in the later stages, as a bit of elective surgery. Suppose a woman had her fifth-month fetus aborted purely out of curiosity as to what it looked like, and perhaps then had it bronzed. Who among us would not deem both her and her actions reprehensible? Or, to go from the lurid to the ludicrous, suppose a wealthy woman, a Wagner addict, got an abortion in her fourth month because she suddenly realized that she would come to term during the Bayreuth Festival. Only an exceptional liberal would not blanch at such behavior. Of course, in both cases one might refuse to outlaw the behavior, but still, clearly we do not respond to these cases as we would to the removal of an appendix or a tooth. Similarly, in my experience few of even the staunchest conservatives consistently regard the fetus, at least in the earlier stages, in the same way as they do a fellow adult. When the cause of grief is a miscarriage, the object of grief is the mother; rarely does anyone feel pity or sorrow for the embryo itself. So too, it is most unusual for someone to urge the same punishment for a mother who aborts a young fetus as for one who murders her grown child.

THE PRO-ABORTIONIST APPEAL

Both sides of the abortion controversy make extravagant claims as to what can ultimately happen if abortion becomes a matter of personal choice. The anti-abortionists argue that it would signal the abandonment of the respect for life. If individuals make this life and death decision, "there can be no criterion of the right to life, save that of personal taste" (St. John-Stevas, 1964:15). In effect, the failure to protect the innocent, weak fetus sets a dangerous precedent, "for the issue is life itself and if we fail the child in the womb, we can hardly be assured that we shall succeed in our defense of the defective child in an institution, of the insane in an asylum, of the senile in a hospital, or of the politically undesirable in a concentration camp" (Rice, 1969:50). Nazi Germany is frequently presented as the prototype of what can happen. Carroll (1968:161) deplores "the German medical community's subordination of its ethics" to state demands, so that its members become "healers, on the one hand, 'respectable murderers,' at best, on the other—moved by fiat in the years 1933–1939 from voluntary, to compulsory, to mass sterilization, and—during the war years—to compulsory abortion. Let us not forget the desire of women can become the demand of the state—if not for racial, then for socioeconomic reasons."

The future envisioned by the pro-abortionists presents a different world indeed. Personal choice in contraception and abortion heralds an age of positive control over fertility and ultimately the "Century of the Wanted Child." Lawrence Lader (1966:155, 166) calls up a vision of a world in which personal control over reproductive functions promises much:

> When nations are ready to assume their ultimate responsibility, this age, once characterized as the Century of the Common Man, must become the Century of the Wanted Child. For too long our only concern has been with the rights of the embryo and the endless creation of rivers of humanity. Now, in our revolt against servitude to uncontrolled fertility, and a reckless flood of children born as accidents and out of ignorance, we at last have recognized that survival of the embryo is not enough. Our laws must not demand that conceptions be brought to term without being equally concerned about the child who is born. As crucial as his right to be born is his welfare as a human being. . . . [By not passing] legislation allowing individual conscience and free choice in abortion, the core of our democratic system is crippled. The right to abortion is the foundation of Society's long struggle to guarantee that every child comes into this world wanted, loved, and cared for. The right to abortion, along with all birth-control measures, must establish the Century of the Wanted Child.

Let us speculate on the reasons for the appeal of the pro-abortionists' vision. Potter (1969:96) points out that the anti-abortionists' argument has the disadvantage of taking place "in a dimension of existence unknown or unexplored by their fellow citizens." They deal with the ultimate harm to society if abortion laws are changed, and they speak of the unseen, unfamiliar fetus as a human being. In contrast, the arguments of the pro-abortionists have an immediacy, practically, and identification that the anti-abortionists lack. It is much easier to empathize with an adult woman who strongly wants an abortion or with a woman who has been injured as a result of a criminal abortion than it is to identify with an unseen fetus and understand how its destruction could lead to general harm for society. In order to counteract this advantage of the pro-abortionists, the anti-abortionists emphasize that the fetus looks as human as an adult woman. Referring to New York Right to Life Committees, Fred Shapiro (1972:36) observes that "speakers rely on a visual argument, buttressing their contention that the unborn child is alive and entitled to the protection of the laws with still photographs of fetuses and film strips." As an example of the potential effectiveness of this approach, anti-abortionists in Michigan saturated the state with printed material and TV appeals showing the fetus in various stages of development and stressing how human it was. Until this campaign, polls showed 56 percent of the voters favoring the 1972 referendum, but as the campaign progressed, opinion shifted and polls showed a majority disapproving of repeal. As a direct result of the massive, visual campaign by the anti-abortionists, the referendum was defeated by a vote of 61 percent to 39 percent.

The pro-abortion argument also provides reassurance that people can and will use technology to create a better world. In a complex society filled with remote and uncontrollable forces, the promise of total and individual control over an important part of life appeals to many. Most are aware of the awesome power of science and technology to bring about destruction and of the individual's limited control over these forces. People want and need to be reassured that technology will create a better world for them; they do not want to be presented with a vision of a Nazi state that uses technology to enforce its will. Given the growing prominence of a scientific and secular world view, a changing set of sexual standards, and an increasingly recognized need for family planning, it will be little wonder if a vision of the Century of the Wanted Child wins out over a vision of a Nazi state.

Ralph Potter (1969:101) poignantly describes the change from a sacred to a secular world which the abortion debate exemplifies for many:

> At stake in the abortion debate is not simply the fate of individual women or even the destiny of individual nations and cultures. . . . But if abortion is not an actual threat to minimal public order it may nevertheless be a symbolic threat to the moral order espoused by Christians for two millennia. Abortion does not merely contradict specific mores and moral teachings pertaining to sexuality, marriage, and procreation or endanger a system of law built upon "respect for life." It implies the rejection of a world view which has sustained a way of life, a mode of being in the world, a pattern of response to the human condition.
>
> Abortion is a symbolic threat to an entire system of thought and meaning. The willingness to practice abortion, or even to condone resort to abortion by others, signals that the high Christian vision of selfless charity has become despised and rejected of men. The Christian portrayal of the true man as one characterized by selflessness, sacrifice, concern for the weak and the unlovely, and a willingness to accept and transcend allotted afflictions through the power of redemptive suffering has faded in public consciousness to the point that it can seldom induce willing imitation. For many people there is simply no meaning in putting up with an unwanted circumstance when recourse is available without a high probability of temporal retribution.
>
> For Christians, an entire system of meaning may be at stake in the abortion debate; but is anything at stake for a secular, pluralistic state?[6]

One other advantage of the pro-abortion position relates to the practical difficulty of holding that the original laws should stand. Both sides typically declare that much can and should be done to lessen the need for abortion. Proposals include more extensive birth control and sex education, easier availability of acceptable contraceptives, more and better health care, better welfare programs, and so on. But for those against any changes in the original laws, these proposals represent the only concrete solutions they can offer to the problem of criminal abortions. Anti-abortionists tend to play down the number of criminal abortions (giving low estimates of 10,000 to 200,000 per year) while the pro-abortionists dramatize the amount of harm done to the many who have criminal abortions (giving high estimates of 200,000 to 1.5 million per year). Here, too, the pro-abortionist has the advantage. Regardless of whether the estimate is high or low, it is acknowledged by all that criminal abortions take place and that they present a serious problem. Further, it appears that even if the need for abortions is lessened through other policies, abortion may still be a necessary part of a total program.

Another complication for the anti-abortionists is the difficulty of seriously and forcefully pushing for the enforcement of restrictive abortion laws—legal authorities seem unwilling, the public does not demand enforcement, and the laws are essentially unenforceable. The woman who gets an illegal abortion is relieved and is not about to testify against the abortionist. Moreover, to insist that the laws be strictly enforced would require the questioning of practices and policies related to hospital abortions, and few are willing to take on the medical profession in a battle that is doomed to failure.

CHAPTER THREE

ABORTION LAWS AND MEDICAL PRACTICES IN THE UNITED STATES

Abortion laws throughout the world vary from highly restrictive ones which allow abortion for few or no reasons to highly permissive laws which permit abortion for any reason. But the law on abortion hardly ever tells the whole story on who does and does not receive an abortion. Under restrictive laws, skilled and unskilled "abortionists" perform "criminal" abortions outside of hospitals, and they are permitted to operate by law enforcement agencies and are well patronized by women seeking abortions. "Reputable" physicians do "therapeutic" abortions in hospitals for selected patients, even though these abortions may be illegal. Under moderate or liberal laws, abortions may be done primarily in one area of a state or only certain hospitals in a city. Thus, depending upon the attitudes and practices of the woman's physician and hospital or depending upon who she is and whom she knows, she may find it easy or difficult to obtain an abortion regardless of how restrictive or permissive the laws are.*

Whatever the abortion statute says and whatever practices have evolved, the split between the law and practice has become an outstanding feature of the abortion controversy in many countries. As this law-practice gap became part of the controversy in the United States, the proponents of abortion denounced the hypocrisy of the situation and called for legal changes to bring the laws into line with medical practices; the opponents contended that changing the abortion laws would not strike at the root of the underlying problem. Opponents felt that reform efforts could eliminate the need for abortion if services such as adoption, sex information and education, contraception, and facilities for children with birth defects were expanded, and the public was educated in the use of alternatives to abortion. The rapid changes in abortion laws that took place in the United States between 1967 and 1970 involved many legislatures and courts, altered many political careers, and deeply influenced the lives of many individuals as the availability of abortion literally changed overnight. The situation in the United States remains especially unpredictable and confusing because abortion legislation is the province of state legislatures and because medical practices regarding abortion have in many cases been set by each hospital within a state. In spite of some actions at a national level—U.S. Supreme Court involve-

* For support of the claim that hospitals have been doing abortions that do not comply with the law see Gold et al. (1965); Hall (1965, 1967, 1967a); Simon et al. (1967); Spivak (1967); and Tietze (1968). Studies of hospital practices in the United States prior to 1966 produced three general findings: 1) the overall incidence of hospital abortions decreased; 2) the indications for abortion changed, with psychiatric and fetal (especially rubella) indications having higher rates relative to medical indications; and 3) the inequalities of practice persisted with respect to geographical regions, ethnic and racial groups, type of hospital, and type of service. See also Overstreet and Traut (1951); Russell (1951, 1952, 1953); Moore and Randall (1952); Stephenson (1954); Packer and Gampbell (1959); Boulas et al. (1962); Hammond (1964); Guttmacher (1967); Mandy (1967); Wilson (1967); and Eliot et al. (1970).

ment, Nixon's anti-abortion statements, a President's Commission pro-abortion statement—the kind of abortion practices that are found in any hospital at any time depends largely upon an array of local factors such as the organization and activity of pro- and anti-abortion groups, whether local medical groups generally support, ignore, or work against abortion, and the predisposition of influential and powerful members of state legislatures and the medical community toward abortion.

THE ORIGINAL LAWS

"Original" laws refer to the first state statutes passed along with any revisions up to 1966, since many abortion statutes went through one or several revisions over the years. But the legislative changes that occurred between 1967 and 1970 were more dramatic than a hundred years of all the revisions put together and "original" has therefore become synonymous with "restrictive." Indeed, a glance at Part A of Table 1 shows that with little variation, the original U.S. abortion laws strictly forbid abortion except for one "therapeutic" exception. The typical wording of this exception, from the Michigan statute, is: "unless the same [abortion] shall have been necessary to preserve the life of such woman." Original statutes not following this pattern are few: Alabama, the District of Columbia, and Oregon included life and health; Colorado and New Mexico contained life and serious or permanent bodily injury; the Maryland statute's only exception was "that no other method will secure the safety of the mother"; and the Massachusetts, New Jersey, and Pennsylvania laws gave no therapeutic exception.

In addition to stating a therapeutic exception which provided a justifiable reason for abortion, some of these statutes also set certain conditions or procedural requirements to regulate abortion. Although consultation requirements and procedural requirements regarding who performs abortions appeared in only a few of the original laws, they came to play a key role in the administration of the original laws and in the post-1966 legislation. Eleven of the pre-1966 statutes specified that a physician or surgeon do the operation, and sixteen states required that "prior consultation with one or more physicians is necessary before a claim of justification can be made" (George,

TABLE 1: ABORTION LAWS IN THE UNITED STATES (January 1, 1973)

	Ala.	*Alaska 1970*	*Ariz.*	*Ark. 1969*	*Calif. 1967*	*Colo. 1967*	*Conn. 1972*	*Del. 1969*	*D.C.*	*Fla. 1972*	*(1*
Part A.											
Original Laws											
Grounds											
life	×	×	×	×	×	×	×	×	×	×	
health	×								×		
other						×					
Part B.											
Reform Laws											
Grounds											
life				×	×	×	×	×		×	
health				×						×	
physical health					×	×		×			
mental health					×	×		×			
fetal deformity				×		×		×		×	
forcible rape				×	×	×		×		×	
statutory rape					15 y.	16 y.					14
incest				×	×	×		×		×	
Procedural requirements											
time limit					20 w.	16 w.		20 w.			
residency				4 m.				4 m.			
M.D. approval				3 *C*	2–3 *B*	3 *B*		1*C-RA*		1 *C*	2 *C*
other consent						×				×	
Part C.											
Repeal Laws											
Procedural requirements											
physician		×									
hospital		×									
time limit		n.v.f.									
residency		30 d.									
other consent		×									

waii 970	*Idaho*	*Ill.*	*Ind.*	*Iowa*	*Kan. 1969*	*Ky.*	*La.*	*Maine*	*Md. 1968*	*Mass.*	*Mich.*	*Minn.*	*Miss. 1966*
×	×	×	×	×	×	×	×	×			×	×	×
									×	×			
					×				×				×
					×				×				
					×				×				
					×				×				
					×				×				(×)
					16 y.								(×)
					×								
									26 w.				
					3 *C*				*RA*				
×													
×													
v.f.													
0 d.													

Table 1 (continued)

	Mo.	*Mont.*	*Neb.*	*Nev.*	*N.H.*	*N.J.*	*N.M. 1969*	*N.Y. 1970*	*N.C. 1967*	*N.D.*	*Ohio*	*O*
Part A.												
Original Laws												
Grounds												
life	×	×	×	×	×		×	×	×	×	×	
health												
other						×	×					
Part B.												
Reform Laws												
Grounds												
life							×		×			
health									×			
physical health							×					
mental health							×					
fetal deformity							×		×			
forcible rape							×		×			
statutory rape							16 y.					
incest							×		×			
Procedural requirements												
time limit												
residency									4 m.			
M.D. approval							2 *B*		3 *C*			
other consent									×			
Part C.												
Repeal Laws												
Procedural requirements												
physician								×				
hospital												
time limit								24 w.				
residency												
other consent												

e.	*Penn.*	*R.I.*	*S.C.*	*S.D.*	*Tenn.*	*Texas*	*Utah*	*Vt.*	*Va.*	*Wash.*	*W. Va.*	*Wisc.*	*Wyo.*
9[a]			*1970*						*1970*	*1970*			
		×	×	×	×	×	×	×	×	×	×	×	×
	×												
			×						×				
			×						×				
			×						×				
			×						×				
			×						×				
y.													
			×						×				
d.													
			90 d.						120 d.				
C			3 *C*						*B*				
			×						×				
										×			
										×			
										4 m.			
										90 d.			
										×			

Sources: Harper (1958:188–92); George (1967:5–7); Means (1968:429); Association for the Study of Abortion; and National Association for Repeal of Abortion Laws.

Key: A date under a state indicates the year a new law was passed; Part B or C indicates the principal contents of the new law.

y. = years and refers to the legal age of consent for statutory rape.

d. = days; w. = weeks; m. = months; n.v.f. = non-viable fetus.

C = consultant and number required; *B* = therapeutic abortion board and number required; *RA* = hospital review authority required.

[a] The Oregon statute contains the additional explanatory phrase: "In determining whether or not there is substantial risk [to the woman's physical or mental health] account may be taken of the mother's total environment, actual or reasonably foreseeable."

1967:7, 9). As an example, the original Georgia law states that "unless the same shall have been necessary to preserve the life of the mother, or shall have been advised by two physicians to be necessary for such purpose."

Fowler Harper (1958:187–92) points out the variation regarding who had the burden of proof in abortion cases, the state or the defendant, but only a few statutes are specific on this point. This means that either the state assumes the burden of "proving non-compliance with law beyond a reasonable doubt" or the doctor-defendant must establish the medical necessity of the abortion (George, 1972). If the statutes are silent on this matter, it becomes a question of judicial interpretation, and George (1972) finds that the courts most often place the burden "on the state to plead and prove the want of medical justification, provided the defendant is shown to be a licensed medical practitioner." These rulings in favor of physicians help to explain why no prosecutions have resulted even though physicians have written and talked about hospital-performed abortions which do not comply with the law. As George (1972) describes the task when the burden rests with the state: "if the prosecutor has to attack the medical judgment of a doctor, particularly one who performs an abortion in a hospital or public clinic under the supervision of his peers on a special committee, and sustain that attack in court subject to a burden of proving non-compliance with law beyond a reasonable doubt, it is unlikely that he will proceed at all."

A few of the original statutes hold the woman guilty of a crime if she aborts herself or submits to an abortion, and at least one state, Vermont, in considering new abortion legislation in 1972, debated a provision for punishing the woman who aborts herself (George, 1967:13; Means, 1968:492; *Burlington Free Press,* Feb. 2, 1972). B. James George (1967:13–14) discusses the legal effect of these provisions:

> . . . the fact that the woman is deemed to have committed a criminal act means that the woman may claim privilege [against self-incrimination] when she is summoned to testify for the state. However, because of the importance, in many instances, of the woman's testimony in establishing the abortionist's guilt, . . . immunity against prosecution is conferred upon the woman when she testifies for the state. This brings the matter

around full circle to about where it would be if the woman were not considered a criminal in the first place.

Although these provisions to punish the woman result in a rather ridiculous legal situation, they symbolically fulfill the need of some to punish the aborting woman for her moral transgression against society.

Treating the fetus differently according to the period of gestation assumed greater importance in the post-1966 legislation, but some of the original laws prohibited the killing of the unborn quick child and regarded it as manslaughter. George (1967:11) contends that the meaning of this prohibition against killing the unborn quick child is not clear, but a "target is probably the person who intends to cause a pregnant woman to abort without her consent and who uses physical violence against her body to achieve the purpose. Conceptually these statutes clearly accord independent personality to the fetus, for the killing of the fetus under these circumstances is called manslaughter and the sections themselves are usually found with other homicide sections." Louisell and Noonan (1970:225–26) explain this provision by arguing that both the original anti-abortion statutes and the sections in the homicide statutes dealing with abortion were intended to protect the fetus.

Abortion can also be regulated by what George calls "administrative sanctions." This refers to the control of licensed medical personnel and hospitals through licensing statutes. George (1967:17–18) finds that performance of or participation in a "criminal" or "unlawful" abortion constitutes grounds for license revocation in most states. Even where no statutory provision exists for revocation of license, "there is statutory authorization for revocation based on conviction of a felony or unprofessional conduct in general" and "since abortion has been declared a form of unprofessional conduct, it is clear that there is no state in which a proven abortionist can continue to practice without his license being subject to revocation" (George, 1967:18). Although the loss of license for performing criminal abortions is a relatively rare occurrence, the fear inspired in professionals by labeling the practice of unlawful abortion as unprofessional conduct should not be underestimated. Jethro Lieberman (1970:104) reported that of 208 medical licenses revoked in 1967 in thirty-one states, twenty-three related to professional competence which included only abortion and narcotics violations.

One of the reasons for the small number of license revocations due to abortion stems from the liberalization in medical thinking that accompanied the growing gap between the law and medical practice. Although the original abortion laws are restrictive, they came to be administered liberally by some members of the medical profession. The Finkbine case stands as a classic example of a hospital's liberal administration of restrictive laws and of how the fear of legal action hovers over the medical community when these policies are publicized.

Though less widely cited, a study published in 1959 revealed more information about the liberal administration of restrictive laws. Herbert Packer and Ralph Gampbell (1959:422) investigated "medical standards and practices viewed in the light of current legal norms." They mailed a two-part questionnaire to the chiefs of the obstetrical services of twenty-nine representative hospitals in the San Francisco and Los Angeles areas. The first part of the questionnaire collected information about such things as the hospital's procedures in deciding which abortions to do, the number of abortions performed, and the attitudes of the physicians. The second part of the questionnaire described eleven hypothetical cases of women requesting an abortion and asked each hospital to treat the cases as if they were actually being presented for approval. Twenty-five of the twenty-nine hospitals answered part two, and twenty-two gave a hospital decision on the hypothetical cases. Table 2 summarizes six typical cases from the eleven, evaluates each case's legal standing, and shows the decisions of the hospitals. Clearly in many cases the indications for abortion accepted by the hospitals did not coincide with the therapeutic exception of California's law at that time.

Until the 1940s "therapeutic abortion was a relatively common procedure, well accepted by the majority of physicians as properly indicated for the preservation of the mother's life or immediate health in certain complicated pregnancies" (Russell, 1953:108). During the last few decades an "extensive realignment of indications for therapeutic abortion" took place within the medical community, and as the Packer-Gampbell cases illustrate, physicians disagree about acceptable indications for an abortion. Guttmacher (1967:16) sums up the reasons for such disagreement when he writes in answer to the question "Who should be aborted?": "Two authors of equally good intent could give different answers, since their judgment in large measure would be affected by their training, experience and social background, and by the institutions in which they have worked."

The net effect of this disagreement, confusion, and controversy among physicians was the establishment of separate therapeutic abortion policies and procedures by each hospital. In the absence of agreement within the larger medical community and in view of the increasing discrepancies between the law and medical practice, each hospital set up its own regulations. Various approval systems developed, and the therapeutic abortion committee, started in 1945 by Alan Guttmacher (1970:73), soon became the most popular method of deciding who receives an abortion. Keith Russell (1964:353) enumerated the "manifold values" of a review committee: "1) they serve as deterrents to the indiscriminate use of therapeutic abortion; 2) they act in the best interests of the patient: 3) they are a medicolegal safeguard for the physician; and 4) they serve as repositories for the accumulation of data concerning the utilization and outcome of cases submitted for the therapeutic interruption of pregnancy."

Although physicians have objected to the committee system, Russell's evaluation represents the prevailing attitude of the early to mid-1960s. The committees control the number and kind of cases approved and thereby "serve as deterrents to the indiscriminate use of therapeutic abortion" by those physicians considered to be too liberal in dispensing abortions. In addition, by sharing the responsibility for the decision, rather than placing it in the hands of the individual physician, the committees provide a "medicolegal safeguard" against the ever-present threat of legal action. That committees "act in the best interests of the patient" has been questioned. Phelan and Maginnis (1969:91) give one of the shortest and most critical descriptions of the purpose and workings of the committee system: "The hospital abortion committee is a completely unnecessary medical precaution, and is simply a smokescreen behind which sexual discrimination flourishes and individual doctors protect themselves against criticism

TABLE 2: THE PACKER-GAMPBELL HYPOTHETICAL CASES[a]

Indication	*Medical Description*	*Legal Standing*	*Number of Hospitals*	
			Approve	*Disapprove*
Medical	"Rheumatic heart disease with aortic stenosis and insufficiency and mitral stenosis. Auricular fibrillation and moderate heart failure are secondary to her rheumatic heart disease."	Legal—"appears to us to qualify under the strict legal standard."	21	1
Medical-Fetal	Hodgkins Disease	Questionable—"Although the accepted forms of X-ray therapy may have a most deleterious effect on the fetus, the indicated disease does not present any special hazard to it, nor does the continuation of the pregnancy appear to influence the course of the maternal disease. . . . The legality of a therapeutic abortion in this case is, at best, questionable. The danger to the fetus from X-ray treatment is irrelevant to any justification based on averting a threat to the life of the mother. However, the presence of the fetus may well inhibit the vigor of the measures required to combat the mother's disease; and on this basis, it might be concluded . . . that the pregnancy should be terminated in order to permit effective therapy in the interest of preserving the life of the patient."	10	11(6)[b]
Psychiatric	Suicide threats and one suicide attempt since pregnancy was diagnosed. Psychiatrist sees suicide threats as "genuine."	Questionable—"A genuine threat of suicide probably comes as close to presenting a justification under the existing legal standard as is possible for a psychiatric indication. Nonetheless, if the patient is kept under restraint in a mental institution, the possibility of a successful attempt at suicide may be greatly decreased. . . . The result of an uninterrupted pregnancy will probably be confinement in a mental institution. However, the addition to a case of psychosis of a genuine threat of self-destruction may be enough to bring the case within the legal standard. The	17	4(2)

		peutic abortion under these circumstances is, at best, questionable."		
Psychiatric	"Severe anxiety neurosis with hysterical physical manifestations (vomiting, dehydration)."	Illegal—"This case presents a psychiatric indication for termination of pregnancy which, in our judgment, is plainly unjustifiable under the provisions of the California Penal Code. There is no suggestion that the patient's life is endangered. The prospect that an existing neurosis may be intensified by the birth of another child is one which probably characterizes a substantial proportion of all such pregnancies. The threat to mental health, while very real, appears to be irrelevant to the considerations underlying the narrow legal justification provided for termination of pregnancy."	10	12(7)
Fetal	Tay-Sachs Disease (amaurotic family idiocy); 3 children, first 7 yrs. and apparently healthy, second child died aged 2 of Tay-Sachs, third 1½ yrs. diagnosed as having Tay-Sachs.	Illegal—"The indication presented is purely fetal and consequently does not afford a justification for termination of pregnancy under the current legal standard."	8	14(7)
Socioeconomic	5 children, one with fibrocystic disease; husband tubercular and about to be readmitted to sanatorium; woman working and has become "tense and apprehensive" since discovery of pregnancy; family physician recommends abortion; obstetrician willing to operate if approved.	Illegal—"we think that [an abortion] is plainly outside the existing legal justification."	1	20(3)

Source: Packer and Gampbell (1959).

[a]Quotation marks indicate direct quotes from the article. See Packer and Gampbell (1959:431–44) for the full case descriptions, authors' comments, and hospital decisions, including individual responses.

[b]Numbers in parentheses indicate those who thought "the case would stand a good chance of approval at another reputable hospital."

by having this anonymous committee sanction their dereliction of duty towards their female patients."

Whether one favors or disapproves of the committee system probably depends upon one's belief about who should have the ultimate decision-making power. But abortion committees clearly serve a purpose for hospitals and physicians in a situation where little consensus can be achieved and where the law leaves the decision in medical hands. Discussing the composition and workings of committees, Karl Schaupp (1964:353) noted that a committee could be set up to "make it do anything you want" resulting in an abortion rate "all the way from zero up to almost no restrictions." Committee decisions were influenced by those physicians who wanted legal changes and reasoned that these changes would come about only by showing legislators that the incidence of abortion would not soar and could be controlled by the medical profession's committee system. In 1964 Howard Hammond (1964:355) concluded a paper and discussion on hospital committees with the remark: "I hope that the presentation of a paper like this will help Dr. Overstreet in his testifying before the legislature to show a conservative trend and a responsible trend among the medical profession so that the lawyers and the legislature will turn the problem back to doctors where it belongs."

REFORM LAWS

To start with an oversimplification, while the original laws generally permitted abortions only to save the pregnant woman's life, the reform laws added health, fetal deformity, and felonious intercourse as indications for a legal abortion. The reform laws were passed during and after 1966 and attempted to clarify or expand the pre-1966, original laws. In all instances where we refer to reform laws without further qualification, we are referring to these liberalized laws as documented in Table 1, Part B.

The reform laws therefore go beyond the original laws, almost without exception, to expand the indications for a legal abortion. But there have also been pressures in some states to go beyond the original laws by strengthening their restrictive features against constitutional attack. The first anti-abortionist reform law came with the passage of the 1972 Connecticut law. Shortly after a U.S. District Court declared the original Connecticut abortion law unconstitutional, the state legislature passed a new law which contained the same therapeutic exception—to save the woman's life—as the original law, provided a tougher penalty for performing or advising an unlawful abortion than the original law, and stated in a preamble to the new law that "it is the intent of the Legislature to protect and preserve human life from the moment of conception" (*New York Times,* June 28, 1972, p. 21-C). This preamble was carefully prepared in order to prevent further court debate about the intent of the legislature and in order to reform the original law by strengthening its constitutional basis. But this strengthened law was also ruled unconstitutional by a federal district court.

Reform legislation, however, has most often, and especially from 1966 through 1969, been associated with the pro-abortionists and with the kind of moderate law proposed in the American Law Institute's Model Penal Code. The Code states that,

> A licensed physician is justified in terminating a pregnancy if he believes there is substantial risk that continuance of the pregnancy would gravely impair the physical or mental health of the mother, or that the child would be born with grave physical or mental defect, or that the pregnancy resulted from rape, incest, or other felonious intercourse. All illicit intercourse with a girl below the age of 16 shall be deemed felonious for purposes of this subsection. Justifiable abortions shall be performed only in a licensed hospital except in case of emergency when hospital facilities are unavailable. (American Law Institute, 1962:189–90)

Mississippi quietly altered its abortion law in 1966 by adding a provision for rape, without specifying whether statutory or forcible rape or both was meant. The first big, noisy wave of legal changes came in 1967 when California, Colorado, and North Carolina passed laws based upon these American Law Institute recommendations.

As Part B of Table 1 shows, these reforms expanded the grounds for abortion along the lines suggested by the American Law Institute and added procedural requirements or conditions for abortions which were not mentioned by the American Law Institute. The reform laws all included life, health, and either rape or incest or both as a justifiable ground for abortion, but these statutes are far from uniform. Some statutes used the words "life and health" while others specified life and physical and mental health. Statutes having no provision for fetal deformity presented an interesting problem because "before reform many [physicians] did an abortion if the woman had rubella in the first trimester. Now, unless danger of 'fetal defect' is specifically mentioned in their state law, they do not always grant an abortion" (Irwin, 1970:80). Each law specifies the proof required and the procedures necessary to bring a valid claim of rape or incest. Some states set age limits on abortion for statutory rape which led to a peculiar inconsistency in some cases. In California, for instance, "sexual intercourse with an unmarried girl below the age of 18 constitutes statutory rape, but if pregnancy results, it can be terminated only if the girl is below the age of 15" (Roemer, 1971:501).

The procedural requirements apparent in the original laws became greatly elaborated in the reform laws. Almost without exception, the reform statutes require abortions to be performed by physicians in hospitals. The concept of treating the fetus differently according to the period of gestation appeared in some original laws as a distinction between a quickened and unquickened fetus, but the reform laws make more extensive and specific use of the time limit. Some statutes set a time limit beyond which abortion is not permitted or is permitted only if necessary to preserve the woman's life (Delaware and Maryland, for example). Or, as another example, in Colorado the time limit only applies to cases of rape and incest. In addition to these conditions, two new procedural requirements appeared in some of the reform laws—residency regulations and consent clauses. A residency requirement means that a woman cannot apply for abortion in the state until she has been a resident for a specified period of time. Consent refers to statutory requirements of consent from a husband, parents, or guardian and is connected with the age or marital status of the woman. For example, Alaska requires consent from a parent or guardian if the woman is under eighteen and unmarried, and in Colorado if the woman is under eighteen consent is required from the husband if she is married or a parent or guardian if unmarried. The South Carolina statute calls for the husband's consent in cases of fetal deformity only.

The greatest elaboration of previous provisions and the key to the administration and interpretation of the reform laws resides in the medical approval systems set up in the statutes. A certain number of consultants (*C*), a therapeutic abortion board (*B*), or a hospital review authority (*RA*) is mandatory (see Part B, Table 1). These approval systems are highly flexible. A hospital review authority for instance can consist of one, two, three, or more members, and the approval bodies vary as to whether a unanimous or majority decision is required for approval. One report from California, using quotations from the chief of the state's Bureau of Maternal and Child Health, shows how the manipulation of the committee system results in a restrictive policy:

> . . . hospitals that want to can make the procedure for obtaining an abortion "complicated, time-consuming and expensive. One method is to require two psychiatrists' statements when the law requires only one."
>
> In many cases, valid requests are turned down altogether. "Free interpretation of the law provides a vehicle for refusing requests in one hospital that would be readily granted in another. . . . For instance, the law requires a hospital committee of at least two physicians to review requests for abortion (up to 13 weeks pregnancy) and stipulates that for committees of three or less a unanimous vote is required, though for larger committees a majority vote is sufficient. Hence, some hospitals will limit the committee to three members and permanently instate one dissident physician, effectively giving him permanent veto power." (Plagenz, 1969:82–83)

Changes in committee procedures can also lead to a more liberal policy. Marder (1970:1232) reports on one California hospital where initially only "overtly psychotic or highly suicidal" patients were even referred to the abortion committee which resulted in the "rejection of a large proportion of early applicants."

> The growing awareness that we were excluding patients who might be more favorably reviewed by the full committee led to a change in procedure that enabled all applicants, regardless of the initial evaluation recommendation, to be presented to the committee for consideration. This liberalized philosophy brought about a more reasonable definition of mental illness for use by the committee: "A disorder of thinking, feeling or behavior producing a breakdown in living so that the individual cannot deal with reality or cannot function in dealing with daily problems of living." (Marder, 1970:1232–33)

Many physicians and observers of the abortion scene see the effect of these reform laws as making physicians "feel more secure in that what they were doing as a matter of course for years has now been sanctified by the legislature" (Walker and Hulka, 1971:444). In essence even before the reform laws were passed many physicians performed abortions to preserve the life or health of women as well as in cases of rape, incest, and fetal deformity; thus, the approval systems evolved informally by some hospitals within the medical community were formally written into the law. By this reasoning, the legislatures that passed reform bills wanted physicians to continue with the medical practices that had evolved and gave them the formal authority, through medical approval systems, to make decisions and set the policy.

Some find this kind of law satisfactory, but most observers have noted the difficulty of interpreting the laws and have attacked the operation of the approval systems. Physicians charge that no common definitions exist for phrases like "gravely impair," "substantial risk," or "mental health." The approval systems set up in law to interpret these legal provisions are "cumbersome, time-consuming, and expensive," and the "operation of the committee itself is highly vulnerable to individual prejudice on the part of members, and the process is far from scientific or rational" (Whittington, 1970:1228). The burden placed upon hospital committees to interpret the law when judging abortion requests has brought the system under attack in other countries, too. In Canada, since 1969, an abortion committee is required at each hospital, and Smith and Wineberg (1969–70) criticize the system because it is arbitrary and capricious in its operation, because appeal procedures are lacking, and because the variations among committees in their interpretations of the law has a discriminatory impact upon the population.

In spite of the criticisms leveled against the reform laws, they initiated the trend toward liberalization and were seen as the most politically feasible course of action since they embody a compromise between retaining the original, restrictive laws and passing a permissive repeal law.

REPEAL LAWS

By 1970 twelve states had passed reform laws, but these laws did not eliminate the abortion problem as seen by the pro-abortionists —many women wanting abortions were being delayed or denied.

there were dire prophecies that the state and, more particularly, an repared New York City would be subjected to social and medical ca- rophe. . . . Women from all over the country would seek abortions in w York City hospitals and clinics in the first year, monopolizing pre- ous hospital beds and the time of scarce medical manpower, with the esult that medical care for other urgent health problems—particularly of New York City's poor population—would suffer. It was predicted that overburdened medical facilities and physicians would be unable to handle the hordes of abortion applicants, whose abortions would be dangerously delayed because of crowded operating room schedules, only to be hastened finally through the procedure by pressured and weary practitioners. The resultant high costs of abortion and high rates of morbidity and mortality associated with the procedure could well create a situation, it was said, as bad as, if not worse than, the one women found themselves in when the old law restricting abortions to life-threatening situations forced women into the hands of illegal abortionists. (Pakter and Nelson, 1971:5)

After the first five months under the New York law, Pakter et al. (1971:196) could report that "on the whole, hospitals have been most cooperative in developing in an amazingly short time the necessary services and staff to care for women requesting abortions. However, anxiety and concern engendered by the large influx of nonresidents and the possibility of overtaxing facilities are not entirely dispelled." Nowhere has the strain on facilities and staff been as severe as a lot of people predicted, but the uneven application of services, the attitudes of personnel, and the cost of abortion continue to be problematic for most states with new abortion laws.

Table 3 gives a good picture of the uneven application of abortion laws. After reviewing abortion ratios in ten states, Kahn and his associates (1971:430) concluded that "the status of a given law regulating the performance of abortions does not bear a predictable relationship to the actual number of abortions performed. States with similarly worded laws have widely divergent performances." Furthermore, a look at the percentages aborted for mental health reasons suggests that the states with higher abortion ratios interpret the mental health provision the most liberally. In addition to the interstate maldistribution of abortions pictured in Table 3, some investigators have reported maldistribution within a state: from March 13, 1970 through July 15, 1970, "three hospitals in Honolulu performed 96.1% of the state's abortions" (Smith et al., 1971:531); in 1968 the

Legislators in some states that passed reform laws, as well as legislators in states with original laws, therefore introduced repeal legislation. The legislatures of Alaska, Hawaii, and New York passed repeal bills in 1970 while the Washington state legislature passed a repeal referendum which the voters approved.

The "repeal" in these laws refers to the elimination of the grounds for abortion and therefore eliminates the need for physicians to agonize over what constitutes an "indication" for abortion that is medically sound and at the same time legal. Instead, as Part C of Table 1 shows, these laws concentrate on procedural requirements to regulate abortion. In consequence, as long as they adhere to the procedural requirements, a woman can request and a physician can perform an abortion without having to give any reasons, or indications, or justifications for it.

The passage of these laws caused a considerable stir among the opposing forces. Most anti-abortionists received them as signals of the beginning of the end of respect for life in the United States. Some pro-abortionists celebrated their passage as a major breakthrough. Other pro-abortionists called them "reform" bills or "fake repeal" bills. In reference to a "licensed hospitals" requirement, one critic wrote:

Hawaii's new law has this kind of restriction, and hospitals there are already busy setting up a new catechism of "guidelines," none of which insure that women will get more abortions and all of which insure that they will have to ask a lot of strangers for "permission" before they are allowed to spend the considerable amount of money that hospitalization inevitably costs. Maryland's recent bill [which was vetoed] and the legislation and "guidelines" proposed in several other states—like New York—contain the same provisions that essentially shift the locus of control over women's decisions from the state to the hospital bureaucracies and their quasi-legal "regulations." (Cisler, 1970:20)

This is a more accurate description of the reform statutes than it is of the repeal laws. The committee procedures written into the reform statutes turned the abortion decision over to hospital bureaucracies. This criticism of the repeal laws does, however, highlight a major issue with respect to the repeal laws—the role of health agencies in controlling abortion.

> The two major opposing points of view are: 1) Having succeeded in getting criminal laws repealed, the imposition of any restrictions by health agencies is a step backward in making abortion freely available, and the introduction of innovative techniques in a fast moving field is likely to be inhibited; 2) the legislatures that have taken the most radical steps in removing the prohibition against abortion from their criminal laws have done so by narrow margins. They have allowed matters relating to abortion to be handled in much the same way other health matters are handled in the community. The use of official health agency mechanisms to protect the health and safety of the population in its jurisdiction is responsible public health practice and is likely to minimize the chance of "backlash" among legislators. (Harting and Hunter, 1971:2091)

Instead of merely shifting the locus of control over women's decisions from the state to the hospital bureaucracies, "the action of the State Legislature in removing entirely the restrictions of the past on abortions has created an entirely new and unprecedented situation. These local health departments have acted in the face of this vacuum of control. Was it the intention of the legislature that such controls *not* be exercised? Was it their intention that any licensed physician [in New York] should be allowed to perform an abortion for any reason at any place as long as it was during the first 24 weeks?" (Curran, 1971:624) In Alaska and Hawaii the statutes restrict abortion to hospitals, in Washington to hospitals or approved facilities, and in New York no restrictions are enumerated in the legislation. In Washington and New York local health agencies stepped in to fill the "vacuum of control" and issued regulations for abortion facilities. Although public health departments still deliberate over procedural requirements and standards, and although some final rulings may be settled in court, it appears that public health agencies have fallen heir to the regulation of abortion and to the view that abortion is a public health issue. William Curran (1971:624–25) voices the opinion that

> health departments should be given the authority unmistakably to enact regulations to control abortion practice in the interest of the public health. The lack of precedent or tradition in such fields should not be an obstacle. In fact, it is the very lack of clear, acceptable, common practices in medicine and public health concerning abortion which makes it essential that the public agencies charged with protecting the people's health take proper action to establish and to enforce adequate standards.

The legal restrictions in this field are lite
a field in which the strict law has been vi
commercial, nonmedical vendors and by le
and hospitals. But much of the medical pract
under various thinly veiled euphemisms. The d
dards of care and treatment has been greatly ha
of the practice itself in the past.

LEGAL CHANGE IS NOT ENOUGH: THE ORGANIZATION AND DELIVERY OF SERVICE

The legal changes that have taken place since 1970
ably improved women's access to desired abortions,
changes are not enough. Improved and more equitable
vices also have to be provided, and among other things th
changes in the way health care is paid for. When reports star
ing in from the states with reform and repeal laws, it became o
that "the development of proper standards of care and treatm
needed attention. As Elizabeth Elkind, director of the Abortion
form Association, predicted, "the repeal movement's job will fir
begin after the laws have been changed" (*New York Times,* March 12, 1970, p. 21).

Generally, fear that one's state would become an abortion mecca was the first reaction to a new law. Most people don't yet see this as desirable or respectable. Residency requirements in states with repeal laws and the combination of residency restrictions and hospital policies in states with reform laws prevented an influx of out-of-state patients. Only New York has in fact become an abortion mecca.

Along with the "abortion mecca" emotionalism, the medical community very practically asked how they were going to deal with an expected flood of abortion patients. This was particularly dramatic in New York City where estimates of the annual number of requests from local women ranged from 50,000 to 100,000 and estimates of requests from out-of-state residents ranged up to 400,000. The possibility of half a million abortion requests annually for New York City staggered the imagination, especially when compared with the 850 abortions done citywide in 1969. The gloomy predictions made after the passage of the New York law express a concern that has been voiced in every state which has passed a new abortion law.

TABLE 3: HOSPITAL ABORTION RATIOS

	Time Period	*Type of Law*	*Residency Requirement in Statute*		*Percentage Aborted for Mental Health*	*Hospital Abortions per 1,000 Live Births*
			yes	*no*		
Alaska	July 29–Sept. 29, 1970	repeal	×			96
California	Jan.–June 1970	reform		×	97.3	135
Colorado	Jan.–June 1970	reform		×	86.7	41
Georgia	Jan.–June 1970	reform	×		76.8	5
Hawaii	Mar. 13–July 15, 1970	repeal	×			192
Maryland	July 1, 1969–June 30, 1970	reform		×		102
New York City	July 1, 1970–Mar. 31, 1971	repeal		×		448
North Carolina	Jan. 1–Aug. 31, 1970	reform	×			7
Oregon	Jan.–June 1970	reform	×		92.1	165
South Carolina	Feb. 1–June 30, 1970	reform	×		78.6	7
Virginia	Jan.–June 1970	reform	×		70.3	13

Sources: Kahn et al. (1971:425); Pakter and Nelson (1971:12) for New York City; and Smith et al. (1971:523) for Hawaii.

San Francisco Bay area performed a disproportionately large number of the state's abortions and although by 1972 the discrepancy between northern and southern California largely disappeared, the rates for rural areas were low (Russell and Jackson, 1969:760; K. Russell, personal communication); in Maryland a few hospitals in Baltimore carry most of the load but this shows signs of improving "as more and more hospitals are recognizing their own community obligations which will enable the Baltimore hospitals to narrow their geographical confines to the neighborhood areas and to the patient populations whom they ordinarily serve" (Barnes, 1969:763); and after one year under the Colorado law, "the great majority of patients requesting legal termination of pregnancy were referred to Denver physicians. The hospitals in the small and medium-sized towns are performing very few therapeutic abortions" (Droegemueller et al., 1969:697).

One result of the interstate maldistribution shows up most clearly in New York City, where substantially more than 50 percent of the abortions were performed on nonresidents during the first two years of their repeal law. Only a small percentage of New York City abortions were done on New York State women who lived outside of the city; it appears that the New York State hospitals outside New York City serve their local areas while New York City facilities bear the brunt of the entire U.S. maldistribution.

> The states from which the greatest number of patients were referred to the city are as follows: a) New Jersey, b) Massachusetts, c) Ohio, d) Illinois, e) Florida, f) Michigan, and g) Pennsylvania.
>
> Every state in the union as well as Canada and other countries were represented. The need for national rather than statewide reform is evident from this finding. (Pakter et al., 1971:184)

Some remarkable figures turn up: from January through June 1970 "for every 1,000 live births in Georgia, five women had abortions in Georgia hospitals" while during July and August 1970 for every 1,000 live births "another five Georgia women had abortions in New York City hospitals" (Kahn et al., 1971:430).

In a hardhitting attack upon physicians' attitudes, Robert Hall (1971:517) charged that "the major effect of abortion liberalization on the medical community has been not to broaden its views but to polarize them. On the obstetrical service of every hospital, no matter how large the staff, there seem to be two or three doctors who do more than half of the abortions." For the first few months under the Hawaii repeal law, Smith and his colleagues (1971:534) found that 23 percent of the abortions were done by three physicians and 60 percent were done by fifteen physicians. After the second year of the North Carolina reform law, Walker and Hulka (1971:443) found from a study of obstetricians that 43 percent did no abortions, 80 percent reported "no substantial increase" in the number of abortions performed under the new law, and 54 percent commented "that the law has had very little or no effect on obstetrical practice in North Carolina." Residents in some teaching hospitals complained that the heavy load of abortion cases distorts their teaching program (Overstreet, 1971a:497), and some nurses complained of increased workloads and suffered from emotional stress and fatigue (McDermott and Char, 1971:622). Medical personnel have been known to harass abortion patients (Marder, 1970:1232). A large majority of medical and paramedical personnel have had little or no training in the areas of human sexuality, family planning, contraception, or abortion (David, 1972:64), and they find it difficult to understand or identify with abortion patients (Marder, 1970:1232; McDermott and Char, 1971:623). Many expect, however, that liberalized laws and the increased demand for abortion services will inevitably bring about attitude changes. Greenhouse (1970a:30, 32) quoted a physician just before the New York repeal law took effect:

> "I didn't do more than whisper about abortion four months ago," said . . . a Manhattan gynecologist and obstetrician who has practiced for 30 years, performed about one abortion a year and had to turn down requests for about 40 a year. "Neither did most of my friends. But now it's all we talk about—morning, noon, night and in between. Whether we're seeking this or not, it will fall into our laps, so what else is there to talk about?
>
> "I will do abortions. Everybody I know will do abortions. But, while I am intellectually ready, willing and able, I will still have an emotional reaction. I've been so emotionally attuned to this attitude toward abortion throughout my whole career that it will be difficult. It's a challenge. We've all been frustrated all these years by having to refuse so many, so no one will say no now. But I would not want to be known as an abortionist. Maybe the next generation wouldn't consider that a stigma, but with me it will persist until I die."

With increasing numbers of women having abortions, private health insurance carriers and Medicaid are being asked to cover the cost. Medicaid is assuming some of the cost for the medically indigent "in such cities as San Francisco, San Diego, Baltimore and New York where hospitals to which the poor have access are willing to perform the procedure and where there is some advocate structure to which a woman can turn to establish her eligibility promptly before the pregnancy is too far advanced." The presence of "advocates" such as Planned Parenthood or the social service division of a hospital or health department seems crucial; without them "there is evidence that . . . welfare clients find it difficult or impossible to obtain medical abortions even where restrictive laws have been reformed or repealed." Great hopes for paying abortion costs should not be held for Medicaid because of the limited population it covers and because it is becoming more restrictive in most states—"it is thus, even potentially, a source of abortion cost reimbursement for no more than 14 percent of medically indigent women of childbearing age" (Muller, 1970:12).

If abortion coverage exists in private insurance plans, it is generally found within the maternity provisions. A national survey of twelve companies that lead the country in writing group health insurance revealed that eleven cover abortion, but there were a lot of restrictions: coverage may not be specified in the contract, single women may not be covered, benefits may be restricted to a hospital, the size of benefits may be less than current fees, and so forth (Muller, 1970:13). Blue Cross and Blue Shield usually cover surgical and hospital expenses for abortion, but in some areas Blue Shield covers abortion and Blue Cross does not (Muller, 1970:16). Perhaps the most discomfiting finding of all regarding insurance coverage is that "it appears to be underutilized because a payment arrangement to cope with privacy problems in filing claims has not evolved" (Muller and Jaffe, 1972:15). Most health insurance companies have already faced, or will shortly face the question of abortion coverage, and some major changes have already occurred. In June 1970 New York City Blue Cross extended coverage to single women and unmarried dependent children but confined the benefit to hospitals (Muller, 1970:16).

Just as there are tremendous variations in abortion rates, so too are there tremendous variations in how abortions are paid for. Overstreet (1971a:497) generalized that "the indigent patient is fairly well served in California, although county hospital therapeutic abortion committees tend to be somewhat more rigid in their attitudes than their private hospital colleagues. But the lower middle-class woman, just above welfare eligibility, is in a parlous position when she seeks legal abortion." In Hawaii, abortions paid for by individuals accounted for the largest percentage of payment (64 percent), with insurance covering 23.1 percent of the cases, welfare 6.9 percent, and the military 4.1 percent (Smith et al., 1971:534). The authors conclude from their study of cost distribution that "the costs of abortion (both hospital and medical) are higher than women in the middle and marginal (medically indigent) income categories might be expected to afford" (Smith et al., 1971:541).

One way of lowering the cost of an abortion is to do it on an outpatient basis. This approach also relieves much of the strain on staff and facilities while providing safe abortions up to the twelfth week of gestation. By not admitting women as inpatients, the cost of abortions decreases and "professional personnel time, including that of the physicians, may be efficiently utilized" (Smith et al., 1971:539). Due to the "innovative organization of new facilities" and economic competition, the cost of early abortions has dropped. Harting and Hunter (1971:2103) observe that "The usual physician willing to arrange an abortion under hospital circumstances or the skilled physician abortionist operating in his office can no longer charge $500 for a D & C. The cost for early abortions in areas such as New York and the District of Columbia is now in the range of $150–200, a significant reduction. The costs for abortions at later stages of pregnancy have not changed as much."

From New York City Joseph Rovinsky (1971:341) speaks of abortion as entering "the *mainstream* of medical care" and that "patients seeking abortion are entitled to the same medical safeguards, scientific benefits, protection of privacy, and preservation of personal self-esteem as are any other patients." Rovinsky also emphasizes the need for counseling before and after abortion and though quarrels have developed about the qualifications and training of counselors and the purpose of counseling, most stress the desirability of counseling. Harting and Hunter (1971:2097–98) report perhaps the ultimate view of the place of counseling in abortion expressed by H. G. Whittington, a Denver physician, who considers abortion without counseling unethical and hopes that abortion without counseling will someday be considered malpractice.

Emphasis on contraception has always been a part of most discussions on abortion, and many feel, along with Rovinsky (1971:341), that the most successful abortion program "is one which, through education and motivation, makes itself obsolete and unnecessary." To this end family planning counselors are assigned to abortion programs, and abortion services have been set up in family planning clinics (Harting and Hunter, 1971:2092).

Another innovator in the organization of services pinpoints pregnancy testing as a "critical bridge" linking a range of services (Oettinger, 1971:15–18). Incredible as it seems, until recently most women had to visit a private physician to get a pregnancy test which can be made by a paraprofessional, costs relatively little, with results available in about two hours. Recently, and "often in response to changes in abortion laws," several pregnancy testing centers have been set up, and some public health departments are making tests available. In March 1971 a Pregnancy Testing and Counseling Center opened in Baltimore with volunteer counselors and funding from religious groups and other sources. Women receive pregnancy tests, contraception, and referral to appropriate services (Oettinger, 1971:16). In effect, through making something as simple as a pregnancy test readily available, women can be steered toward a variety of related services (Rains, 1971:180–81).

As an example of the kind of services that should be tied together, Planned Parenthood of New York City "opened a new, comprehensive family planning clinic where, in addition to contraceptive consultation, services include venereal disease screening, pregnancy testing and abortion, all on the premises of the clinic" (Oettinger, 1971:15). Other "fertility-related" services would include prenatal care, genetic counseling, male and female sterilization, and help with infertility problems. To provide such comprehensive services on a large scale obviously requires public funds, administrative imagination and energy, and a massive educational effort directed at medical personnel and the public. Whether the lawmakers, health professionals, or the public like it or not the demand and need for these services exist and show signs of increasing. This can ultimately change medical attitudes, make fertility-related services a part of the mainstream of medical care, and force health insurance carriers to include these services as part of their standard coverage.

CONSTITUTIONAL ISSUES: RIGHTS OF THE WOMAN V. RIGHTS OF THE FETUS

Prior to 1969 occasional judicial involvement in abortion cases established that the threat to the life of the woman need not be imminent or certain for abortion to be justified, and courts in

Massachusetts and New Jersey, where the statutes had no therapeutic exception, added life or health provisions (Lucas, 1968:740; George, 1967:6). The thalidomide scare and the rubella epidemic of the early 1960s, along with the American Law Institute's proposals for legal reform, initiated a dialogue among lawyers on the merits of abortion law reform. The 1965 *Griswold v. Connecticut* Supreme Court decision overturning an anti-contraceptive statute led to speculation on whether this decision applied to the abortion laws.

In 1968, while the reform movement was gathering momentum, Roy Lucas published a landmark article which laid out the grounds for a constitutional attack on the abortion laws. Lucas wrote that "the constitutional issues implicit in the enactment and application of abortion laws have received scant judicial attention." He explains further that "in the constitutional context [abortion] is a problem bearing few factual similarities to any decisions in the 150-year expanse of pre-*Griswold* history" (Lucas, 1968:753, 754). In a very short time the first decisions on the constitutionality of abortion laws were handed down: *People v. Belous* in September 1969 by the California Supreme Court and *U.S. v. Vuitch* in November 1969 by the U.S. District Court for the District of Columbia. Both of these decisions declared parts of the original abortion statutes unconstitutional.

Optimism ran high in the pro-abortion camp, and many looked to the courts to strike down the original restrictive statutes and thereby dispense with time-consuming, state-by-state legislative change. As more cases were decided by federal and local courts, however, the hopes of the pro-abortionists were cooled by several decisions which upheld the constitutionality of the original abortion laws. In the fall of 1970, Ruth Roemer (1971:502) counted five cases on the U.S. Supreme Court docket, over twenty cases before three-judge federal courts, and eleven states with cases in local courts. By 1972 many cases were still before the courts, and the judicial and legislative situations were unpredictable. As Justice Douglas aptly wrote in his opinion on *U.S. v. Vuitch:* "The subject of abortions—like cases involving obscenity—is one of the most inflammatory ones to reach the Court. People instantly take sides and the public, from whom juries are drawn, makes up its mind one way or the other before the case is even argued." From 1969 to 1972 the phenomenal number of abortion cases brought before all levels of courts across the country singled out several constitutional issues as most salient and dramatized the sharp cleavage in positions between pro-abortionists and anti-abortionists.

Vagueness. To declare a law unconstitutional because of vagueness rests essentially on due process requirements of the fourteenth amendment. Constitutionally, the law must be specific enough so that individuals know what is and is not a crime. In the case of abortion, physicians face criminal prosecution if their interpretation differs from that of law enforcement agencies. Lucas (1968:767–68) argues that no medical agreement exists regarding the meaning of phrases in the original laws like "without lawful justification" and "except to save the life of the mother"; he further notes that the medical community is not in agreement on cases of abortion for physical or mental health, rape, incest, or fetal deformity. The opposition argues that the original statutes had been in operation for many years "without the court ever before adverting to the difficulty of understanding these words," and "by the standard customarily invoked to measure definiteness, the usual statutory phrase 'necessary to preserve life' is clear enough" (Louisell and Noonan, 1970:238, 240).

The rulings of the several courts on the vagueness argument have been mixed. *People v. Belous,* decided by the California Supreme Court in 1969, gives a good example of a court's declaring an original abortion statute unconstitutionally vague. The Court ruled that

> the term "necessary to preserve" . . . is not susceptible of a construction that does not violate legislative intent and that is sufficiently certain to satisfy due process requirements without improperly infringing on fundamental constitutional rights. . . . Dictionary definitions and judicial interpretations fail to provide a clear meaning for the words, "necessary" or "preserve." There is, of course, no standard definition of "necessary to preserve," and taking the words separately, no clear meaning emerges. . . . Various possible meanings of "necessary to preserve life" have been suggested. However, none of the proposed definitions will sustain the statute.

In contrast, the District Court rejected the vagueness argument in a 1970 Wisconsin case, *Babbitz v. McCann.* The Court declared that they had examined the challenged phraseology and are persuaded that it is not indefinite or vague. In our opinion, the word "necessary" and the expression "to save the life of the mother" are both reasonably comprehensible in their meaning. . . . In *People v. Belous,* . . . the California court found that the words "necessary to preserve her life" in that state's abortion statute were unconstitutionally vague. While the Wisconsin statute uses slightly different language ("necessary to save"), we doubt that the distinction between the words used in the two statutes is significant. However, we do not share the view of the majority in *Belous* that such language is so vague that one must guess at its meaning.

A district court was persuaded that the Wisconsin statute was not "so vague that men of common intelligence must necessarily guess at its meaning and differ as to its application," while the California Supreme Court thought that the interpretation of the statute would require guesswork.

Privacy. The ninth amendment, which has only rarely been cited in court cases, holds that the enumeration of certain rights in the Constitution "shall not be construed to deny or disparage others retained by the people" (Mabbutt, 1972). One of these unenumerated rights is the right to privacy, and several recent court cases have established the right to privacy in the area of sexual activity. The essential issue is that these rights are considered of "fundamental" personal interest, and that state law may not infringe upon these individual rights. The most famous of these decisions, *Griswold v. Connecticut,* declared Connecticut's statute forbidding the use of contraceptives unconstitutional and asserted that it violated the right to marital privacy. The right also stems from the Fourteenth Amendment.

The proponents of abortion argue that the rights of parents to plan the number and timing of children falls within the scope of marital privacy, and therefore "*Griswold,* on its facts, protected a general interest in planning a family without state interference" and includes a right to abortion (Lucas, 1968:764). The opposition argues vehemently that this overextends the meaning of *Griswold* and other cases. Abortion is not a fundamental personal right, and the state has a "compelling" interest in protecting the fetus. For instance, forbidding the use of contraceptives violates the privacy of husband and wife in the sexual relationship since "enforcement of the statute would have required invasion of the marital bedchamber." But abortion laws do not interfere with the sexual relationship, and their enforcement does not involve "invasion of the conjugal bedroom" (Louisell and Noonan, 1970:233).

Court decisions on the abortion laws generally acknowledge the fundamental individual right to privacy in sexual activity and the right to determine family size, but opinions differ as to whether these rights include abortion. If these rights include abortion, the state may not infringe upon them, and statutes regulating abortion are unconstitutional. If abortion is not included in these rights, the state may have a compelling interest in protecting the fetus, and abortion statutes represent this state interest and are not unconstitutional. In 1970 a district court in the case of *Rosen v. Louisiana State Board of Medical Examiners* expresses this problem and also shows how court involvement in the abortion controversy has placed the familiar moral issues before the bench.

We deal in this case, however, not merely with whether a woman has a generalized right to choose whether to bear children, but instead with the more complicated question whether a pregnant woman has the right to cause the abortion of the embryo or fetus she carries in her womb. We do not find that an equation of the generalized right of the woman to determine whether she shall bear children with the asserted right to abort an embryo or fetus is compelled by fact or logic. Exercise of the right to an abortion on request is not essential to an effective exercise of the right not to bear a child, if a child for whatever reason is not wanted. Abstinence, rhythm, contraception, and sterilization are alternative means to this end. . . . Before the "moment" of conception has occurred, . . . the choice whether or not to bear children is made in circumstances quite different from those in which such a choice might be made after conception. . . . The basic distinction between a decision whether to bear children which is made before conception and one which is made after conception is that the first contemplates the creation of a new human organism, but the latter contemplates the destruction of such an organism already created. To some engaged in the controversy over abortion, this distinction is one without a difference. These men of intelligence and good will do not perceive the human organism in the early part of its life cycle as a human "being" or "person." In their view, the granting to such an organism of the right to survive on a basis of equality with human beings generally should be delayed until a later stage of its development. To others, however, the "moment" of conception or some stage of development very close to this "moment" is the point at which distinctively human life begins. In their view the difference between the decision not to conceive and the decision to abort is of fundamental determinative importance. Thus the root problem in the controversy over abortion is the one of assigning value to embryonic and fetal life.

The Court concluded that the abortion laws of Louisiana protected the embryo or fetus and that the state had an interest in protecting life before birth. The law was not declared unconstitutional because the Court did "not recognize the asserted right of a woman to choose to destroy the embryo or fetus she carries as being so rooted in the traditions and collective conscience of our people that it must be ranked as 'fundamental.' " In sharp contrast to this ruling, another district court in the 1970 Wisconsin case, *Babbitz v. McCann,* found that "a woman's right to refuse to carry an embryo during the early months of pregnancy may not be invaded by the state without a more compelling public necessity than is reflected in the statute in question. When measured against the claimed 'rights' of an embryo of four months or less, we hold that the mother's right transcends that of such an embryo."

Rights of the Fetus. The opinions in *Rosen* and *Babbitz* set forth the dilemma the courts face: the firmly established "fundamental" rights of privacy and self-determination guaranteed to the woman versus any "compelling" state interest in abridging these rights. The "compelling" state interest refers to protection of the fetus and forms the core of the anti-abortionists' position. Against the cases which assert an individual's right to personal privacy in the area of sexual activity without state interference, the anti-abortionists emphasize a series of court decisions which point to the ascendancy of the rights of the fetus. It is argued that these decisions "help establish the intent of legislatures to give [the fetus] a right to life" (Charles and Alexander, 1971:160), and abortion, except for "the necessary self-defense of the mother," deprives the fetus of its constitutional right to life (Louisell and Noonan, 1970:255–56). In order to determine if the fetus has constitutional rights, "a court must ascertain what the word 'person' means in the Federal Constitution, in which this word is used many times . . . and in the Bill of Rights in the fourth, and the fifth, amendments" (Means, 1971:402). Summarizing the court decisions in favor of the fetus' rights, David Louisell and John Noonan (1970:246) give the case for restrictive abortion laws and suggest that any other solution confronts us with serious legal inconsistencies:

It would be strange if a fetus had rights to support from his parents, rights enforceable by a guardian and sanctioned by the criminal law of neglect, and yet have no right to be protected from an abortion. It would be incongruous that a fetus should be protected by the state from willful harm by a parent when the injury was inflicted indirectly but not when it was inflicted directly. It would be odd if the fetus had property rights which must be respected but could himself be extinguished. The decisions recognize that where a choice must be made between the life of the fetus and the convenience or deep desires of the parent, the law will make the parent subordinate his rights in order to preserve the life in the womb.

The opposition, as exemplified by the ruling on this issue in *People v. Belous,* answers either that "statutes classifying the unborn child as the same as the born child require that the child be born alive for the provisions to apply" or that the statutes "reflect the interest of the parents." The pro-abortionists also argue that no evidence exists that the framers of the original Constitution and Bill of Rights thought of the fetus as a person (Means, 1971:403).

Anti-abortionists' attempts to establish a fetal right to life have been relatively unsuccessful. For instance, the anti-abortionists have succeeded in being appointed as guardians to represent all unborn fetuses, but the courts have ultimately rejected these attempts to establish a fetal right to life. The abortion statutes of two states, Georgia and Connecticut, contain provisions which suggest a fetal right to life. As B. James George explains, the Georgia reform statute "gives the local prosecutor, or anyone who would be a relative of the child if born, the power to seek a declaratory judgment as to whether the abortion would 'violate any constitutional or other legal rights of the fetus' " (*New York Law Journal,* Aug. 23, 1972). In spite of this phrase in the Georgia law, the United States District Court in *Doe v. Bolton* denied a motion to appoint a guardian for the fetus declaring that "the Court does not postulate the existence of a new being with federal constitutional rights at any time during gestation." The phrase in the 1972 Connecticut law that "it is the intent of the Legislature to protect and preserve human life from the moment of conception" did not save the law from being declared unconstitutional.

One possible solution, or at least compromise, of the serious dilemma between the woman's rights and the fetus' rights, is to grant the states the right to exert a compelling interest in the protection of the fetus only after a certain period of gestation. This explains in part why time limits have become an important part of reform and repeal legislation. While this provides a compromise for the courts and the legislatures, it displeases pro- and anti-abortionists alike. Anti-abortionists charge that it places an arbitrary, meaningless date on when a fetus is entitled to its right to life while the pro-abortionists agree about the arbitrary nature of the time limit and claim that "it constitutes an arbitrary limitation on medical practice" and "invites constitutional attack on equal protection grounds" (George, 1972).

Equal Protection. This is an argument used primarily by the pro-abortionists and involves the right to receive proper and lawful medical care. Due to cost, procedural requirements, residency requirements, and differing hospital policies, the same medical services for abortion are not as available to blacks and the poor as to whites and the affluent. This argument does not require that the court assert a woman's right to abortion or a state's interest in regulating abortion, but "expressed as an equal protection right, the interest in receiving an abortion on the same terms as others receive them may more easily be considered 'fundamental' " (Charles and Alexander, 1971:162). The opponents of abortion contend "that not every inequality in fact is denial of equal protection of the law" (Louisell and Noonan, 1970:237). As a district court said in *Doe v. Bolton:* "the mere fact that physicians and psychiatrists are more accessible to rich people than to poor people, making abortions more available to the wealthy than to the indigent, is not in itself a violation of the Equal Protection Clause." The anti-abortionists further argue that if the state permits abortion for any reason other than to save the woman's life, it constitutes a denial of equal protection to one group—the unborn (Louisell and Noonan, 1970:246). To date the courts have been relatively silent on the merits of the equal protection argument.

These few arguments form the basis of most attacks upon the abortion laws, regardless of whether we are dealing with original, reform, or repeal laws, or whether the attacker is pro-abortion or anti-abortion. In addition, the procedural regulation of abortion practices by the medical community has raised other legal problems requiring judicial clarification. The question of the constitutionality of the delegation of authority to medical approval bodies such as hospital abortion committees, and the authority of health departments to decide where abortions may and may not be performed, has arisen. Many statutes provide freedom of conscience exemptions so that doctors, nurses, other hospital employees, or hospitals do not have to participate in abortions, but as legal controls on abortion loosen, questions arise as to whether these individuals or hospitals, especially public hospitals, "can refrain from participation." George (1972) refers to a need to work out "the delicate balancing of the interests of private practitioners and hospitals, women who desire abortions and governmental apparatus . . . through the judicial process." The question of consent also needs clarification. The courts may be called upon to resolve conflicts between husband and wife if the law requires the husband's consent. In the case of unmarried minors, physicians dealing with young women seeking an abortion often find it difficult or impossible to obtain parental consent, and they risk a civil suit if the abortion is performed without parental consent. It has also been suggested that consent could be obtained coercively from the poor by the threat to withhold public benefits if consent to an abortion is not given (George, 1972).

CRIMINAL ABORTIONS

One aim of the liberalized abortion laws has been the elimination of illegal or criminal abortions. With restrictive laws and tight medical control on the one hand and a tremendously high demand for abortion on the other, it was not surprising to find an extensive, flourishing traffic in criminal abortions. Estimates of the number of criminal abortions in the U.S. have ranged up to 1.2 million per year. The change in abortion laws has apparently begun to make a dent upon the number of criminal abortions in some jurisdictions. Harting and Hunter (1971:2101) assume "that the first measurable changes will appear in those jurisdictions that have larger populations and the greatest functional availability of legal abortions." Indirect evidence already points to a reduced number of criminal abortions—abortion-related maternal mortality rates are down, and septic and incomplete abortion rates are down (Stewart and Goldstein, 1971; Overstreet, 1971a; Harting and Hunter, 1971; Health Services Administration,

1972). If the trend toward greater availability of abortions continues, the importance of criminal abortions will diminish still further, and discussions of criminal abortion will have historical rather than contemporary relevance.

Given the "inherent unenforceability of a statute that attempts to prohibit a private practice where all parties concerned desire to avoid the restriction," it is little wonder that there is a substantial discrepancy between the number of criminal (nonhospital and hospital) abortions committed and the number of offenders apprehended and convicted (Williams, 1957:207). The lack of a complainant and therefore the difficulty of obtaining evidence presents the greatest obstacle to enforcement. If evidence is obtained, it comes primarily from abortions resulting in death or hospitalization, from a well-planned raid which coincides with an abortion in progress, or from complaining witnesses (Bates and Zawadzki, 1964:6; Schur, 1965: 36–38). Assuming that enough evidence is gathered, the state may still have to prove that the operation was performed and that it was not medically necessary (Schur, 1965:38). Finally any discussion of the difficulties in enforcing abortion laws must take into account the fact that some practitioners of criminal abortions make payoffs to the police and other officials to ensure their safety (Dr. X, 1962:202; Bates and Zawadzki, 1964:69; Schur, 1965:34–35). In addition, a large part of the estimated $350 million spent each year for criminal abortions ends up in the crime syndicate, and abortion ranks as the "third largest criminal racket in the United States" (Bell, 1971:142).

As this chapter amply documents, criminal (some might prefer illegal or extralegal) abortions also occur in hospitals. The situation with regard to legal interference in hospital abortions reported at the 1958 Arden House conference still holds today: "it is virtually unknown for an abortion performed in a hospital under proper jurisdiction to be questioned" (Lidz, 1958:40). The aura of respect that surrounds physicians and hospitals, as well as the comparative safety of hospital abortions, work to the advantage of those physicians or hospitals that break the laws. Any practice carried out in a hospital receives the approval and acceptance of the community. This community sanction combined with the mutual professional support among medical personnel would present a formidable task to any authority who might question hospital practices or procedures. Regarding abortion, where the laws are somewhat vague and the physician is responding to a widely recognized need, the possibility of a criminal conviction is practically nil.

All of these obstacles to the enforcement of restrictive abortion laws, along with a basic public ambivalence toward abortion, add up to a policy of token enforcement. Any efforts at enforcement focus upon illegal nonhospital abortionists—the police might build up a case against the more notorious offenders or they might conduct raids if pressured for a "clean up." For the most part no action is taken unless a complaint is filed.

In general usage, an "abortionist" means a criminal abortionist and refers to a person who does abortions usually to the exclusion of any other medical practice and usually outside of a hospital. Along with this goes the culturally instilled connotations of an illegal, sordid, back-street operation. From a variety of sources, it is possible to sketch a picture of who these practitioners are, how they operate, and how contact with them is made.

As a result of a survey and interviews, Lader (1966:54) presented a chart of "skilled" abortionists, as of 1964, which covered twenty-nine states and the District of Columbia. Lader (1966:42–51) also interviewed a retired Baltimore abortionist, Dr. G. Loutrell Timanus, and a practicing abortionist, Dr. S. (Dr. Spencer). A 1962 publication, *The Abortionist,* related the experiences of another skilled abortionist. Yet these men and women are probably in the minority since a large number of the people performing illegal nonhospital abortions are by no means as skilled. For instance, Bates and Zawadzki (1964:35) distinguished the following five major types of criminal abortionists based upon an examination of court records:

1) The physician-abortionist; 2) The abortionist with some medical training. This group includes registered and licensed practical nurses, chiropractors, physiotherapists, licensed masseurs, dentists, midwives and so forth; 3) The "quack" doctor. . . . A "quack" doctor is defined as an unlicensed general practitioner of medicine with little or no formal medical training who comports himself in the community as a duly licensed physician; 4) The amateur type. These persons, the records show, enter the abortion field from extremely diverse prior activities. They include salesmen, elevator operators, prostitutes, barbers, and even unskilled la-

borers; and 5) The self-abortionist. While self-abortion is not uncommon both historically and in the contemporary scene, no record could be located of anyone being convicted for this offense at the Court concerned.

Abortionists may operate primarily from one location or they may move around. Drs. Timanus, S. (Spencer), and X, the previously mentioned skilled abortionists, stayed in the same place. Sometimes the abortionist goes to the patient's home or some other place to perform the abortion, perhaps in addition to having a fixed location. An abortion mill and an abortion ring are two kinds of highly organized operations. The abortion mill "might be defined as an abortionist or several abortionists working steadily in a fairly permanent location and aborting a dozen or so women daily," while the abortion ring "may be viewed as a number of interacting abortionists or mills working intermittently at several occasionally changing locations and aborting an even more considerable number of women daily" (Bates and Zawadzki, 1964:51). The mill and ring usually have fairly large staffs (including the abortionists, receptionists, nurses, and perhaps an apprentice abortionist or other employees), are run quite efficiently, and may be very professional in matters of setting, appearance, and manner (Bates and Zawadzki, 1964:51–75; Schur, 1965:31, 34; Ball, 1967:296).

Like any other illegal activity, the communication network surrounding illegal nonhospital (and to a limited extent hospital) abortions is largely by word of mouth. Until the mid-1960s neither the abortionist nor the patient had access to formal channels of communication, but both relied upon physicians, druggists, former patients, taxi drivers, bell hops, and their own acquaintance networks for information (Bates and Zawadzki, 1964:54–55; Lee, 1969). These people may charge for this information, and/or they may be paid by the abortionist for referring someone. In short,

> We can specify some of the factors that are involved in leading some women to competent practitioners and others to incompetent and dangerous ones: an unconflicted desire for abortion, personal qualities of skill and persistence, access to money, and most of all, access to friends who are willing and able to help.
>
> In obtaining illegal abortion, to use the old cliche, it is not what you know but who you know that matters. . . . Competent doctors make their services discreetly available to their middle-class patients, and the

informal networks circulate this information among people similar in background, while poor women find only nonphysicians or self-induced methods available to them. Even two wealthy women of identical background with identical reasons for seeking abortion may find that while one is only temporarily inconvenienced by the unwanted pregnancy, the other must endure a difficult and humiliating search, fear, and despair in being forced to deal with unknown, inconsiderate abortionists, severe pain, and the risk of serious injury or even death. (Lee, 1969:167–68)

LEGAL TRENDS

From 1967 through 1970 twelve states passed reform laws and four states passed repeal laws. It therefore seemed easy to conclude that abortion laws and practices throughout the United States would liberalize rapidly. During 1971, however, not one additional state joined the ranks of those with liberalized laws. And in 1972, while several states became more liberal through judicial or legislative action, Connecticut passed a more restrictive law and New York's repeal law was almost retracted. Several factors contributed to the cooling off in the movement toward liberalization: 1) those supporting reform laws of the Model Penal Code variety realized the inadequacy of these laws; 2) those opposed to any change from restrictive laws became better organized to exert public pressure; 3) the availability of legal abortions in New York relieved some of the pressure for change, while legislatures marked time to observe what happened in Alaska, Hawaii, New York, and Washington; and 4) everyone waited for legal clarification from the U.S. Supreme Court.

The long-awaited decision of the United States Supreme Court was delivered on January 22, 1973. In a sweeping 7 to 2 decision both an original statute (Texas, *Roe v. Wade*) and a reform statute (Georgia, *Doe v. Bolton*) were declared unconstitutional. The Court ruled that a state could not intervene in the abortion decision between a woman and her physician during the first three months of pregnancy. During the second trimester, when abortion is more hazardous, the state's interest in the health of the woman permits the enactment of regulations to protect maternal health, such as statutes specifying where abortions may or may not be performed. Beyond such procedural requirements, however, the decision is still the woman's and her physician's. After the fetus has reached the stage of viability, corresponding to approximately the last three months of pregnancy, the state can exercise an interest in promoting potential human life. It may do so by prohibiting abortion except when it is necessary to preserve the life or health of the mother. Although the Court did not accept the pro-abortionist position that a woman has an absolute right to an abortion, regardless of circumstances, its judgment nevertheless renders all original and reform laws unconstitutional, and makes abortion far more available throughout the United States.

The major ground for the United States Supreme Court's decision, based upon the Fourteenth Amendment's "concept of personal liberty," was the woman's right to privacy, which the Court held "is broad enough to encompass a woman's decision whether or not to terminate her pregnancy" (*Roe v. Wade*). In the face of such a comprehensive decision other constitutional attacks upon restrictive abortion laws become less germane. For example, the Court struck down the residency requirement of the Georgia law (*Doe v. Bolton*), but since the Court's decision makes abortion readily available in all states the residency issue is of limited significance. The Court also struck down Georgia's requirements (see Table 1) for confirming justification from additional physicians and for the approval of a hospital abortion committee as infringing upon the woman's and the physician's rights by placing constitutionally unjustifiable obstacles in their way.

A major consequence of the Court's decision is that it greatly restricts the areas of legal maneuvering left to the contending forces. Not all of the constitutional issues, however, were settled by the Court. And the decision still leaves the states some discretion in abortion legislation for the second and third trimesters of pregnancy. In the few days after the Court's decision a bill was introduced by pro-abortionists to remove the remaining restrictions in New York state, and plans were announced by anti-abortionists to strive for a constitutional amendment that would recognize a fetus' right to life. In view of the deep passions generated by abortion, we can expect a continuation of the controversy, not only in the mass media, but also in the legislatures and the courts.

CHAPTER FOUR

THE MEDICAL ASPECTS OF ABORTION

Many differences of opinion have arisen over what is a justifiable indication (reason) for a therapeutic abortion. Many also believe that even the absence of legal indications, as in the case of repeal laws, does "not nullify the moral need to consider the validity of different 'indications,' or reasons, for abortion; that need is independent of different legal solutions to the abortion problem" (Callahan, 1970:26). The consideration of indications takes into account, in varying degrees, medical judgment and practice, the realities of health care costs and facilities, the legal indications, the personal needs of the patient, and the "moral needs" of the physician, patient, and local community. The medical profession has assumed the major responsibility for considering the validity of different indications, and progress in medical science has led to an ever-widening split between the original laws and medical practice.

MEDICAL PRACTICE AND THE LAW

Although Lister published his revolutionary concept of antiseptic surgery in 1867, it was not until the turn of the century that his techniques were well enough understood and widely enough practiced to be considered a major general advance. After the widespread adoption of Lister's techniques, safe procedures for specific operations, including dilation and curettage, were developed. Continuous refinements in the use of general and local anesthesia and the development of antibiotics to control infection also made surgery significantly safer. At the same time that abortion was becoming a safe procedure, abortions became justified when certain strictly medical conditions endangered the life of the woman, and "the accepted attitude of the physician was that, if a pregnant woman were ill, the thing to do would be to rid her of her pregnancy" (Guttmacher, 1967:13). But today, unlike thirty years ago, therapy and cures exist for many conditions which previously would have meant a serious risk to the life of a pregnant woman, and "it is felt that unless the pregnancy itself intensifies the illness, nothing is accomplished by abortion" (Guttmacher, 1967:13). In other words, the whole notion of the "therapeutic" benefits of abortion has undergone change. Nathan Simon (1971:73) asks "therapeutic for whom?" This could involve the woman, her husband, other children, the physician, or the community, and "what is therapeutic for one could be therapeutic for others but the possibility of the contrary situation also exists." Roy Smith and his associates (1971:540) state that the term "therapeutic abortion" now has no consistent usage, but that the term "had been used to give physicians and patients a means of reconciling the inconsistencies of the law and medical practice."

A broader definition of health and therapy, along with medical advances in controlling many physical diseases, explains why so-called psychiatric indications have increased relative to medical indications. The meaning of "the preservation of life" and the concept of "a healthy person" have expanded. From mere physical and organic survival, we have moved to a consideration of the total human being when we speak of a healthy person. This means that "health and emotional integrity are considered keystones in the arch of life as important as a pulsating heart or a breathing lung" (Guttmacher, 1969:214). Another change is that "an age-old lack of appreciation for psychiatric disease becomes an acute recognition of its prime significance in a modern world" (Trainer, 1965:152). This leads some to the idea that "distinctions between physical and mental health are meaningless" (Ryan, 1967:68). Thus, despite the elimination of traditional reasons for abortion in cases of heart disease, some kidney disorders, tuberculosis, and some neurologic diseases, a woman and physician may still be aware of the difficulty or impossiblity of caring for a child and the attendant threats to the health of a woman. In consequence, new reasons for abortion have arisen.

MEDICAL INDICATIONS

Heart disease (rheumatic, congenital disorders, chronic hypertensive disease). It was long thought that heart diseases in pregnant patients involved a great risk to the life of the patient. Keith Russell, writing in 1953, considered heart disease an important indication for abortion and stated that some clinics reported it as the leading cause of maternal death. He also indicated that at Los Angeles County Hospital one-half of the abortions during the period 1946–1950 were done because of cardiac disease. Today, improved care, better surgical procedures, and advances in anesthesia have greatly decreased the threat to life, and therapeutic abortions due to heart disease are now rare compared to twenty or thirty years ago when heart disease was the leading indication (Guttmacher, 1969:215). Some physicians still accept a severe cardiac disorder as a medical indication. As Alan Guttmacher (1967:18) states: "if the severe cardiac patient cannot avail herself of proper care, or is resistant to undertaking the risk pregnancy implies, abortion is justified." Others believe that heart disease or any other medical condition serious enough to indicate an abortion might indicate sterilization as well. Donald Christian (n.d.:56–57) points out that "permanent sterilization must always receive consideration as an accompanying procedure. If the heart disease or other medical indication is not only chronic and progressive but does not appear to be amenable now or in the foreseeable future to any possible advances in treatment, a sterilization procedure should accompany the abortion or be carried out shortly thereafter." Still others, however, doubt the validity of heart disease as an indication. According to Connor and Aydinel (1970:133), "any patient with heart disease seen early enough to be aborted was seen early enough to be carried successfully through the pregnancy if she would abide by certain rules."

Renal (kidney) disease. Pyelitis (inflammation of the pelvis or kidney) frequently necessitated the termination of pregnancy before the introduction of antibiotics but seldom does today. Niswander (1967:43) and Guttmacher (1967:19) see no need for abortion of a patient with only one kidney if it functions well. Patients afflicted with chronic nephritis (a prolonged and progressive form of kidney inflammation or deterioration) might actually risk a shortening of their lives due to the effects of pregnancy on the disease, and abortion is therefore indicated (Niswander, 1967:42). Guttmacher's opinion (1967:17) is that patients with hypertensive renal disease with evidence of renal impairment would do badly during pregnancy and might be worse after pregnancy. The situation is by no means clear with respect to kidney diseases as an indication for therapeutic abortion, but as with cardiac disorders, the more severe cases or the cases with complications would probably be acceptable.

Pulmonary disease. Pulmonary tuberculosis has also become a less important indication for therapeutic abortion. In former years pregnancy was thought to adversely affect the course of the disease and in some cases to increase the risk of death. In the average case today pregnancy does not affect the course of the disease nor is the course of the disease improved by abortion (Connor and Aydinel, 1970:133). Guttmacher (1967:18) believes that occasionally extensive bronchiectasia or severe emphysema provides an indication for termination of pregnancy.

Diabetes. In the past diabetes also indicated an abortion. The present situation would rarely call for an abortion on a diabetes indication although poor medical control or complications (arteriosclerosis affecting retina, heart, or brain) may be exceptions.

Malignancy. The situation here remains foggy. Guttmacher

(1969:215) lists cancer of the breast, thyroid, or genitals as a relatively common indication for abortion since these are the most likely to be stimulated to grow by the normal chemicals produced by the placenta. Gold et al. (1965:969) found that abortions for malignant neoplasms (abnormal growth) declined only 10 percent from 1951–53 to 1960–62—the second lowest rate of decrease of all indications. New information will no doubt clarify the situation, but in the meantime the effect of pregnancy on neoplastic diseases is unpredictable (Niswander, 1967:45).

Neurologic disease (multiple sclerosis, epilepsy, muscular dystrophy, post poliomyelitis paralysis, various congenital disorders). Kenneth Niswander (1967:43) reported that multiple sclerosis and epilepsy are sometimes made worse by pregnancy (effect unpredictable), but little evidence exists that they actually increase the risk of death during pregnancy. Connor and Aydinel 1970:133) place neurologic disorders in a category of "now uncommon indications."

Miscellaneous (rheumatoid arthritis, hyperthyroidism, lacerated cervix, severe vomiting of pregnancy [hyperemesis gravidarum], varicose veins, essential hypertension with renal involvement). This list covers some conditions that previously indicated therapeutic abortion, but are now fairly well under control, although severe cases *might* still indicate abortion.

Callahan (1970:31) provides a good summary of the present situation with respect to the medical indications for abortion. He reviewed the literature thoroughly and could find only one person arguing that strictly medical indications for abortion were still of importance. "But this is not to say that the issue is totally irrelevant. Since there always remains, as mentioned, the possiblity of unusual medical situations, the issue continues to have some life in the formulating of laws and in posing difficult moral questions. Hence, while one can safely say that medical indications are increasingly nonexistent, one must also cautiously add that they are not necessarily totally nonexistent. Moreover, to be sure, the quality of medical personnel and facilities will make a difference; medical indications could well exist in underdeveloped countries where therapeutic facilities are nonexistent."

Even though physicians may not agree on each particular case or may not agree upon the importance of certain medical indications, all evidence indicates that the "triad of heart, lung and kidney has been replaced in primary importance by psychiatric conditions, potential abnormalities of the fetus and malignancy previous to or concurrent with pregnancy" (Guttmacher, 1967a:10). In the final analysis all medical indications are "relative: relative to the severity of the conditions; relative to the chance that the pregnancy in question will further impair the health or life of the mother; relative to the maternal desire for the given pregnancy; and relative to the psychological impact the patient will experience with interruption of pregnancy. The physician involved in any therapeutic abortion situation must bring the strength of his experience and best professional judgment along with all available medical knowledge to bear in making his decision" (Christian, n.d.:59).

PSYCHIATRIC INDICATIONS

Some of the dilemmas faced by the physician evaluating psychiatric indications for abortion parallel the dilemmas confronted when considering medical indications. A few physicians contend that there are no medical or psychiatric indications for abortion. The reasoning goes something like this: No medical or psychiatric conditions will be *cured* by abortion. Therefore, a pregnant woman with medical or psychiatric complications can be handled in such a way as to bring the pregnancy to term. In case of medical complications "it is possible for almost any patient to be brought through pregnancy alive unless she suffers from a fatal illness such as cancer or leukemia and if so, abortion would be unlikely to prolong, much less save life" (Guttmacher, 1967a:9). This implies excellent medical care and may involve keeping patients in the hospital for six or seven months (Hellman, 1958:95). Similarly, regarding psychiatric indications, it is not claimed that severe psychiatric difficulties do not exist in pregnancy but rather that with "psychotherapy, intensive care, and social and family support" a woman could in all probability carry the pregnancy to term (Callahan, 1970:63).

Most physicians, however, are prepared to accept certain psychiatric indications for abortion. As with medical indications, many clinicians have attempted to set forth guidelines for evaluating psychiatric indications. These evaluations entail several problems which do not occur when looking at medical indications. The most frequent problem seems to be that the psychiatrist is called upon to evaluate a patient he has never seen before and who is determined to have an abortion. Under these circumstances, a tremendous strain may develop between the physician and patient. The psychiatrist feels pressured to evaluate the woman in one or two visits, and the patient wants only to convince the psychiatrist that she needs an abortion. As Alexander Aarons (1967:747) notes, "a psychiatric evaluation based upon an initial interview is tentative and awaits confirmation. To conduct such an interview with a patient who is committed to the ulterior motive of obtaining consent for an abortion is to do so against odds; too much must be left to the opinion and value judgment of the psychiatrist." Leon Marder (1970:1231–32) observes that another complication psychiatrists face is with the "markedly agitated, depressed, suicidal, or . . . borderline psychotic" patient whose symptoms have been alleviated by the promise that they would be referred to a therapeutic abortion committee. These patients do not appear as seriously disturbed as anticipated when referred to the psychiatrist, but "rejection by the evaluator or the committee has immediately reinstituted the previously noted overt, emotional malignant condition and has produced deepening depression with serious and near-fatal suicidal attempts." *

Another major difficulty in psychiatric evaluations involves the lack of knowledge about how a pregnancy (or an abortion) will be affected by a particular condition and how a particular condition will be affected by a pregnancy. The psychiatrist must weigh and contrast the consequences to a woman's mental health of bearing a child or of having an abortion, often based upon a single interview. Added to these particular problems is the more general difficulty that "in an emotional illness, be it neurosis or psychosis, the psychiatrist cannot think in terms of a precise prescription because the number of pertinent conflicting emotional factors that may have a determining influ-

* See Bolter (1962:3131); Aarons (1967:747); Peck (1968); Callahan (1970:62–64); Marder (1970:1230–31); Senay (1970); and Stone (1970:32) for a good overview of the problems of psychiatric evaluations of patients requesting abortions.

ence on the case is not immediately or easily predictable" (Aarons, 1967:747). In practice many feel that the reform laws require "physicians to make judgments that are difficult to make, impossible to prove and of crucial importance to the patient's welfare and the welfare of those dependent on her and intimately involved with her. The burden of responsibility on the psychiatrist and the gynecological surgeon are great, particularly with the time pressure of advancing pregnancy" (Pike, 1969:319).

In spite of the problems inherent in a psychiatric evaluation of a woman requesting abortion, many have tried to enumerate psychiatric grounds for therapeutic abortion.

Suicide. A psychiatrist obviously takes a threat of suicide or an attempted suicide seriously. But with a woman who wants an abortion, suicide may take on a special meaning and present a difficult problem to the psychiatrist. Under a law which forbids abortion except to save the life of the woman, a psychiatrist's opinion that suicide was possible would insure the legality of the abortion. A woman therefore has reason to fabricate or exaggerate suicidal tendencies in order to make the abortion possible. Psychiatrists complain of pressure from gynecologists and pregnant women to endorse an abortion when no legitimate medical grounds can be found. Sidney Bolter (1962:313) claims that the referring physician has already decided the woman should have an abortion and passes her along to the psychiatrist since he "can find no good medical reason for it." *

Studies show a low incidence of suicide among pregnant women which suggests that "not many pregnant women attempt suicide and only a few attempts are successful. Thus, although human happiness and well-being can scarcely be measured by such a coarse statistic, it seems improbable that the risk of successful suicide is sufficient to justify the legal requirement of a hazard to the life of the patient" (Sloane, 1969:1207). This does not mean that threatened or attempted suicide is never a psychiatric indication for abortion. Robert White (1966:551) and Alan Guttmacher (1958:139) suggest that a past history of suicidal attempts or threats or a highly depressed patient threatening suicide might possibly indicate termination of preg-

* See also Taylor and Kolb (1958:139–40) and Murdock (1967) for remarks on this point.

nancy but that each case must be individually assessed. Marder (1970:1232) presents the following "criteria for establishing the severity of suicidal indications:"

1. Slight—a history of previous suicide attempt or if the patient is more than mildly depressed;
2. Moderate—a history of multiple suicide attempts without major improvement in the life situation or demonstrable intrapsychic change or if there is a new stressful situation (unwanted pregnancy);
3. Severe—a history of multiple suicide attempts and a recent major setback or a history of having made a near-fatal suicide attempt and current preoccupation with suicide.

This is an exact quote of Marder's criteria. Although it is an attempt to clarify the situation, it is still highly subjective, and the "ors" in No. 2 make it especially ambiguous. This example of an attempt at clarification that is itself vague is fairly typical.

While attempts to set up criteria for evaluating the validity and severity of suicidal threats continue, some psychiatrists are suggesting that the threat itself might better be viewed as an indication of how desperately a woman wants an abortion. Alan Stone (1970:29, 32) observes that a "useful clinical dichotomy exists between suicidal 'gestures' aimed primarily at manipulating the environment (either consciously or unconsciously) and suicidal behavior based on the conviction that life no longer provides any prospect of gratification. Women requesting abortion rarely fit into the latter, far more serious, category. The real alternative is more often not suicide, but, 'I am desperate. I don't care what happens to me, I have to have an abortion.' The rarity of suicide among pregnant women and the plenitude of criminal abortions would seem to confirm that this clinical constellation is fairly typical." Some physicians are aware that a threat to obtain an illegal abortion can pose a threat to the life or health of a woman. Anderson (1966:82) considers threats to obtain an illegal abortion frequent and more serious than suicidal threats, and Natalie Shainess (1970:20) comments that she has "seen women take desperate suicidal chances to obtain abortion."

Other psychiatric indications. A neat list of psychiatric indications for abortion is impossible. Unlike the literature on medical indications, clinicians do not all use the same diagnostic categories when discussing mental illness. Some clinicians discuss the general factors that should enter into the psychiatrist's evaluation rather than giving specific criteria or dealing with particular conditions. Some give the illness for which a patient could be aborted on psychiatric grounds, but they are not specific about the degree of severity that would indicate an abortion. These variations in approach show why it is impossible to present a set of psychiatric indications; it is possible, however, to give examples of how various psychiatrists have dealt with the dilemma.

One of the earliest attempts to set up criteria came in 1929 when Hart briefly stated the categories of illness that warranted an abortion: "for preexisting psychosis terminate only very rarely; for schizophrenia arising in pregnancy and for recurrent psychosis not related to former pregnancy, no termination; for recurrent psychosis of pregnancy and puerperium, terminate; for severe active anxiety and depressions stemming from pregnancy, termination depends on a question of degree" (quoted in Callahan, 1970:59). Similar categories have been used by later psychiatrists who suggest termination in all of these cases. White (1966:551–52) writes that "the usually accepted criteria are suicidal tendencies, any serious suicide attempt, recurrent psychotic reactions to previous pregnancies, impending psychosis that seems reasonably linked to the occurrence of the pregnancy, and perhaps, the exacerbation of a severe neurosis that seems reasonably linked to the occurrence of the pregnancy." Aarons (1967:750) attends to "considerations of obvious and overt emotional malignancy where *seemingly* there is no doubt about the deleterious and threatening effect of prolonging a pregnancy. Cases in point are psychotic depression, a history of so-called postpartum psychotic reactions, or acute psychotic episodes, whether or not attendant upon pregnancy or childbirth."

In spite of the frequent mention of certain mental illnesses with respect to abortion, most clinicians are reluctant to state that these illnesses always require an abortion; a few clinicians dispute the notion that abortion is indicated for any of these conditions. For example, the literature contains frequent conflicting discussions of mental illnesses related to childbirth: puerperal and postpartum psychosis or psychosis of the puerperium. Anderson (1966:81) rejects puerperal psychosis as an indication for abortion and states that it, "in itself, practically never constitutes an indication for termination." He adds that "the notion of specific 'puerperal psychosis' dies hard and it is difficult often enough to persuade colleagues, as well as the patient and her husband, that this association might have been fortuitous, that the patient might very well go through this pregnancy to term without mishap only to develop a similar illness later, unassociated with childbearing. In any case the patient can be reassured that even if symptoms should develop treatment may be expected to bring about fairly speedy relief" (Anderson, 1966:82). Sloane (1969:1206) takes essentially the same position on puerperal psychosis as Anderson since he emphasizes that the prognosis is good when adequately treated. Anderson's and Sloane's discussions of puerperal psychosis point to an increasingly important position in the writings on psychiatric indications: that there are few psychiatric indications for abortion, and that with proper treatment most pregnancies can be brought to term without impairing the life or mental health of the woman. According to this position, pregnancy becomes the precipitant rather than the cause of most cases of psychosis, and treatment of the illness is indicated rather than termination of the pregnancy (White, 1966:551).

Psychiatrists clearly have several special problems when faced with a request for an abortion, and this is reflected in the controversy about appropriate psychiatric indications for abortion. One problem is the difficulty of determining to what extent pregnancy, childbirth, and childrearing will affect an illness. Second, besides dealing with this purely medical question, the psychiatrist may be confronted with the problem of translating the medical condition into legal terms. Finally, the psychiatrist faces a dilemma of personal conscience and ethics when he meets women who desperately want an abortion, but who do not suffer from what he would interpret as a "real" psychiatric indication. Theodore Lidz (1967:278–79) comments upon the difficulty of writing a law clear and precise enough so that the physician has no doubts about what is legal, but he also underscores the fact that the major difficulty lies with the medical evaluation when he states: "Unrestricted by regulation, the decision to recommend therapeutic abortion for psychiatric reasons would remain just about as difficult as at present."

Jerome Kummer (1955:1318) presents his view of the elements that should enter into the psychiatrist's evaluation and decision:

> Therapeutic interruption would then be considered when the findings give strong reasons to believe that the pregnancy, if permitted to continue, would result in a mental illness of a serious nature. As to what constitutes a serious illness, some of the criteria are: (a) The possibility of the patient's injuring or killing herself; (b) the possibility of her injuring or killing others, particularly the newborn; (c) the problems related to management (hospitalization, restraint, care of the newborn and others in the immediate family, etc.); (d) extremes in anguish as seen in some obsessive-compulsive neuroses; (e) the length and reversibility of the illness, either spontaneously or with treatment; (f) and the effect of the illness on the child through heredity and environment.

Kummer's approach offers more latitude to the psychiatrist than the more traditional indications stated by Hart, White, and Aarons. It would be much easier for a woman who wanted an abortion to meet one of Kummer's criteria.

This brief review of psychiatrists' thinking reveals much discussion but little agreement on what, if indeed anything, constitutes a valid psychiatric indication for abortion. The following quotations clearly point out the present situation: decisions made on psychiatric grounds often reflect the personal beliefs of the psychiatrist more than his medical judgment; data on the relationship between mental illness and pregnancy are lacking; and the formulation of valid psychiatric criteria must await more research.

> It is a wise obstetric practice to insist, in general, that therapeutic sterilization accompany therapeutic abortion for psychiatric indications unless unequivocal and acceptable reasons are presented to contraindicate the sterilization. (Connor and Aydinel, 1970:134)

> The psychiatrist's personality, school of thought, and anxieties concerning humanitarian, social, economic, and religious considerations rather than any definite psychiatric criteria play a definite role in his objections or consent to legal abortion. (Friedman, 1962:254)

> On the one hand there are no unequivocal psychiatric indications for therapeutic abortion. The risk of exacerbation or precipitation of a psy-

chosis is small and unpredictable, and suicide rare. On the other hand, emotional instability is alleviated (for a time) by interruption of the pregnancy. (Sloane, 1969:1209)

The recent wave of "reform" in the abortion area has produced new laws in several states and more generous interpretation of old statutes in other states. What results, in either circumstance, are more abortions based on *psychiatric grounds*. But, a thorough review of the psychiatric literature on the criteria for abortion strongly indicates that there now exist almost no reliable clinical data on which valid psychiatric criteria might be based. In fact, there has to this date been no *controlled psychiatric* study which compares the effects of abortion vs the effects of forced maternity. Without such careful long-term studies, the clinician must rest on his own experience and intuition which, though valuable in this area, are far from infallible. . . . Physicians, it can be shown, demonstrate marked variation in their interpretation of statutory language, and hospitals have vastly differing abortion rates, more often reflecting religious and political policies than solid medical judgment. (Stone, 1970:29)

RAPE AND INCEST

Although these so-called "humanitarian" indications are often enumerated separately in the laws, they are frequently considered psychiatric indications in the medical literature. Referring to rape and incest of girls under sixteen, Anderson (1966:83) notes that "the effects on the development of the girl's personality may be serious, even if these are indirect, such as the disturbance of family relationships, loss of career prospects in a schoolgirl, the responsibility of a child before she is ready for it, and relative social isolation. Even if the child is adopted, the girl may in later years become guilt-ridden at having parted with the child. The situation is even graver in cases of incest." Sloane (1969:1208) is far more tentative about the effects of pregnancy in cases of rape and incest: "The psychological effect of a continued pregnancy resulting from rape or incest does not seem to have been much studied. Most would agree that it is psychologically undesirable." Others discuss the emotional consequences of the rape itself. At a panel on "Rape and Its Consequences," Charles Hayman remarked that "follow-up will get victims to clinics and private physicians for comprehensive evaluation, re-treatment of injuries, and in decreasing frequency of gonorrhea, pregnancy, and syphilis." He continues, however, that "the most important aspect is emotional trauma, which cannot be predicted, since it depends on the female's life history, sexual experience and cultural milieu, and the character of the rape itself, whether a weapon was used as a threat, and whether physical violence and brutality ensued" (Hayman et al., 1972:31).

Speculation abounds on the consequences of rape or incest. Many are concerned and agonize over how to determine the validity of a claim, and the role medical and legal bodies should play in the decision. While debates about how to determine validity continue, it has been pointed out that 1) some physicians do not completely fill out the examination form, thus jeopardizing cases due to lack of "medical corroboration"; 2) some physicians are reluctant to appear in court; 3) the woman, not the rapist, is the one who is often suspect; and 4) rape is one of the most difficult crimes to prove (*National Observer,* Oct. 9, 1971; Paris, 1971; Hayman et al., 1972; Lear, 1972; Williams, 1972). It is hardly surprising that rape is the most underreported crime—"in 1970, 37,270 rapes were reported, and an estimated four or five times that number were committed" (Lear, 1972:11). Debates about determining the validity of rape and incest indications for abortion and whether abortion is the "answer" for women who become pregnant as a result of rape or incest seem rather absurd when one considers the infinitesimal number of abortions performed for rape or incest, and the enormous amount of red tape necessary to obtain an abortion for these humanitarian indications. Lana Phelan and Patricia Maginnis (1969:77), with biting sarcasm, tell us:

> There seems to be an irrational public fear that women will "abuse" the law and claim rape when they need an abortion. As everyone knows, a nice woman will die before she permits a rape. Therefore, a thorough investigation into the moral character of this allegedly "raped" woman is necessary to be sure she is not lying, and also to determine why she is not decently dead.
>
> Let us gently remind the raped woman who must deal with district attorneys and courts: Pregnancy resulting from rape is an emergency to *no one but yourself.* Old and new abortion laws respectfully allot district attorneys any length of time from five days to infinity to establish that rape did indeed occur before allowing the raped female citizen to have a ten-minute D&C.

FETAL INDICATIONS

Like the humanitarian indications of rape and incest, fetal indications are often stated separately in the laws but are sometimes included under psychiatric indications in the medical literature. On fetal abnormality and its psychological consequences for the woman, Sloane (1969:1208) writes that "it seems reasonable, in deciding the advisability of abortion, to weigh not only the statistical risk of malformation but also its emotional effect. What evidence exists indicates that psychoneurotic or unstable women do less well both during and after pregnancy than healthy ones. This suggests that the health of a woman who *seeks* abortion through fear of fetal abnormality is aided by termination of her pregnancy." The problem for the psychiatrist in cases of fetal deformity is much the same as it is in cases of rape and incest and other psychiatric illnesses—more research is needed in order to learn how various emotional states relate to unwanted pregnancies.

More research is also badly needed on fetal deformity. Much of the research has been done relatively recently and the etiology or probability of deformation is not well understood. Harold Goodman (n.d.:45), referring to the 1967 North Carolina law, writes of the physician's difficulties in interpreting a provision for fetal deformity:

> . . . abortion is a felony unless a doctor of medicine can reasonably establish that ". . . there is a substantial risk that the child would be born with grave physical or mental defect. . . ." The law as written clearly places the responsibility of decision on the physician because it does not define what constitutes either "substantial risk" or "grave physical or mental defect."
>
> Further, if the words ". . . the child would be born with . . ." are interpreted literally, only those defects present at birth would be included. The literal interpretation of these last words is at variance with current application of therapeutic abortion and possibly with the intent of the legislators. Many inborn metabolic errors producing grave physical and mental defect, for example, gargoylism and Tay-Sachs disease, are not manifest at birth though the genetic potentialities for these diseases are determined at conception. How far one can extend the words "born with" remains a moot question. For instance, would a pregnant woman with Huntington's chorea be eligible for therapeutic abortion on the basis that there is a 50:50 chance that an unborn would ultimately develop the same disease?

At the present time, there are five general categories under which the usually accepted fetal indications for abortion can be placed.

Infectious agents—protozoa, bacteria, viruses. This refers particularly to the rubella virus, the most common fetal indication. In 1943 "it was firmly established that anomalies occurred in infants whose mothers had rubella during the first trimester of pregnancy, but the actual percentage risk to the infant could not be accurately assessed" (Yow, 1970:107). In 1962 the rubella virus was first isolated which led to the development of amniocentesis to determine the presence of the disease. The difficulty with this test is that the procedure is not carried out until the fourteenth week of pregnancy at the earliest, and it takes an average of an additional thirty days to perform the analysis on the cultured fetal cells. This time factor is also a problem in some of the techniques used to determine maternal infection in that it may take longer than four weeks to obtain evidence of infection.

The rubella epidemic in 1964 and 1965 led to many studies of the effects of the disease and the incidence of malformations. Yow (1970: 109) reports that these studies showed that "when there is maternal infection early in pregnancy there is a high risk of fetal infection," while Goodman (n.d.:50) notes that "more recent prospective and retrospective studies indicate that the risk that a child will have congenital defects resulting from fetal rubella is between 10 and 20%" and that the severity of defects varies greatly. Connor and Aydinel (1970:133) report an overall risk of defect of 20 percent with the greatest risk approaching 60 percent during the first four weeks of pregnancy and falling to about 7 percent at thirteen to sixteen weeks. A rubella vaccine is now available although pregnant women cannot be immunized since the vaccine causes fetal malformations.

In addition to the rubella virus, Martha Yow (1970:107) observes that in the last twenty-five years evidence has accumulated which points to the importance of other viral agents in the production of congenital anomalies. Among these viruses are the cytomegaloviruses and recent evidence suggests that the herpes simplex virus, the virus of the common fever blister, may cause congenital anomalies. The protozoal agent, *Toxoplasma gendii,* causes serious abnormalities in the fetus and is hard to diagnose, but "to date this disease has not been sufficiently prevalent in the United States to result in large numbers of damaged infants" (Yow, 1970:106). The *Treponema pallidum* of syphilis is the most common bacterial agent causing congenital abnormalities, but fortunately it is easily diagnosed, sensitive to therapy, and the child "should not be seriously damaged if early therapy is given" (Yow, 1970:106–7).

Drugs. The thalidomide babies born in the early 1960s to women in Europe and elsewhere brought the category of harmful drugs as a fetal indication to public attention. As Kenneth Niswander points out, this is not the first drug known to cause fetal abnormalities nor will it be the last. "The folic-acid antagonists, employed in the treatment of leukemia, had previously been found to produce severe anomalies because of their metabolic action. Certain other drugs are suspected of teratogenicity, although none is as well established in this regard as thalidomide or the folic-acid antagonists. As the field of developmental pharmacology progresses, however, there seems little doubt that other drugs will be implicated" (Niswander, 1967:46).

Radiation. "It is generally agreed that when radiation is given in therapeutic doses to the mother in the first few months of pregnancy, malformation or death of the fetus may result" (Niswander, 1967:47). Such therapeutic radiation would be given particularly to treat cancer of the cervix, and in these cases spontaneous abortion often occurs. Women may also be exposed to lesser doses of radiation if extensive diagnostic X-ray is used during the early weeks of pregnancy, but "in most instances [this] does not cause fetal malformation. When extensive diagnostic X-ray is used during the earliest weeks of an undiagnosed pregnancy, some physicians recommend therapeutic abortion" (Niswander, 1967:48; Connor and Aydinel, 1970:133). Some evidence exists to suggest that radiation from atomic fallout may become a future risk (Nadler, 1971:94).

Rh Incompatability. Due to Rh antibodies produced by the maternal organism, the fetus becomes anemic (destruction of red blood cells) and may die in utero. This fetal indication, however, is likely to diminish and altogether disappear "given the development of exchange transfusion techniques and the advent of a gamma-globulin injection which forestalls Rh complications from the outset" (Callahan, 1970:92). Rhogam is now being used immediately after delivery or abortion in order to prevent maternal sensitization, but it has no value for a woman who has previously been sensitized.

Hereditary defects causing genetic abnormalities. Of all the fetal indications, the least is known about genetic defects, and "it is not anywhere a commonly employed ground even when legally available" (Callahan, 1970:92). Harold Goodman observes that while fewer abortions are performed for genetic reasons than for rubella the frequency of genetic diseases is far greater than the frequency of rubella and in some genetic disorders the defects are "as severe or more severe than those observed in congenital rubella." The low incidence of abortion in cases of genetic disorders can be explained in part by the greater publicity given to the 1964 rubella epidemic and by the fact that in cases of rubella a single abortion would eliminate the fetal danger thus making the decision to abort easier than in cases of genetic disorders with a "fixed and continuing risk." Further "many genetic disorders are not manifest until subsequent children have already been conceived or born." As techniques for detecting genetic defects are refined and more is learned about medical genetics requests for abortion may increase. Goodman contends, however, that "genetic considerations are unlikely to become a major source of requests for therapeutic abortion in a society which has a widely disseminated knowledge of birth control and which has liberal legislation on sterilization" (Goodman, n.d.: 52, 53).

At the present time tests have been developed "which permit precise identification of the parents at increased risk of having a child with a genetic defect," and amniocentesis is making it possible "to detect a number of significant genetic and birth defects in utero" (Nadler, 1971:95). The refinement of these techniques may make genetic counseling a precise field in which late abortion is a choice for those pregnancies where it is definitely known that the fetus is affected. Medical technology is also advancing in the treatment of birth defects, but many defects still do not have any successful therapy. In consequence, and despite the close scrutiny and testing of drugs before marketing is permitted and the development of new vaccines to control infectious agents, abortion for fetal indications will remain the most feasible alternative for some women.

SOCIOECONOMIC INDICATIONS

The simplest way of classifying abortion indications is in the two categories of medical and nonmedical. All of the indications discussed so far are primarily medical. It is a medical matter to determine how severe a heart condition is, what might precipitate psychosis, or what is the likelihood (in some cases the certainty) of a baby being born abnormal. When factors such as low income, financial insecurity, "too many" children, or a woman's marital status enter the picture, it is no longer a strictly medical matter. These involve social or economic issues.

In Eastern Europe, the USSR, and Japan abortions are legally done solely for social indications, or for "personal reasons" as they are sometimes called. In the Scandinavian countries the laws allow abortions for medical, psychiatric, humanitarian, fetal, and a mixed social and medical indication and

> official comments point out very explicitly that "purely social" indications cannot be accepted . . . according to any of the present Scandinavian laws. The borderlines between medical, sociomedical, and social indications are, however, not clearly defined in the laws but left to the judgment of the deciding physicians and committees. . . . The impossibility, however, of understanding uniformly such vague terms [in the laws] as "serious danger," "particularly difficult," and "potential weakness" in connection with the evaluation of social influences on health has allowed rather wide individual and local variations in interpretation, and also changes from one period of time to another. (Geijerstam, 1970:316–17)

Except for the 1969 Oregon law, no U.S. statute has established this mixed social and medical indication. Either the law allows medical indications only (original laws), provides for medical, psychiatric, humanitarian, or eugenic indications as in the case of the Model Penal Code (reform) laws, or eliminates indications from the law altogether as in the case of the repeal laws. In this last case, of course, abortions can be done for purely social reasons. The relative absence of social or mixed social and medical indications in the law does not mean, however, that U.S. physicians have not taken social factors into consideration. The medical literature frequently mentions the influence of social factors on an abortion decision even though the abortion must be officially justified for a different reason. For example, after discussing psychiatric indications for abortion, Rosen (1967:86–87) states that the indications he mentioned "are the ones stressed on certificates forwarded by physicians to hospital abortion boards. Nevertheless, in most cases these are mere rationalizations. The medical, including the psychiatric, indications must be utilized if the abortion is to have legal justification. However, in most cases, the socioeconomic factors are pronounced; and whether the interruption of the pregnancy is legal or extra-legal the actual indications are, for the most part, socioeconomic."

The medical profession increasingly realizes the importance of taking social factors into account in all medical judgments. This philosophy, along with the knowledge that most abortions are desired for social reasons, has contributed toward the movement for the repeal of abortion laws. With repeal each woman makes the abortion decision for herself, and physicians do not need to split medical and social hairs. Ruth Roemer (1967:1914) writes that a virtually uncontroverted premise today is that "it is impossible to separate social factors from physical and mental health. Substandard housing, living on the edge of poverty in crowded conditions, the support and care of many children affect health no less importantly than physical or mental conditions." Fox adds that "if there is one lesson to be learned from fifty years' research it is that social and mental health are inseparable" (quoted in Roemer, 1967:1914). Questions arise from inside and outside the medical community as to a physician's competence and willingness to assess the social considerations in abortion cases. If such considerations become necessary due to legislative changes that introduce social or sociomedical indications for abortion, some ancillary profession might share the task. More likely, however, social factors will continue to be taken into account informally. This will be done by the woman in states where the abortion laws are repealed and by physicians in states which pass reform laws.

ABORTION TECHNIQUES

A wide variety of largely ineffective and sometimes dangerous techniques have been used to try to induce abortion. Ergot, knitting needles, quinine, chopsticks, lye, starvation, papyrus, magic, and hard work have all been tried. A Kgatla woman takes a drug after coitus to expel the semen. A woman of the Loyalty Islands might drink boiled seawater to abort. The Romans inserted papyrus into the cervix (Devereux, 1967). Some women ask a druggist for "something to bring my period down" and receive a catheter, quinine, and penicillin. The lore about abortion methods is ancient, extensive, and often horrifying. George Devereux (1967:123–33) distinguishes sixteen categories of techniques in his study of abortion in 350 primitive, ancient, and preindustrial societies. Some of these categories are applicable to techniques still used in the United States.*

Effort and Jolts. Effort includes the lifting of heavy objects, climbing, and hard work; jolts would result from such activities as jumping up and down several times, jumping from high objects, and horseback riding.

Mechanical. This refers to any method which attempts to damage the fetus through the abdominal wall. Weight placed on the belly, or squeezing, massaging, rubbing, pinching, or twisting the belly would be examples of abortion attempts by a mechanical method. Mechanical methods as well as effort and jolts can cause injury to the mother or fetus, but they rarely cause abortion.

Instrumentation. Inserting an instrument into the uterus is quite common, and a variety of implements have been used including coat hangers, knitting needles, pens, artist's paintbrushes, curtain rods, and telephone wires. This method involves the danger of perforation (bursting) of the uterus and bladder and subsequent death from infection or hemorrhage.

Inserting foreign bodies and leaving them in place. Packing the opening of the cervix with gauze and leaving it in place causes the cervix to dilate and either a curettage can then be performed or the fetus is expelled through a spontaneous labor-like process. Similarly, a rubber catheter inserted as far as possible and left in place causes the cervix to dilate and the fetus to be expelled. Along with these techniques goes a high risk of infection, hemorrhage, or perforation of the uterus.

* Devereux (1967:123–33) was especially useful in classifying the many methods of abortion. Also useful were Bates and Zawadzki (1964); Schur (1965:28–29); and the *Fifth Estate,* September 13–16, 1970, p. 15.

Fluids inserted into the uterus and injections into the uterine wall. Boiling water and soap suds, potassium permanganate, Lysol, alcohol, lye, and pine oil are a few of the preparations women insert into the uterus. They can result in severe burning of the tissue, hemorrhage, shock, and death. Ergot, pitocin, and sodium pentothal have been known to be injected into the uterine wall but are poisonous and overdoses can result in death.

Drugs taken orally. Drugs taken to produce abortion are of infinite variety. If taken in large enough doses to induce an abortion these drugs can cause damage or death to the woman. For example, an overdose of ergot compounds is poisonous and can result in fatal kidney damage, and quinine sulphate can cause deformities in the fetus or death to the woman. Estrogen and castor oil are simply useless. Other drugs or preparations commonly taken include calomel, herbs, lead salts, pennyroyal, oil of wintergreen, kerosene, and a variety of strong purgatives and irritants. The use of drugs to produce abortion is widespread, and Bates and Zawadzki (1964:80) quote an advertisement appearing in a "Hollywood" or "confession" type magazine which offers a doctor's prescription to bring prompt relief from a delayed period. Women who fear an unwanted pregnancy but whose periods are delayed due to psychosomatic or physical reasons take these drugs with "success" and the folklore that these drugs are effective is perpetuated (Bates and Zawadzki, 1964:81).

The above methods are used for illegal abortions performed by nonmedical personnel and for self-induced abortions. Four other methods of abortion are medically accepted procedures used by physicians doing hospital or clinic abortions. This does not mean, however, that these procedures are not also used for illegal abortions. A fifth technique is gaining in popularity although it is not accepted by all physicians. One final method of abortion is still in the early stages of research.

Dilation and curettage (*D. and C.*). This was the most popular and familiar technique in the United States until recent years, and it is still in use for the early termination of pregnancy. "The opening of the cervix, or lower portion of the uterus, is dilated with a series of instruments in graduated sizes to allow the insertion of a curette, or scraping instrument, into the uterus. The pregnancy is then scraped from the uterine wall. . . . It can be done under a local anesthetic, which is injected alongside the cervix" (Greenhouse, 1970a:26).

Suction curettage (*vacuum aspiration*). This technique for terminating pregnancies came to the United States from the People's Republic of China and the USSR (Novak, 1970:74–75). Although it was not introduced in the United States until 1966, it has now become "the procedure of choice for early termination in hospitals and clinics doing large numbers of abortions" (Harting and Hunter, 1971:2094). Using this method, "the cervix is dilated as in a D. and C., and then the uterus is evacuated by means of vacuum suction machine. . . . Like a D. and C., suction can be performed under local anesthesia" (Greenhouse, 1970a:26). The suction method, compared with D. and C., reduces the risk of perforation, reduces blood loss, and lessens trauma (Novak, 1970:77–78).

Hysterotomy. This method is used for pregnancies during the twelve-to-sixteen-week period "or in pregnancies of lesser or greater duration when a concomitant tubal sterilization is planned which accounts for many more than half of the hysterotomies" (A. Guttmacher, personal communication). A hysterotomy is "actually a Caesarian operation in which the uterus is opened from above and the fetus removed," and usually the woman needs to spend several days in the hospital (Greenhouse, 1970a:26).

Salting out (*saline induction*). This technique is used after sixteen weeks and has largely replaced hysterotomy. The Medical Committee of the National Association for Repeal of Abortion Laws states that hysterotomy is "more dangerous and subject to more complications than saline induction" with the result that physicians are telling patients twelve to sixteen weeks pregnant to wait until after sixteen weeks for the safer salting out technique. "In this procedure, a hypodermic needle is inserted through the abdomen and uterine wall into the amniotic sac, which contains the amniotic fluid and the fetus. About 200 cc. of amniotic fluid are removed, and are replaced by no more than that amount of a 20 percent saline solution. The saline solution kills the fetus and induces labor. Labor begins from 12 to 36 hours after the injection, and the woman expels the fetus in a normal delivery" (Greenhouse, 1970a:26). Salting out is done under local anesthesia, and sometimes women go home and return to the hospital when labor begins.

Menstrual extraction or regulation. Women's liberation groups and some physicians accept menstrual extraction or regulation as the newest, safest, least expensive method for early abortion. A woman usually has to wait at least ten days after a missed menstrual period before a pregnancy test can be given. Instead of waiting until the pregnancy test can be given, a woman goes to a physician's office for a menstrual extraction. A Karman cannula, invented by Harvey Karman of Los Angeles, has made this procedure safe according to advocates of the procedure. The Karman cannula is a thin, flexible plastic tube which bends under pressure and thereby reduces the incidence of perforation and makes it easier to abort women who have never given birth. *Newsweek* (July 24, 1972, p. 69) describes menstrual extraction using a Karman cannula: "Because the tube is only 4 millimeters in diameter, it can easily be inserted into the hard, undilated cervix that is characteristic of the very early weeks of pregnancy. Attached to the tube is a small syringe that is used to suck out the contents of the uterus, including the fertilized egg" if it is present. Critics of the procedure claim that it is not safe, but this remains to be proven. The obvious question arises as to whether this procedure falls under a state's abortion laws since the menstrual extraction is performed without evidence that the woman is pregnant.

Experimental drugs. One group of drugs merits special attention —the prostaglandins. Early research on the prostaglandins holds open the promise of developing a safe, effective, simple abortion inducing drug that might be taken orally, administered intravenously or by local application to the vagina or uterus. During 1971 several countries, including the United States, initiated clinical trials on the prostaglandins (Bergström et al., 1972:1280). Even if the prostaglandins prove unsatisfactory, other effective drugs may be developed. It will no doubt be several years before an abortion pill or shot or uterine insert is widely available, but this method of abortion may eventually replace other methods mentioned above as the medically accepted technique of abortion.*

* See the *New York Times,* January 28, 1970, p. 26-C and September 20,

NEW ROLES, CHANGING ROLES

Euthanasia and abortion are receiving more and more attention in the medical literature. As has been pointed out time and again by anti-abortionists, lay and medical, these practices violate the basic tenet of medical ethics and practice—the preservation of life. The performance of an abortion, by definition, confronts the medical profession with a basic dilemma. Pro-abortionists point to a physician's responsibility to preserve and protect a woman's life against incompetent abortionists and suggest that physicians need to rethink just what preserving and protecting life means. With several different kinds of abortion laws in the United States and an increasing demand for and incidence of abortion, today's physician belongs to "a generation in transition." Russell and Jackson wrote an article on physicians' experiences with the California reform law, and Keith Russell concluded on a very personal note.

> I have often wakened in the middle of the night wondering how I became so involved in a problem that is basically distasteful and disturbing —the interruption of pregnancy. And, at the same time, I have had the visions of the many daughters and wives of colleagues and patients who have subjected themselves to the most inferior medical care because we had nothing better to offer them than platitudes and high-sounding phrases. And my disturbance is eased a bit in the certain knowledge that here is a challenge and a problem upon which none of us as physicians can turn his back, and from which none of us can walk away. Society expects far more from us, as those special practitioners of obstetrics and gynecology. (Russell and Jackson, 1969:765).

Physicians in general, and obstetricians and gynecologists and psychiatrists in particular, play a special role in abortion decisions. Some prefer their position under the original laws which now provide few reasons for doing an abortion since medical skills can bring almost any woman through a pregnancy without threat to her life. Others dislike these restrictive laws because they interfere with a physician's best judgment about when an abortion is indicated. Still others resent medical practices that take place under the original

1970, p. 30; Engström (1970); Segal (1970); Speidel and Ravenholt (1971); and Bergström et al. (1972) for accounts of the research and clinical efforts with drugs.

laws—physicians disregard the law or disregard women pleading for an abortion, psychiatrists are manipulated by patients and colleagues, and women with money and connections obtain access to abortion facilities that are unavailable to other women.

Some physicians' dilemma is solved by the reform laws based upon the American Law Institute's Model Penal Code. These laws sanction and extend what has been practiced for years, and the physician can feel secure that what he does is legal. Further, the committee, board, or consultation approval system divides responsibility for decision-making about abortions and relieves the physician from the burden of individual responsibility. Other physicians, however, find the reform laws abominable. Vague provisions are impossible to interpret, the laws are unevenly applied, and the approval systems encumber medical decisions with bureaucratic red tape. Some find the reform laws equally intolerable because too many abortions are done for pseudo-psychiatric reasons, and they resent this as an evasion of the law.

Many physicians are dissatisfied with the original and reform laws and wish to see the laws repealed. Once the law is repealed, the physician's role in decisions about who receives an abortion is very substantially changed. Rather than playing the paramount role in decision-making, the physician plays a secondary role. It is therefore important to examine what "repeal" means, and what implications it has for the role of the physician. Sanford Meyerowitz and John Romano (1969:261) speak of proposals to repeal all restrictive laws "so that the question of abortion can be resolved between a patient and her physician as are other medical decisions." They continue that "although . . . liberal reforms appear to be minor concessions compared to the repeal of all restrictions, there may be little difference in practice. The most liberal interpretation of the new laws, however, will hopefully stop short of 'abortion on demand' in one major way: the important obligation of the physician to look beyond the face value of the demand." The authors mean that there are "complex factors motivating requests for abortion," and in some cases women may have mixed feelings about the pregnancy which can be resolved with a physician's help. A woman may be pressured by others to have the abortion, or "a strong disinclination to carry the child may prove to be a manifestation of psychotic thinking." The important obligation of physicians is to study these complex facts and attitudes so that "informed and appropriate decisions in the study and care of their patients" can be made. In other words, even when abortion is presumably available on demand, these clinicians argue that the physician still has the role, indeed the obligation, of having a say in who does and does not receive an abortion.

Physicians accede to patients' requests for cosmetic surgery or other types of elective surgery without any problem, but some of them appear to balk when responding to a request for an abortion. Part of the problem stems from the controversy about taking a life, and part of the problem stems from the drastic role change the physician faces when he switches from playing God (Augenstein, 1969) to playing second fiddle to his patient. Perhaps with time to adapt to the new role will come less concern about being labeled an abortionist and less of a tendency to further stigmatize the abortionist with the label of technician. Participants at the 1968 international conference on abortion wrestled with what it means to say the abortion decision should be between physician and patient and with the question of the physician as technician:

GUTTMACHER: I am a little bit confused, and I think Dr. Fletcher can help me. I believe that he thinks abortion should be purely a matter between the patient and the physician. And what kind of judgment is the physician to make? What are you endowing us with to make the wise decision? We are not religionists. Most of us are not psychiatrists. We are not social workers. We're just plain doctors. And on what basis are we going to say to a woman, "Yes, you should" or "No, you shouldn't have an abortion," if this is going to be a decision between an individual and her physician?

FLETCHER: Professional servants are educated guessers, and many of the problems of human decision-making are more or less problematic. Presumably a gynecologist or obstetrician who had no awareness of or sensitivity about the social and psychological dimensions of his patients' lives and problems, and focused simply upon the physiology of his patients could not make, in my opinion, a very mature decision with respect to whether to terminate a pregnancy or not.

I would say that abortion should be available to patients if there is no medical contraindication. But, you see, I am quick to add there might be situations you know of in which that generally sound and valid proposition ought not, in fact, to be followed in a given case. And I don't see how it is possible to tie the creative freedom and technical discretion of any professional servant down any more fully than just that. If behind your question, there is some wondering whether we can't establish some prefabricated criteria for when and when not, I would say that you know that's not only probably an unrealizable hope, but potentially quite disastrous.

MOORE: Dr. Guttmacher, I would hope that if the day were to come when this was simply a matter between a woman and her physician that he would neither be in a position to say "Yes, you may" or "No, you may not," nor be in a position to say "Yes, you should" or "No, you should not." He should be there in his role as a physician to tell her about possible medical contraindications.

GUTTMACHER: I was thinking this through when Dr. Fletcher was talking about medical contraindications. There is *no* woman we can't abort, so this idea that a certain proportion of patients cannot be aborted is not a medical concept. So it is not a matter of "Can you?" It is a matter of "Should you?" I don't have difficulty understanding the "can," but I have difficulty understanding the "should."

MOORE: I would hope that it never would be interpreted that it was the physician's role to say, after the consultation, "Yes, I think you should," or "No, I think you shouldn't." I would hope that he would view his role as helping the woman to see what the alternatives are, medically and socially, to make sure that an abortion is what she really wants.

HARDIN: I have a feeling we have a conflict between sovereignties. Miss Moore is asserting the sovereignty of a woman to get what she wants, and aren't you, Dr. Guttmacher, asserting the sovereignty of physicians to refuse to perform their offices?

MOORE: Refusing responsibility is all that you men are saying. This is a decision to be made between the patient and the doctor.

GUTTMACHER: Then, if a woman says that she wants to be aborted and we can't persuade her from this course, then we simply act as a rubber stamp and do it. That's a simple problem.

HARDIN: Then my question is: Would you be willing to accept the role of rubber stamp or do you rebel at that?

GUTTMACHER: I would be unhappy.

HARDIN: Yes, you would be unhappy, and this may be a significant thing. And how can we keep the doctors happy and give the women what they want?

R. HALL: We are talking about two ends of a spectrum really. At one end, people have said that there must be medical indications for abortion, and now we are talking about medical contraindications. There are virtually no medical indications for abortion and there are virtually no medical contraindications against abortion. So, really, you can forget those two extremes and focus on all the areas between them.

I would place the doctor in the role of a technician, simply wielding the curette, but not solely at the insistence of the patient. She should receive some guidance, not necessarily from a doctor, but perhaps from some agency such as the Mothers' Aid Centers they have in Denmark. Through such an agency she could be led to explore the alternatives to abortion—such as getting married and having the child. Then if she still wants the abortion she should have it. When it comes to the doctor, I think he is eventually going to be no more than a technician. This may be humiliating to him. But it is his unavoidable plight if we are to grant women their inherent right to abortion.

SHUR: I wonder whether Miss Moore then would approve a policy under which doctors would be compelled to abort those who had thought through their problems and decided they should have an abortion—but where the doctor considers, on conscientious grounds, that such an abortion would be inadvisable. It seems to me this potentially and theoretically could be the situation into which we would be pushed if this were carried to extremes.

MOORE: I feel that it is difficult to compel anyone to do something that is against his conscience. It is just as wrong to compel the physician to perform an abortion if he feels it is against his moral feelings as it is to compel the woman to complete the pregnancy.

I don't know what you would do in a town where the physicians all felt that way. I hope the woman would be assisted by some societally arranged structure to find what she needed somewhere else. (Hall, 1970:II, 107–10)

When the abortion laws do not restrict abortions to certain justifiable indications, as is the case in the repeal states, abortion becomes available at the request of the woman. To say that these laws make the abortion decision a private matter between an individual and her physician misses the mark. The original laws and the reform laws leave the final decision to physicians, but the repeal laws leave the final decision to the woman. In practice, of course, the physician may be influential in the decision-making process, and he does have the right to refuse to do abortions—in that sense, perhaps, the abortion decision involves the woman and her physician. If we accept the premise that there are virtually no medical indications for or contraindications to abortion, the physician's role could be to help the woman explore her reasons for abortion and alternatives to abortion. But as Guttmacher pointed out, physicians are not religionists, psychiatrists, or social workers, and Hall sees guidance coming from some other agency. The physician is then left with the role of technician—to use his skill in performing the abortion on a woman who has decided that she wants one.

The physician's role can be performed with satisfaction or dissatisfaction, depending upon whether he prides himself in his skill or deplores his loss of decision-making power. Paradoxically some physicians who complained about the agony of decision-making under original or reform laws seem to miss the ecstasy of decision-making once they lose it under repeal laws. The loss of status in being called an "abortionist" goes right along with the contempt for the role of technician. The Walker and Hulka (1971:444) survey of North Carolina physicians indicated that one "broad category of attitudes" concerned the fear of losing the respect of colleagues and patients if they did too many abortions and gained the reputation of being an abortionist. The authors quote a response from a private obstetrician: "A private practitioner in a solo practice has to be extremely careful about performing a therapeutic abortion for the so-called emotional reasons for fear of becoming subjected to the loss of the respect of fellow physicians and patients" (quoted in Walker and Hulka, 1971:444).

Edmund Overstreet predicted that "in the next few years it seems certain that legal abortions will become by far the most common gynecological operation in the United States" (quoted in Phillips, 1970:62). Some are concerned about a possible loss of status for obstetrics and gynecology and fear that this prevalence of abortion will make obstetrics and gynecology a less desirable specialty. In order to relieve the pressure on physicians, especially obstetricians, proposals have been made to train nonphysicians to do early abortions, to require residents and interns in teaching hospitals to do a certain number of abortions, to spread abortion cases out among other specialties, and to get a higher percentage of obstetricians to perform some abortions as part of their regular practice (Roemer, 1971:506; Hall, 1971:519). Although each of these suggestions seems reasonable, they can generate a great deal of resistance. The training of nonphysicians for early, low-risk abortions could relieve much of the physicians' load, but the suggestion is fraught with difficulty. Physicians object overtly because it may subject patients to greater risk, and they object covertly because it impinges upon their territory. It would lower the status of those physicians who continue to do abortions because nonphysician technicians were also doing abortions. And it would raise the question of whether nonphysicians were being trained to carry out abortions on the medically indigent while physicians were being reserved for private patients.

The search for a place to obtain an abortion can be trying for a woman and profitable for an entrepreneur. Before the mid-1960s information on where to obtain an abortion depended on a woman's social contacts, perseverance, resources, and luck. Gradually nonprofit groups such as the Clergyman's Consultation Service, women's groups, and Planned Parenthood offices began to provide information on how to go about getting a medically safe abortion, either legal or illegal. Profit-making referral agencies were also established in various cities in the United States in order to sell packaged abortion trips to other countries where abortions could be obtained. After the New York repeal law these referral agencies mushroomed, some put up billboards to advertise their services, and some charged fees of $50 and $100 simply to give the address of a clinic or physician. Some states, notably New York, outlawed commercial referral agencies, but they continue to flourish in other areas. The need for an extensive public or nonprofit referral system has become glaringly obvious. If, for example, physicians are not going to be compelled to do abortions against their consciences but women are going to be entitled to have an abortion, "some societally arranged structure" for women to find a willing physician, as Emily Moore stated, must be available. A central clearinghouse for abortion appointments could be run by a health department, as is done in New York City for low-income residents (Daily, 1971). Commerical referral agencies which exploit women will continue to thrive until a referral system run by health departments or nonprofit organizations can handle abortion requests.

The decision to undergo an abortion can also be trying, and a new role of abortion counselor is developing to help women who contemplate or have an abortion. The trend toward some form of counseling is a strong one, and the counselor can deal with information and feelings in a variety of areas: subsequent contraceptive use; alternatives to abortion; the reasons for having an abortion; the medical procedures of abortion; and the spiritual and mental well-being of the woman. It is striking that the proposals and programs for abortion counseling do not include the obstetrician or whoever actually performs the abortion. Few can agree on the selection and training of abortion counselors, but the skills needed range from an ability to provide relatively simple information and referral to an ability to help women "for whom pregnancy creates a real life crisis and great ambivalence of feeling" (Harting and Hunter, 1971:2098).

In instances where the pregnancy involves a psychological crisis for the woman or where the abortion situation turns up unrelated problems of mental illness, psychiatrists see themselves as the proper counselors or therapists. Psychiatrists perhaps have a special claim upon the role of abortion therapist under repeal laws (where the woman has the final decision) because they have often borne the brunt of breaching the restrictions of the original and reform laws. They resent the roles they have played "as social decision-makers with respect to abortions" (Pfeiffer, 1970:405), with "no clear moral sanction from society or from [their] professional reference group" (Senay, 1970:408).

Edward Senay also writes that if "the clinician satisfies himself that these [abortion] patients are in a significant psychological crisis, then his role is clarified," and in this role the "psychiatrist functions as a screening and treating person." As Senay explains it, the role derives from the premise that from a psychological point of view indications and contraindications for abortion do exist, and crisis intervention identifies women where abortion is contraindicated, averts abortion, begins treatment, and concludes "in a marriage now stronger for having learned from the crisis rather than becoming weakened by guilt and anger" (Senay, 1970:409, 412–13).

Another psychiatrist believes that abortion may be the best alternative for some to an unwanted pregnancy, but "it is almost never a complete solution to the woman's problem" (Pike, 1969:320). Pike continues that "the underlying psychological problems that have either been involved in her allowing herself to become pregnant, or at least have caused her to be unable to adjust to it, must be treated," and therefore she believes that "by working with the woman in group therapy on a crisis basis for the two weeks before, during and following the abortion, we might guide more of them to continuing therapy. With such a program we might avoid the tragedy of subsequent unwanted pregnancies."

Lydia Rapoport and Leah Potts (1971:254), however, caution against assuming that a woman with an unwanted pregnancy is in a crisis state. They observe that "a closer scrutiny of actual events, with the question posed as to who is actually in a state of crisis, often yielded the proposition that the crisis existed in the family, the community, and even on the part of the professional caretakers." The tremendous concern over counseling women about abortion often shows a mixture of concern for the woman and ambivalence among professionals about their attitudes toward abortion and their role in providing abortion services.

As an example, referring to the Governor's Commission in New York State, Fisher (1970:110) said that "we felt that after the woman had done a great deal of soul-searching and decided that [an abortion] is what she wanted, that before it be committed, we would tell her to take some type of spiritual guidance first, rather than just leave it up to her and the doctor." As another example, one of the District of Columbia's proposed standards to regulate abortion was that each patient be given pre- and post-abortion counseling. A representative of the Metropolitan Washington chapter of the National Association of Social Workers objected on the grounds that counseling should be given by people with "masters degrees in social work and a year of field experience in family life problems" and not just by someone with a degree in social sciences as the regulations suggested. She was quoted as saying that abortion counseling in clinics "is not up to professional standards" with one result being that "we're getting many, many women back for two and three abortions" (*Washington Post,* Feb. 11, 1972 and Feb. 16, 1972). For many the measure of successful abortion counseling is that the counseled women become effective contraceptors. From this perspective "abortion is viewed as, at best, a failure of contraception or, at worst, a failure of the healing and teaching professions to educate Americans effectively about contraception, and of society to make birth control services readily available to all who want them" (Dauber et al., 1972:23).

It is likely that various paraprofessionals as well as professionals —psychiatrists, social workers, nurses, clergymen—will become involved in abortion counseling, with each group establishing its own area of expertise, its own ideology of why and when counseling is needed, and its own criteria of successful counseling. Although some of the overemphasis upon the need for counseling stems from an exaggerated view of the psychological trauma produced by an abortion, abortion counseling can be extremely helpful to some women:

> [The counselor] made sure to be around when she knew I needed to talk —made sure I knew the exact procedures involved—talked about how other women react to their abortions. I thought I was overreacting and couldn't understand the mental pain I felt. We talked about it—I was amazed and relieved to find it is pretty normal to be afraid and sad. Once I realized that—well it all worked out. I kind of learned not to be afraid of being afraid. I would have been completely bewildered without that kind of help. (quoted in Dauber et al., 1972:27)

Abortion services need to be administered and coordinated, and public health professionals are most actively involved in this role. These professionals, through state and local health departments, are apt to play a growing role in the organization, delivery, administration, and surveillance of abortion services. Public health professionals are also working to standardize the collection of data. From the Center for Disease Control in Atlanta, James Kahn and his associates (1971:423) report that their data gathering went from "a modest enterprise of hospital sampling to a program that at present includes reports from health departments in all States where abortion is legal." A sense of urgency pervades many data gathering projects so that practitioners and health planners can deliver safe, inexpensive, and humane abortion services. For example, while abortion bills were being considered by the legislature, the Michigan Department of Public Health and the University of Michigan Center for Population Planning held a conference to plan abortion facilities (Harting and Hunter, 1971:2098).

The changing abortion situation in the United States is bringing about new roles and changing roles. Although the medical literature on abortion focuses principally upon the problems of patients, or how the health professionals view the patients' problems, some are emphasizing the need to counsel "hospital personnel" or "staff," principally nurses. Caring for large numbers of abortion patients can precipitate a "crisis" among the nursing staff, threaten their professional identities, and affect the quality of care given to abortion patients (Felton and Smith, 1972; Kibel, 1972). Physicians face these same problems. Role changes are far from over, both with regard to abortion services and health services generally, while the implications of these changes are just beginning to be recognized by health personnel.

CHAPTER FIVE

PSYCHOLOGICAL AFTEREFFECTS AND PARTISAN PSYCHIATRY

Does the abortion experience do physical or psychological harm to a woman? The incidence of physical and psychological aftereffects is a major subject for dispute. Those who advocate restrictive laws often argue that abortion is a harmful procedure and that the laws must protect women against such harm. Those who advocate permissive laws often argue that abortion is beneficial to the woman who wants it and that in any case the laws should not interfere with what is a medical issue. Both sides cite "facts" about the aftereffects of abortion to support their positions, but these facts and the studies they come from are seldom examined critically. An anti-abortion climate has prevailed in the United States for a very long time, and it is only in recent years that it has begun to give way to a pro-abortion climate. The meeting of these two climatic conditions still produces a great deal of turbulent weather. Psychiatrists, in particular, are often caught up in the eye of the storm, and they may be forced into the role of "dispensator from the law" (Levene and Rigney, 1970) or "bootlegger of humanistic values" (Szasz, 1962).

THE ANTI-ABORTION CLIMATE AND ADVERSE REACTIONS

Even though attitudes toward abortion are changing, the anti-abortion sentiments still exert considerable pressure. They are seen in moral and legal codes that prohibit abortion, in punitive attitudes of physicians and other medical personnel, and in the way a woman's social role is viewed by herself and others.

The general cultural prohibition against abortion stems from Judaic-Christian teachings which were eventually carried over into statute law. The original U.S. abortion laws thus "express a responsibility ethic which lies very deep in the psychosocial structure of our society. They say, in effect, that individuals are and must be responsible for the consequences of their acts; that whether or not they are, they ought to be" (Cooke et al., 1968:60–61). As Stephen Fleck (1970:45) puts it, "to be pregnant and not to want to become a mother is contrary to Western ethics, i.e., an event that is supposed to be a blessing is resented." These cultural attitudes have a pervasive influence throughout society, and they are therefore apt to influence the way a woman reacts to an abortion. The degree to which she is influenced will of course be largely determined by the degree to which she upholds these cultural attitudes (Dietz, 1970:16). Another factor to consider is that for some women abortion still involves breaking the law, and "they inwardly respect the law they transgress, and they suffer from this transgression, they suffer still more from having to find accomplices" (de Beauvoir, 1949:461). Nancy Lee (1969:106) points out that "many women reported that they had been far more depressed before the abortion was performed, during the period of making the decision and searching for an abortionist, than they were afterward," a major reason being the "involvement in an illegal activity."

Many feel that the psychological aftereffects of hospital or therapeutic abortions are apt to be very different from those of abortions done illegally under medically and emotionally inadequate circumstances. Laidlaw (1958:132) compares the "trauma connected with a cold and frightening commercial atmosphere" of an illegal abortion and the "long-lasting deleterious results" this can have to "the therapeutic atmosphere of a hospital" where "the results are entirely different."

Yet in spite of the general feeling that a hospital abortion leads to fewer ill effects, the ambivalent or negative attitudes of physicians and other hospital personnel can influence a woman's reactions to an abortion. Marder (1970:1236) writes about one California hospital in which "hostility and resentment toward the patient by staff and nursing personnel have been responsible for some of the emotional disturbance experienced by patients." He gives several examples of harassment of abortion patients and points out that on some occasions "nurses, interns, and residents, as well as medical students, demonstrated anger and resentment toward a patient by voicing an old theme: 'You've had your fun and now you want us to take care of it for you' " (Marder, 1970:1232). In addition to this kind of treatment, certain hospital policies are highly punitive. The best example of such a policy is found in those hospitals which in certain cases will do an abortion only if the woman agrees to be sterilized at the same time.

Certain attitudes and assumptions about the appropriate social role of a woman can also contribute to adverse psychological aftereffects. Bolter (1962:314) expresses a fairly prevalent view of what the role of women is:

> Despite protests to the contrary, we know that woman's main role here on earth is to conceive, deliver, and raise children. Despite all other sublimated types of activities, this is still their primary role. When this function is interfered with, we see all sorts of emotional disorders and certainly the climax of these disorders is reached at the menopause when women recognize that they no longer can reproduce their kind and interpret the menopause as the end of life rather than the change of life. This is not just textbook theory, as all who practice psychiatry very well know.

Galdston (1958:118, 120) holds a similar attitude with respect to how abortion affects women:

> A woman is a uterus surrounded by a supporting organism and a directing personality. In advancing this proposition I am neither facetious nor deprecatory of womankind, nor superior in masculinity. I am biologically objective. In elaboration of this proposition, I would add that from the psychiatrist's viewpoint the strivings that animate the female can best be understood in terms of the functioning of the uterus. The uterus is the main rationale of the *biological female,* and this is not new or novel, but is very ancient knowledge. . . . Drawing upon my experience I would summate the major psychological effects in three terms: frustration, hostility, and guilt. . . . I would subsume abortion as a "form of sterility associated with profound biological and socioeconomic pathology."

Bolter says in effect that the biological functioning of a woman determines her social value and social role; she is subordinated to the demands of the species "to conceive, deliver, and raise children." Thus, any interference with a woman's reproductive functions results in profound damage to her biological and emotional make-up. The logical extension of this position is that *all* women suffer serious effects as a result of abortion. Galdston recognizes that abortion may be desired in cases where socioeconomic factors are relevant. Accepting the proposition that abortion "runs counter to the biological stream of life," he puts forth the logical corollary that "if and when a so-called adult woman, a responsible female, seeks an abortion, unless the warrant for it is overwhelming—as say in the case of rape or incest—we are in effect confronted both with a sick person and a sick situation" (Galdston, 1958:119). Galdston does not seem to recognize that a woman might choose to have an abortion in order to control her biological functions. He implies that a woman can only be "so-called" adult and responsible if she seeks an abortion and that this betrays a "sick" personality. If a woman believes, along with Bolter and Galdston, that her sole purpose in life is to bear and raise children, then her chances of suffering aftereffects from an abortion are greater than a woman who sees her role differently.

Anti-abortion pressures can create emotional difficulties for a woman unless she can tap into recent challenges to traditional and restrictive attitudes and assumptions. One such development is the change toward more permissive laws and attitudes toward abortion. In addition the increasing availability and use of nonjudgmental abortion counseling brings the issue out in the open and provides information and support which can relieve some of the fear and guilt. Attacks have been directed at the medical profession's treatment of women, and traditional sex roles have been questioned. Finally, several investigators have begun to make comparisons which suggest that post-abortion reactions are no more severe and possibly less severe than other psychological states which women commonly experience. For instance, are the psychological aftereffects of an abortion or of bearing an unwanted child more severe? Research-based evidence for a definitive answer to the question is not available, but partisans on either side of the abortion controversy have their ideologically based answer. Several recent investigators have forcefully pointed out the contrast between the weak research data and the dogmatic positions taken on abortion (Beck, 1971; Pohlman, 1971; David, 1972). Others have compared post-abortion and postpartum depression. Stephen Fleck (1970:44) observes that "the postpartum blues are a well known, almost universal occurrence known to all [obstetricians] as typical depressive stress manifestations to the end of pregnancy and the beginning of nursing tasks, whereas post-abortion reactions of the same type have been observed to be brief and mild, unless there was a serious mental disorder before the pregnancy." And again, as with post-abortion reactions, some have asked how the hospital experience might relate to postpartum depression. Particularly concerned with early signs of maternal rejection, Marian Morris (1966:10) describes some of the hospital experiences which she feels might in part contribute to postpartum depression: "Mothers say they are isolated and humiliated. They say that in addition to their own anxieties they must worry about what their doctors think, and be careful to please and propitiate the staff members, who may have power of life and death over them and their babies. They say that they are kept in stirrups for hours—shackled in what reduces them to something sub-human—yet afraid to complain."

Stephen Fleck (1970:44) also reminds us that abortion, like "every surgical operation, every inroad on a person's body, has psychological elements or sequelae which may leave psychological scars." His comparison of abortion to other surgical procedures suggests certain unexplored research possibilities. Most importantly the psychological aftereffects, hospital practices, and medical personnel's attitudes associated with uniquely female surgical procedures—especially abortion, hysterectomy, and mastectomy—should simultaneously be investigated. The psychological reactions associated with these procedures might also be compared to reactions to other surgical procedures, including those most typically performed on males.

The warring assumptions about a woman's role and about the morality of abortion create a highly complex situation within which the question of the psychological aftereffects of abortion must be considered. Perhaps for most women the situation can be summed up in one word—conflict. For a woman at one of the two polar ends of this controversy, there is little problem. If she strongly believes that abortion is wrong and that she ought to bear the child, or if she strongly believes in her right to have an abortion, then her course of action may be clear and unconflicted. But if she falls somewhere between, then regardless of whether she decides to have an abortion or to bear the child, she will experience the conflict.

THE EVIDENCE OF IDEOLOGY

> . . . the findings presently available constitute a rather persuasive body of evidence pointing to the fact that the psychiatric "sequelae" of abortion can be bad—sometimes extremely so. (Shaw, 1968:112)

> From such conclusive evidence, it seems obvious that psychic damage from abortion is mainly the product of myth. (Lader, 1966:23)

> The author has never seen a patient who has not had guilt feelings about a previous therapeutic abortion or illegal abortion. (Bolter, 1962:314)

> Never have I seen a case of genuine guilt or regret after abortion. (Shainess, 1970:20)

These declarations about the psychological aftereffects of abortion are beautiful illustrations of how ideology is wedded to evidence. It is not hard to guess that the first writer, Shaw, opposes abortion, that Lader is a campaigner for abortion law reform, that Bolter is a psychiatrist opposed to abortion, and that Shainess is a psychiatrist who favors abortion. These statements also suggest the two kinds of evidence usually cited to support or deny a claim of post-abortion psychological damage—research studies and clinical experience. The partisan use of evidence forms one of the most colorful chapters in the abortion controversy.

During the 1940s and early 1950s hardly an article on abortion in the medical journals failed to conclude that abortion resulted in more or less damaging psychological aftereffects. One of the first signs of a crack in this attitude showed up in the 1954 publication of Rosen's *Therapeutic Abortion*. The following two excerpts from Rosen's book express the prevailing attitude of that day:

> It may be said that those who commit or request abortion and those who suffer or endure abortion appear to have a similar post-abortion hangover. Whatever the differences in conscious or unconscious motivations for abortion, the experience of abortion inevitably arouses an unconscious sense of guilt. (Dunbar, 1967:31)

> Certainly, many mothers who during the first weeks [of pregnancy] feel terrified at the thought of having a child, later bless the doctor who refused to allow them to proceed with their plans for abortion. It is also true that the woman who experiences an abortion, whether therapeutic or criminal, is traumatized by the act to such a degree that the memory becomes a potent factor in her future behavior pattern. (Wilson, 1967:196)

In contrast to this prevailing position of the inevitability of guilt and trauma, two other physicians in the same volume suggest that ill effects have been overemphasized:

> The discussion of the dangers inherent in voluntary abortion may seem to be overaccentuated, for a great many women have abortions with great relief and with little if any subsequent disturbance. The psychiatrist, however, is usually called upon when there is evidence of emotional instability, and it is in just such cases where the adverse results are likely to ensue and where it is particularly difficult to be certain that the outcome will not be deleterious. (Lidz, 1967:280)

> From psychiatrists themselves have come statements which frequently tend to discredit psychiatric recommendations. An example in point is the exaggerated and frightening warning of the frequency with which serious depressions may follow induced abortions. To my knowledge, there is no valid support for drawing such general conclusions from limited data. It may be true that a depression can follow an induced abortion but . . . it may also follow a spontaneous abortion. And no attempt has been made to gather data on the thousands of women who have had one or more induced abortions without suffering any ill effects. In an obstetrical practice, one sees little evidence to justify the alarm created by psychiatrists in this regard. We have seen in our clinic a number of patients who admitted to as many as fifteen or twenty self-induced abortions without

any evidence of guilt or serious depression consequent to these acts. (Mandy, 1967:291–92)

The phrase "post-abortion hangover," coined by Dunbar, and Mandy's declaration that some women induced fifteen or twenty abortions without guilt or depression, have been quoted many times on both sides of the ideological fence—either as strong evidence to support a partisan position or as faulty evidence that called for criticism.

Probably the most quoted evidence on psychological aftereffects comes from Ekblad's study, published in 1955, of Swedish women who had abortions. This still stands as one of the most thorough and careful pieces of research in this area, and it is the most quoted to support *and* deny claims of adverse reactions. In part Ekblad's thoroughness and attention to the ambiguities and subtleties inherent in the question of psychological aftereffects has made it easy to quote his study for either position.

Another major display of the controversy on aftereffects stems from the 1958 publication of Calderone's *Abortion in the United States*. Bard Brekke reported on two Scandinavian studies that had opposite results. "The Swedish study shows a fairly high proportion of rather severe psychological reaction to legal abortions. The Norwegian study shows practically no psychological reaction." * It is amazing—or alarming—that many subsequent investigators have quoted one of these studies and ignored the other, especially since they are reported together and that Brekke says that "if any conclusion can be drawn from this it is that we should show a certain degree of caution in evaluating data we obtain in this way, since there may be factors involved that we are unable to analyze completely at the moment. There may be differences in the indications in the two countries, or in Norway we may have been extra careful in weighing the counterindications, or perhaps the social workers who carried out the two studies were different in their approaches" (Brekke, 1958:135, 136).

Three articles published in the early 1960s have provided good

* The Swedish study was published by Malmfors in 1951 in a Swedish journal and has not been translated into English. Brekke (1958:133–36) summarizes Malmfors' study and also presents the details of his own Norwegian study.

ammunition for partisans in the controversy about psychological aftereffects. Bolter's article appeared in 1962 and his conclusion that he had never seen a woman who did not feel guilty about an abortion was quoted above. He (1962:315) states further that "in most of the requests which are made to us concerning an interruption of pregnancy, the pregnancy can be carried to term and the patient can be handled either in office treatment or in a hospital until the baby is delivered." Sim (1963:418) reports on 213 mentally ill patients whose request for an abortion was rejected and who accepted the offer of psychiatric supervision or treatment. He reports that none deteriorated as a result of continuing the pregnancy and bearing the child and therefore concludes that "there are no psychiatric grounds for the termination of pregnancy." In sharp contrast, Kummer (1963:982) concludes "that abortion, as a precipitating stress towards moderate to severe psychiatric illness, is of only very minor significance, probably similar to any number of non-specific factors, such as a disappointment in love, an accident, loss of job, etc. This stands in vivid contrast to pregnancy, childbirth and child-rearing, which have been found to be substantially significant stresses in susceptible females."

Since Martin Ekblad's lengthy study (1955) is one of the most quoted to support both anti-abortion and pro-abortion positions, we present our own summary of the study below, and follow it with various quotations to show how his study is used for partisan purposes. Ekblad drew his sample from women who had a legal abortion at a Stockholm hospital during 1949 and 1950. All 479 women in the final sample were interviewed in the hospital a few days after the abortion and interviewed again two to three years later.

The researchers collected extensive data on the women, including an evaluation of pre-abortion "mental status." A psychiatric diagnosis of pre-abortion status placed 42 percent of the sample in the normal category and 58 percent in the abnormal category. Ekblad (1955:46) comments that the latter represent "symptoms of chronic neurosis or deviating personality" which existed before the pregnancy in question, and that the "corresponding frequency in a normal population probably amounts to at most 15 percent."

Table 4 shows the aftereffects reported. The categories of "satis-

TABLE 4: THE EKBLAD STUDY OF PSYCHOLOGICAL AFTEREFFECTS

Longer-Term Attitude	*Normal Personalities* no.	%	*Abnormal Personalities* no.	%	*Total* no.	%
Satisfied, no self-reproaches	149	74	163	59	312	65
Considered abortion unpleasant, but no self-reproaches	19	9	28	10	47	10
Mild self-reproaches	21	10	45	16	66	14
Serious self-reproaches	12	6	42	15	54	11
Total	201		278		479	

Source: Ekblad (1955:170–71)

fied, no self-reproach" through "serious self-reproach" are based upon the women's statements, in an open-ended interview, of their attitudes toward the abortion. Ekblad devotes about forty pages of his monograph to case reports of the fifty-four women who reported serious self-reproaches two to three years after the abortion. He comments that: "A closer study of the case-histories of these women with serious self-reproaches shows that even if their subjective sufferings due to the abortion were severe, their depression must from the psychiatric viewpoint be designated as in general mild. The woman seldom needed to consult a doctor on account of these mental troubles" (Ekblad, 1955:212).

The researchers used working capacity to measure the degree of severity of illness in these fifty-four women. Five of them (representing 1 percent of the total sample) experienced impaired working capacity in connection with the symptoms of psychic insufficiency after abortion. With respect to the severity of aftereffects in his sample, Ekblad (1955:212) concludes that "it is obvious that a legal abortion entails feelings of guilt and self-reproach in many women. On the other hand, it is seldom that these undesirable psychic sequelae are so serious that they may be described as morbid or that they adversely affect the woman's working capacity."

Ekblad examined the following social and psychological variables for their possible association with feelings of self-reproach: personality type (normal-abnormal), age, intellectual level, new pregnancy after abortion, previous pregnancies, influence of others to apply for abortion, sterilization either with abortion or later, childhood environment, occupation, and relation to male partner. Of these, only personality type and influence of others turned out to be related to feelings of self-reproach. Women diagnosed as abnormal, and women who had been influenced by others to submit to an abortion were likelier to experience serious self-reproach. The bottom two rows of Table 4 show the significance of normal-abnormal personality type in the occurrence of self-reproach—16 percent of the normal group felt mild or serious self-reproach compared to 31 percent of the abnormal group; 6 percent of the normal group reported serious self-reproaches compared to 15 percent of the abnormal group. Ekblad's comment on this finding has become perhaps the most frequently quoted conclusion of his study: "This implies that the greater the psychiatric indications for a legal abortion are, the greater is also the risk of unfavourable psychic sequelae after the operation" (Ekblad, 1955:213).

At the end of the monograph, where the results of each chapter are summarized, Ekblad (1955:234) elaborates: "In the cases in which [severe psychic sequelae have] occurred in the present material the woman's psychic state and situation at the time of the unwelcome pregnancy were such that they would probably have entailed equally unfavourable psychic sequelae even if the pregnancy had not been terminated with legal abortion."

Ekblad's report contains several loose ends that could have contributed toward misleading those who use his findings to support their ideological stance. For example, he refers to his figures of women admitting self-reproaches as minimum figures, and yet he later comments that "the desire to present themselves in as favourable a light as possible may have led some of the women to admit to self-reproaches that they had not felt" (Ekblad, 1955:170–71). But he does furnish many different figures in his study that can be used in partisan fashion, and a few examples will illustrate this technique. Shaw (1968:112), an anti-abortionist, points out that Ekblad "found that 14 percent experienced mild reproach and regret, 11 percent serious reproach and regret, and 1 percent serious post-abortion psychiatric illness." Ekblad (1955:170), however, refers only to self-reproach and not to regret for the mild category, and he refers to self-reproach *or* regret for the serious category. Further, the 1 percent figure is not additive, but refers to that portion of the 11 percent whose illness was severe enough to impair their working ability. Sim (1963:147), also an anti-abortionist, reports "that 11 percent had undesirable sequelae of a psychiatric nature." In contrast, the pro-abortionsts who cite Ekblad are likelier to mention the large majority who experience no self-reproach or regret, using the figures of 65 or 75 percent. They are also likelier to use the 1 percent figure, sometimes alone, and sometimes emphasizing that figure while citing others. Finally, they are much likelier to cite qualifications to the figures, even including qualifications to the 1 percent. Lader (1966:21) and Osofsky and Osofsky (1972:50) respectively cite the 75 and the 65 percent figures. Lader (1966:21), Niswander and Patterson (1967:702), Kummer (1963:981), and Peck and Marcus (1966:418) all use the 1 percent figure, and the last two use that figure only; they all further qualify these figures. To illustrate, the full reference to Ekblad's work in Peck and Marcus (1966:417–18) is cited below:

> Ekblad examined 479 women two or three years after they had legal abortions for psychiatric indications. He found that guilt and self-reproach were common, but mild. The few—one percent—who were significantly disabled by depression all had shown marked psychiatric illness prior to their abortions and had broken with their male partners by the time of follow-up examination. Ekblad stressed that guilt was greatest in women influenced by others to submit to abortion and least in those who clearly wanted abortion themselves.

None of these quotations does gross injustice to Ekblad's work, but taken together they indicate the subtle bias that can operate in areas of controversy and partisanship. They also further document the rather confused and contradictory nature of the medical literature on the aftereffects of abortion during the mid-1960s. The lack of conclusive data and the partisanship were aptly singled out in a review article by Simon and Senturia. They examined twenty-seven books and articles, representing the research and clinical literature from 1935 to 1964, and their conclusion has been widely repeated:

> It is sobering to observe the ease with which reports can be embedded in the literature, quoted, and requoted many times without consideration for

the data in the original paper. Deeply held personal convictions frequently seem to outweigh the importance of data, especially when conclusions are drawn. In the papers reviewed the findings and conclusions range from the suggestion that psychiatric illness almost always is the outcome of therapeutic abortion to its virtual absence as a post-abortion complication. (Simon and Senturia, 1966:387)

The most serious problem in the studies reviewed by Simon and Senturia is the poor methodology. A few case histories, limited clinical experience, and an uncritical use of the literature were often used as the basis for wild generalizations. As Simon and Senturia (1966:378) say, "although Taussig makes only the most cursory references to psychiatric sequelae of therapeutic abortion, he is quoted by nearly every author since 1936 as warning against serious psychiatric sequelae to abortion." Galdston (1958:117), a psychiatrist, aptly points to his limited clinical experiences with the effects of abortion and indicates that "the psychiatrist generally does not have contact with masses of people, but rather with single individuals. Hence, the psychiatrist can report cases but he finds it rather difficult to draw generalizations or broad deductions." A few pages later he overcomes this difficulty, and states, "I think any abortion is likely to have serious traumatic sequelae" (Galdston, 1958:121).

Due to the widely held belief, until the mid-1960s, that abortion had serious psychological consequences, many investigators presented their contrary beliefs or findings with hesitance. Laidlaw's (1958:132) report is an example:

It is my impression that in the therapeutic field the guilt reactions—if such occur and I think they do rarely occur—come more from the type of antecedent psychiatric problem that the patient may present. . . . I do think, however, that the question of guilt is important enough to merit a recommendation that the patient should be seen psychiatrically subsequent to the surgical procedure, even though she may have had no antecedent psychiatric history or treatment.

Since the review article by Simon and Senturia, more attention has been paid to the methodological problems involved in studying the psychological aftereffects of abortion, and less attention has been paid to studies generalizing about serious aftereffects based on limited clinical data. Two recent review articles (Walter, 1970; Osofsky and

Osofsky, 1972) conclude that the available evidence actually suggests that there are relatively few serious aftereffects to an abortion and that women who are refused an abortion have more serious psychological postpartum aftereffects. David (1972) introduces a note of caution, however, pointing out that the research evidence is too meager for any strong conclusion. Pare and Raven (1970) carried out a study that is exceptional in including control groups and in being able to follow up a high percentage of women. They provide information on women who were considered for an abortion in London, England, on psychiatric grounds and on organic grounds; these are further divided on whether they were recommended for an abortion or refused; and the latter are further divided on whether or not they obtained an abortion elsewhere. The authors state:

> This study confirms the opinions of workers in the United Kingdom that the stress of bearing an unwanted child can lead to psychiatric symptoms. In our series such symptoms were not uncommon, were sometimes protracted, and were occasionally severe enough to require admission of the patient: they were especially likely in the overburdened multipara and in the single girl lacking support. On the other hand, patients in whom pregnancy was terminated on our recommendation had remarkably little psychiatric disturbance, provided the patient herself wanted the operation: psychiatric sequelae were much commoner in those patients who were reluctant to have the operation, for example some patients with organic conditions. (Pare and Raven, 1970:637–38)

We are, in fact, now witnessing the growth of a pro-abortion climate. As Marder et al. (1970:661) report for one hospital in California, "where once psychiatric evaluations and recommendations were questioned, now the failure to recommend abortion is questioned." This new climate is partly influenced by recent evidence about a woman's better apparent adjustment to an abortion than to bearing an unwanted child and by the increased emphasis upon a woman's right to make her own decisions about reproduction.

THE PSYCHIATRIST MEETS THE PATIENT

When a woman with an unwanted pregnancy consults a psychiatrist, she typically does so to obtain psychiatric dispensation from a restrictive law. In states with the original laws in force, the psychiatrist's diagnosis that the pregnancy represents a threat to the woman's life may sanction a therapeutic abortion. In states with a reform law, the psychiatrist's diagnosis that the pregnancy threatens the woman's health may legalize an abortion. The psychiatrist clearly plays a key role in abortion decisions under these circumstances. Thomas Szasz (1962:347) says that "he is a legally authorized bootlegger. In this role, the law empowers the psychiatrist to grant permission for otherwise prohibited acts. . . . He is authorized to prescribe abortion as though it were treatment, provided he can find the pregnant woman to be mentally ill (so as to justify his prescription)." A similar point is made by Levene and Rigney (1970:52, 54) who point out that "legislators, in liberalizing existing anti-abortion laws by including mental health provisions, have placed the psychiatrist in the role of dispensator—quite different from his usual role of consultant. . . . In essence, he is able to grant dispensation from the law's restrictive consequences."

The pregnant woman, the gynecologist, and the psychiatrist are all aware of the latter's special position in states with original or reform laws. It can be assumed that the dynamics of the process involved in arranging a therapeutic abortion on psychiatric grounds is a fascinating one, but the psychiatric literature has very little to say on the topic. This is no doubt due to the fact that the psychiatrist, who is in the best position to describe the dynamics of the process, has so much of his personal and professional esteem caught up in the process that he finds it painful to deal with it objectively.

The woman has a vested interest in manipulating the psychiatrist by appearing sufficiently ill to justify an abortion:

> The request for a therapeutic abortion produces a strained doctor-patient relationship in that the patient's motives are to present herself in such a way as to obtain the abortion. The physician's attitude toward the patient is altered in that he feels manipulated and threatened by the pressure of responding to the patient's request. The woman presents herself with considerable anxiety, usually related to the fact that she is pregnant and does not wish to be. When the woman is determined to obtain an abortion, a most difficult situation develops in which to conduct a psychiatric interview because the normal motivation which promotes cooperation is not present. She may consciously exaggerate all of her symptoms and frequently can be considered manipulative and malingering. Her greatest need is to convince the psychiatrist of her inability to continue with the pregnancy. (Marder et al., 1970:658–59)

Eric Pfeiffer says a psychiatrist on an abortion committee reviews two kinds of cases—those with psychiatric indications and those with psychiatric justifications. The women with psychiatric indications experience symptoms that warrant attention whether or not they seek an abortion. These indications for abortion include "active psychosis; serious suicidal risk; severe personality disorders; borderline states; and history of a previous postpartum psychosis." The other women want an abortion and come to the psychiatrist only because they need psychiatric justification for the abortion. Women seeking psychiatric justification include those with "temporary emotional turmoil related to the unwanted pregnancy; the likelihood of upsetting career or marriage plans; economic hardships; family pressures, etc." Pfeiffer continues that the law encourages these women "to feign psychiatric symptoms, to mouth suicidal ideas, and to present themselves generally as emotionally disordered when in fact they are not" (Pfeiffer, 1970:404, 405).

Brody et al. (1971:350, 352) entertain the possibility that "the applicants may have attempted to fake a psychiatric disturbance in order to maximize their chances of being accepted," or as R. F. Tredgold (1964:1252) puts it, "the patient may have an interest in deceiving the doctor." Levene and Rigney (1970:57), in trying to evaluate threats of suicide and of illegal abortion, state that "often the woman seemed to be trying to convince the interviewer that she was sick or desperate enough to qualify under the law." Anderson (1966:82) sees such threats as "attempts at blackmail of the doctor." Phelan and Maginnis (1969:103) offer advice to women on how to acquire an instant psychosis in order to qualify for a legal abortion:

> If rape and incest aren't your speed
> For abortion care, a psychosis you need!
> In order to prove you're as mad as a hatter
> Let's practice a little psychiatrist chatter. . .

In brief, the legal requirements place both the woman and the psychiatrist in an untenable position (Rapoport and Potts, 1971).

Due to lack of clear evidence for making a decision—"we do not have the capacity to predict, with any degree of certainty, which women will experience major psychiatric illness as a result of unwanted pregnancy" (Whittington, 1970:1228)—the psychiatrist is forced to fall back upon his own moral and ideological convictions. Enough strands of evidence are available to enable the psychiatrist, whether anti-abortion or pro-abortion, to wrap them around his nakedness. Or he can forthrightly state that the evidence for a decision is lacking and then proceed to act principally in terms of his values. Myre Sim (1963) refused to recommend abortions for "instability in pregnancy" or "puerperal psychosis" because these did not present "clear psychiatric indications for termination of pregnancy. In its stead, psychiatric supervision or treatment was offered." He tells us that "relatively few accepted the offer," and it took him twelve years to accumulate the 213 patients he bases his report on. He informs us that "no patient suffered permanent mental damage as a result of her puerperal psychosis. Even those who were schizophrenic prior to pregnancy did not deteriorate, and in the vast majority of cases recovery was rapid. The babies thrived and maternity and child-welfare reports showed no handicap." His conclusion is the same as his initial assumption: "There are no psychiatric grounds for the termination of pregnancy." Although his psychiatric textbook mentions other approaches, his own position regarding abortion was not altered (Sim, 1969:895).

The Simian approach is shared by many others who make it clear that women can adapt to the stress of pregnancy and childbirth, and that there is therefore no good reason for terminating a pregnancy. While the mental condition of some women may worsen under the stress of an unwanted pregnancy (or an abortion), no basis exists for deciding which few women may suffer that fate. One relevant finding, however, which was reported by Ekblad (1955) and others (cf. Callahan, 1970:68–69) and has been widely quoted, does provide us with some information: women with the most severe psychiatric symptoms prior to an abortion are likely to show the most severe symptoms after the abortion. Although such a finding is hardly surprising, and is unlikely to have anything to do with the abortion, it has been accepted uncritically by some people as indicative of the psychological aftereffects of the abortion.

Some psychiatrists have used this information to engage women in a game of Catch 22. According to reform law, a healthy woman is not entitled to an abortion—a woman must show serious signs of mental illness in order to qualify for an abortion. But according to the psychiatrist, only a healthy woman can adjust readily to the abortion experience—a mentally ill woman will not be able to make that adaptation. The result, of course, is that no woman is able to qualify. Another version of the game is played as follows. If the woman does not say that she wants an abortion, then she continues with the pregnancy. If she says she wants an abortion, then you cannot take her at face value because "the ultimate fulfillment of a woman is the bearing and rearing of children" (Kleegman, 1958:112). "In the face of all of this evidence for unconscious influences in women's attitudes toward pregnancy, how can we accept a conscious statement from a woman to the effect that she does not want a certain pregnancy" (Bolter, 1962:315). Thus, whether a woman wants an abortion or does not want one, she does not get one.

Other psychiatrists are ready, even eager, to recommend abortions for psychiatric indications and relish their role of providing such dispensations. They deny that this role involves any compromise of psychiatric or scientific principles:

> It is our contention that, if our proper role is to function in the primary prevention of mental illness, there is no compromise by remaining on the scene. To do so will, in itself, help change the law and concurrently allow us to gather more clinical data on this problem. The data already accumulated strongly suggest that to force a woman to carry a pregnancy to term against her will is indeed very likely to be detrimental to her mental health as well as that of her prospective child. (Levene and Rigney, 1970:55)

If we assume that women have an incentive to exaggerate their illness when applying for an abortion, then it appears sensible that some time after the abortion they might speak more honestly to the psychiatrist. Patt et al. (1969) indeed found—three months to four years after the abortion—that the stated reasons of about half of their patients did not meet the psychiatric criteria. But they report "a retrospective effort to deny previous or present illness" and generously conclude "that most of the women in this study qualified for abortion according to the accepted criteria." They report that the short-term and long-term effects of abortion were favorable and that "abortion was genuinely therapeutic."

The psychiatrist who believes that it is a woman's right to make her own decision on abortion may go beyond the spectator's role to playing an active part in the dramatic performance that wins a woman her abortion. Thomas Scheff (1968) provides a fascinating account of how psychiatrists and lawyers can influence patients or defendants during the course of an interview. Through coaching, the lawyer and his client construct a version of reality that provides the latter with an opportunity to make a strong case for his innocence. In the same way, it is possible for a psychiatrist to coach his patient into presenting the strongest possible case for obtaining an abortion. Resnik and Wittlin (1971:14, 19) point out that others besides the psychiatrist may also do the coaching:

> We think that the sympathetic psychiatrist tends to draw from a willing patient indications of suicidal thoughts. Furthermore patients are often schooled by lawyers, ministers, family, friends, and the referring physicians to tell the sympathetic psychiatrist what he professionally needs and "wants to hear." . . . In short, as long as our society refuses to acknowledge reality, threatened suicide will continue to serve as a convenient vehicle for an unspoken collusion between patient and psychiatrist, to circumvent the real issue: a woman's right—with counsel and medical advice—to determine her child-bearing options.

Patt et al. (1969:413) suggest that "the structure of the pre-abortion interviews emphasized psychopathology. . . . The manifest function of the pre-abortion interview is to reveal rather than to suppress pathology." They further note that some patients "inferred the [legal criteria for abortion] from the direction of the psychiatrist's questioning" (Patt et al., 1969:410).

Most observers agree on the difficulty, if not impossibility, of the job that confronts the psychiatrist who must recommend abortion on mental health grounds (Group for the Advancement of Psychiatry, 1969). The psychiatrist who takes a pro-abortionist position finds his role easier to carry out if the woman has been properly coached. Once the woman successfully presents her case, the sympathetic psychiatrist is able to use appropriate diagnostic categories as "window dressings" (Christakos, 1971:108) in order to justify the abortion. This is a rather cumbersome process, and it is not surprising that some psychiatrists prefer a restrictive interpretation of mental health grounds to eliminate psychiatric indications as the major reason for abortion, while most psychiatrists would prefer to see the laws changed so that women could make their own decisions about abortion.

CHAPTER SIX

PHYSICAL AFTEREFFECTS

Like the medical views on the psychological aftereffects of abortion, the literature on physical aftereffects also has its "harmful consequences" tradition. This tradition of the adverse physical aftereffects stems from Russian experience. Until 1920 abortion in Soviet Russia was illegal, even for medical indications. Abortion was legalized from 1920 to 1936, but the policy was changed in 1936 and abortion became illegal except for medical indications. This continued until 1955 when abortion was again legalized, and since 1955 there has been no major change (Field, 1956).

Belief in the harmful physical consequences of abortion came from the 1920 to 1936 period of legalization. As Gebhard and his associates (1958:216) remarked, "most gynecologists in the western world had looked askance at the unorthodox Russian program, and their doubts about its soundness were pleasantly substantiated by this retreat [i.e., the 1936 decree making abortion illegal] of the Soviet social reformers." With a predisposition to believe the worst, the assumption of dire physical complications entered the mainstream of medical literature. A number of articles appeared in the 1930s, 1940s, and 1950s based upon the 1920 to 1936 Russian experience which stressed the harmful effects of abortion. The Rosen anthology, *Therapeutic Abortion,* first published in 1954, contained a lively debate about the relevance of the Russian experience. Psychiatrist Manfred Guttmacher (1967:178) declared that "despite the amazingly low reported mortality rate when the operation was carried out legally, it was found that repeated operations, even when done aseptically, led to sterility in a high percentage of cases, to a great increase in ectopic pregnancies and to complications in deliveries with increased fetal mortality." Taussig, in a 1942 article, stated that "the Russian experiment in legalized abortion, extending over a period of about ten years, proved beyond doubt that when the bars are let down on permitting instrumental evacuation of the uterus, in spite of the relatively low primary mortality, there was a marked deterioration of the physical condition of the aborted woman" (quoted in Rosen, 1967a:178–79). Others, however, questioned whether abortions were still that dangerous. Rosen (1967a:179) takes issue with the Manfred Guttmacher and Taussig position on the grounds that it

> does not take into consideration the advances in medical knowledge during the past eighteen to thirty-six years, the advent of antibiotic therapy, our increased knowledge of those emotional factors which may be involved in such sterility or relative fertility, etc.
>
> I have not been able to find any meaningful statistical or other studies which would imply that Taussig's remarks now hold true for this country in the year 1953, when, after competent physicians and hospital reviewing boards have thought the operation indicated, a therapeutic abortion is performed in the operating room of one of our modern hospitals.

Despite the overwhelming belief that the Russian experience demonstrated, at least for that time period, that abortion was followed by serious physical aftereffects, the reports from Russia were actually quite contradictory. Gebhard et al. (1958:216) inform us that during the 1920s "the reports on the shrinking number of illegal abortions, low mortality, slight morbidity, and lack of serious aftereffects had been enthusiastic and glowing." On the other hand, Rudolf Schlesinger (1949:174) contends that a Conference of Gynecologists on Experiences with Abortion for Social Indications held in 1927 in Kiev "was actually a demonstration against legalized abortion." One of the Resolutions of this Congress stated: "After thorough investigation in which the manifold harm done to women by artificial abortion has become evident, this Congress declares that it is most important to warn the population of its harmful consequences, and against a light-hearted approach to abortion" (quoted in Schlesinger, 1949:187).

Abraham Stone (1958:207) gives the following account of the reports of the mid-1930s:

> The Russians claimed, in 1934, that they had very few complications, and almost no fatalities; one for every two thousand operations was the figure reported.
>
> But soon after the tide began to turn against legal abortions, and *Izvestia,* the official Russian paper, began to speak of abortion as "an instrument of mass mutilation of women." Medical reports began to appear —and I read many of them at the time—of complications resulting from abortions: chronic ill-health, sterility, ectopic pregnancy.

It is difficult, if not impossible, to determine to what extent the attention to the complications of abortion represented strictly medical concerns or political concerns heralding an impending change in government policy (Field, 1956; Heer, 1965).

The idea of extensive physical damage after abortion has not been laid to rest, despite the advances of medicine since the Russian experiences between 1920 and 1936. Callahan (1970:35) says that "it is still possible to discover an occasional article in the medical literature which heavily stresses the hazards of induced abortion even under adequate septic and professional conditions," but "most recent literature does not . . . present such a pessimistic outlook."

There are several reasons for the predominantly favorable, though cautious, assessment of physical complications. Most obvious is the presence of an ever-advancing medical technology to deal with physical complications. Furthermore, experience in performing abortions coupled with the "observance of established surgical and obstetric principles" makes abortion a relatively safe procedure even though, "contrary to prior publicity, abortion is *not* as safe as the proverbial tooth extraction" (Rovinsky, 1971:335). Perhaps the strongest influence on a favorable view of the physical aftereffects stems from information on the hazards of the alternatives to legal abortion. Among psychiatrists, the controversy about the relative psychological aftereffects of a legal abortion or alternatives to it continues. But the physical aftereffects of alternatives to a legal abortion are more clearly delineated. Even the highly critical 1927 Russian Conference on abortion resolved that "The legalization of artificial abortion has resulted in a considerable decrease in the number of secret [criminal] abortions and of the diseases or deaths ensuing thereupon" (quoted in Schlesinger, 1949:187).

Almost universally, where abortion is legalized and made readily available, the maternal mortality rate drops and the incidence of septic and incomplete abortion decreases. This points to the conclusion that legal abortion reduces the incidence of ill effects from criminal abortion and is therefore preferable to criminal abortion. It has also been demonstrated that abortion in early pregnancy carries fewer risks than childbirth. Callahan (1970:34) probably summarizes the prevailing attitude toward the physical aftereffects best when he says, "how much one should be alarmed about these hazards will be very much dependent on the extent to which one thinks an abortion would be medically or socially valuable."

The evidence on physical aftereffects falls neatly into three broad categories—mortality, early complications, and late complications. Figures on mortality rates probably represent the most complete and accurate set of data on any aspect of abortion, and it is rare for anyone to make a case for high mortality from legal abortion. Even the earlier statements of Taussig and Manfred Guttmacher which emphasized the harmful effects also mentioned the low mortality rate.

The data on complication rates, however, are plagued by methodological problems similar to those found in the studies on psychological aftereffects. As David (1970:253) notes, studies on the physical aftereffects lack standard definitions of what constitutes complications, and many more studies are needed of "the frequency of early and late complications experienced with different methods of abortion and different periods of gestations in women of good health."

Early complications of abortion occur immediately after the operation and can include hemorrhage, infection, perforation of the uterus, fever, shock, retained tissue, injury to the cervix, and failed induction in the case of late abortions. In spite of the problems in comparing studies, this category of evidence is fairly extensive, fairly refined, and many investigators tend to see the early complication rates as tolerable or as amenable to improvement if certain medical practices are observed.

The late complications refer to associations between induced abortion and secondary sterility, spontaneous abortion, premature births, cervical insufficiency, difficulties in later pregnancies and deliveries, ectopic pregnancy, and menstrual disorders. The data on most of these complications are scanty and inconclusive. It is in this category of late complications that the tendency prevails to view abortion as harmful to the health of women.

TABLE 5: MORTALITY RATES FOR LEGAL ABORTIONS

		Mortality Rate per 100,000 Abortions	*Number of Abortions*
Denmark	1961–65	41	21,700
Sweden	1960–66	39	30,600
England, Wales, and Scotland	1968–69	21	40,466
U.S.—JPSA[a]	1970–71	8.2	72,988
New York City	July 1, 1970–Dec. 31, 1971	4.3	278,122
Japan	1959–65	4.1	6,860,000
Czechoslovakia	1963–67	2.5	406,000
Hungary	1964–67	1.2	739,000

Sources: Diggory et al. (1970:288, 290) for England, Wales, and Scotland; Tietze (1970:198, 208) for Denmark, Sweden, Czechoslovakia, and Hungary; the Health Services Administration of New York City (1972:2) for New York City; Tietze (personal communication) for Japan; and Tietze and Lewit (1972:98) for the U.S.—JPSA.

[a] The Joint Program for the Study of Abortion (JPSA) includes sixty-six institutions (sixty teaching hospitals and six clinics) with almost one-half of the hospitals and five of the clinics located in New York state.

MORTALITY

Table 5 shows a range of abortion-related maternal mortality rates with the low rates of Czechoslovakia and Hungary setting the standard that others strive for. In a monograph on the socialist countries of Central and Eastern Europe, Henry David (1970:253) concluded that "mortality associated with legal abortion induced in the first trimester of pregnancy has fallen to such low levels that the *risk is less than that of carrying a pregnancy to term*." Even in countries with higher rates, few are alarmed. Diggory and his colleagues (1970:290) compare the 21 per 100,000 abortion mortality rate for England, Scotland and Wales "with a maternal-mortality rate of 24 per 100,000 total births," and continue that "clearly fears that legal abortion would prove dangerous have not proved justified." Similarly from Sweden, Jan-Otto Ottosson (1971:180) compares the legal abortion mortality rate with the mortality rate for delivery and concludes that "the mortality in legal abortions is only slightly higher than in parturition." The higher abortion mortality rates in the Scandinavian countries have been attributed to a greater proportion of late abortions and to the poorer health of the women who are being granted legal abortions (Geijerstam, 1970a:131; Tietze and Lewit, 1971:10). Not only do the mortality rates for legal abortions compare favorably with the maternal mortality rates for births, but the general pattern has been that the longer abortion is legalized, the lower the abortion mortality rate goes.*

Finally, perhaps the most conclusive evidence of all on the low mortality of legal abortion comes from Christopher Tietze's oft-quoted model: "maternal mortality from complications of, or associated with, pregnancy, childbirth, and the puerperium excluding in-

* The Joint Program for the Study of Abortion focuses on early complications and has headquarters at the Population Council in New York City. The Transnational Family Research Institute in Washington D.C. conducts research on abortion and is compiling a Directory of Abortion Researchers. The Family Planning Activity of the Center for Disease Control in Atlanta gathers data on legal abortions from hospitals across the United States. The New York City Board of Health requires a report from all hospitals and figures are available from the Health Services Administration of New York City. Some states, such as Oregon, have compulsory reporting which was written into the reform statute (Harting and Hunter, 1971:2093). Figures for Great Britain can be obtained from the United Kingdom, Office of Population Censuses and Surveys, *The Registrar General's Statistical Review of England and Wales for the Year 1970—Supplement on Abortion* (London: Her Majesty's Stationery Office, 1972). In addition to the references cited in Table 5, see also Muramatsu (1970:122); Rovinsky (1971:333, 335); and Tietze and Lewit (1971:10) for details of mortality rates and their change over time.

duced abortion—20 deaths per 100,000 pregnancies"; a rough estimate (from the United States) of maternal mortality associated with criminal abortion performed "by persons without medical training—100 deaths per 100,000 abortions"; mortality from legal abortion (Eastern European statistics)—3 deaths per 100,000 abortions; and "excess mortality from thromboembolic disease attributable to the use of oral contraceptives [from studies in Great Britain] —3 deaths per 100,000 users per year" (Tietze, 1969).

EARLY COMPLICATIONS

Much variation occurs in the manner of reporting aftereffects and several investigators point to the need for great caution in interpreting the available data because they believe the aftereffects are underreported due to inadequate patient follow-up. A few examples will serve to illustrate the variation in reporting and the attitude toward the data.

Andras Klinger reports complications for Hungary in 1964 as follows: .13 percent perforation of the uterus; .37 percent feverish conditions; .62 percent hemorrhage; .47 percent repeated hospital treatment within four weeks due to fever; and 1.02 percent repeated hospital treatment due to hemorrhage. This gives an overall complication figure of 2.61 percent, but it is not clear whether each woman with complications is counted once only or may be placed in more than a single category. After discussing the low mortality rate, Klinger says that "the complications of induced abortion are, however, more significant. . . . The low mortality suggests that these complications are successfully treated, but the aftereffects of these complications cannot be followed up. At any rate, their frequency indicates the dangers of induced abortion" (Klinger, 1966:474, 475). In the same volume K. H. Mehlan (1966:210) presents figures similar to Klinger's—early sequelae in 5.2 percent of the cases in Czechoslovakia in 1958, 2.3 percent in 1963, and 2.8 percent in 1962 for Slovenia. Based upon these similar figures, Mehlan gives the rather different assessment that "in general, an insignificant number of cases of damage to health is reported, and even this number is declining as physicians become more experienced."

Another possible source of confusion can be shown by examining results that classify aftereffects by their degree of severity. Referring to 1,500 induced abortions in Seoul, Korea in 1964, Sung-Bong Hong (1970:125–26) reports that in 36 percent of these cases some physical complaint was voiced by the woman. This could be reported simply as complications in 36 percent of the cases, but he goes on to add that about one-fifth were described as "very severe," one-fifth as "severe," and three-fifths as "not so severe." Moreover, among the 36 percent with complaints, "88% recovered within one week, including 77% of those with very severe complaints, 82% of those with severe complaints, and 95% of those with not so severe complaints."

Another example of how distinguishing the degree of severity of aftereffects can make a difference comes from the JPSA study. Tietze and Lewit (1972:106–7) report that 9.6 percent of 72,988 women had one or more complications, but this very large figure includes "many complaints of a comparatively trivial nature, such as a single day of fever" and "may produce a quite distorted impression of the risk to health associated with legal abortion." The authors describe what constitutes a "major complication" and note that 1 percent of all patients and 11 percent of all patients with complications fell into this major complications category.

As one final example from the literature reporting on physical aftereffects, Per Kolstad (1957:56) studied 714 women at one Norwegian hospital during the period 1940 through 1953. He found an overall complication rate of 10.3 percent, with 2.7 percent of a serious nature. Kolstad continues that "after interruptions of pregnancy, fever occurred in 2.8% of the cases, hemorrhages in 3.3%, and the total rate of complications was 10.3%. In connection with deliveries, the corresponding figures are 3.7%, 3.7%, and 11.5%, respectively." Kolstad (1957:55) also reviews the literature during the late 1940s and early 1950s and reports a range of 40 percent to 3.8 percent complications. He adds that "a comparison of materials that seem to have been following the same procedure in the registration of complications as the present material . . . reveals that all of these authors mention appr. 10–15% of complications, out of which about 2% are counted as serious."

Since the amount of data available and its comparability is more satisfactory for the physical than the psychological complications of abortion, there is more agreement in the literature about a tolerable standard of complications. This is also aided by the better information that is available on the physical than the psychiatric aftereffects of alternatives to abortion. The tolerable standard appears to be about 10 to 15 percent for "total" complications and about 2 to 3 percent for "serious" complications, but these percentages are far from being fixed because the comparability of the reports on physical complications leaves a great deal of room for improvement. Tietze and Lewit, writing in 1971, thought 10.1 percent a "very high figure" for total complications but stress the trivial complaints that this figure includes. Mehlan, writing in 1966, labeled his reported figures of 5.2, 2.3, and 2.8 percent as "an insignificant number of cases of damage to health." Kolstad, writing in 1957, concluded that with respect to "the frequency of complications [10.3 percent overall, 2.7 percent serious], this study again confirms the experience that artificial abortion is a comparatively harmless operation during the first twelve weeks of pregnancy." One has only to reflect on the controversy that would be generated by a 10 or 5 or 2.8 percent rate for psychological aftereffects to realize the importance of an agreement on a tolerable level of aftereffects in the evaluation of data.

By far the most important aspect of the studies on early physical complications is the analysis of the factors that contribute to these complications.

Gestation Period and Abortion Technique. The abortion technique used is largely determined by the period of gestation with suction curettage and dilation and curettage considered safe up to twelve weeks.* The thirteen-to-sixteen-week period is considered by many too late for safe curettage but too early for saline induction, and ab-

* When reporting period of gestation, there is a distinction between completed weeks and ordinal weeks. Completed weeks is calculated by counting from the first day of the last menstrual period, and "the number of completed weeks is one less than the ordinal number of the week of gestation during which the abortion occurred" (Tietze and Lewit, 1972:101–2). So, for example, gestations of twelve completed weeks correspond to the thirteenth ordinal week. The JPSA data are reported in completed weeks, but this detail of calculation is usually not mentioned in other studies. Since the most important use of these figures is to guide physicians on the preferred abortion technique for various periods of gestation, the lack of a standardized method of calculating and reporting period of gestation is lamentable.

dominal hysterotomy is sometimes used during this period. Since saline induction and hysterotomy are more complicated, more hazardous procedures, it is not surprising to consistently find a strong association between the period of gestation and both mortality rates and early complication rates—data show higher rates for late abortions than for early abortions. With respect to late abortions, the trend in the United States favors saline induction over hysterotomy since higher mortality and complication rates are associated with the latter and hysterotomy, unlike saline, "leaves a scar in the uterus which may make subsequent vaginal births unwise" (A. Guttmacher, personal communication). Some investigators have observed an unusually high complication rate for the thirteen-to-sixteen-week (four-month) period of gestation and have suggested that perhaps the appropriate method was not used (Kolstad, 1957:53; Muramatsu, 1970:122; Ingraham and Longood, 1971:16; Rovinsky, 1971:337; Smith et al., 1971:539). That is, suction curettage and dilation and curettage were performed when another technique or waiting until around the seventeenth week to perform a saline induction would have been more appropriate. In short, even though late abortions carry a higher risk than early abortions, if certain standards are followed and as physicians gain more experience, the complication rates can be reduced.

Some data show a higher complication rate for very early abortions than for those in the seven-to-eight-week period or the nine-to-twelve-week period (Smith et al., 1971:538; Tietze and Lewit, 1972:114). The JPSA data give a total complication rate of 3.8 per 100 women for six or less weeks compared to 3.4 per 100 women for seven to eight weeks. Some think the ideal time for abortion might be around eight to ten weeks, and others hold with the traditional belief of the earlier the better. The settlement of this question awaits further data from larger numbers of early abortions.

Quality of Care. A controversy developed around the question of whether or not abortions done on an outpatient basis are safe. At the Kiev conference on abortion in 1927, Benderskaya speculated on the connection between the quality of care and postoperative complications. He said that "the large number of hemorrhage cases in Kiev can only be explained by the lack of hospital accommodation; it is interesting to note that every year this number almost exactly corresponds to the number of refusals of requests for hospital admission for artificial abortion" (quoted in Schlesinger, 1949:182). In a brief report on Japan called "The Harmful Effects of Induced Abortion," Koya (1966:170) commented on the "remarkable fact . . . that some 70 percent were operated upon on an ambulatory basis without hospitalization." Specifically in regard to the high incidence of fever following abortion, Koya (1966:171) thought it "might well be diminished to a considerable extent if the operation were carried out more carefully and the patient kept under stricter aftercare." Carl Müller (1966:79) generalized that "the risk of post-operative complications is no doubt greater in those countries in which abortion is entirely free and therefore mostly done on ambulant patients."

Some American physicians, however, are beginning to compile data which challenge the idea that outpatient abortions are unsafe. Margolis and Overstreet (1970:480–81) stress the need to conserve facilities and personnel and therefore "to emphasize the simplicity and the safety" of performing early abortions by suction on an outpatient basis. They consider it significant that none of the post-abortion complications developed earlier than two days after the abortion and would therefore not have been prevented or discovered if the patients had been hospitalized for the "conventional twelve to forty-eight" hours. Strausz and Schulman (1971:204) make a plea for early abortions by suction and under local anesthesia on an outpatient basis as "the procedure of choice." The strongest evidence for the safety of early outpatient abortions comes from the JPSA data. Complication rates for abortions by suction were lowest for outpatient clinic patients and lower for hospital outpatients than for hospital inpatients. Another factor relevant to quality of care was the JPSA finding that "nonprivate patients had significantly higher complication rates than private patients, especially for abortions in the second trimester" (Tietze and Lewit, 1972:98).

In short, the evidence points to the safety of outpatient abortions by suction on relatively healthy women. The consistently higher complication rates for nonprivate than private patients may be associated with poorer health among nonprivate patients, poorer medical care, and "inadequate aftercare in their home environment" (Tietze and Lewit, 1972:111).

Preexisting Complications and Sterilization. Although common sense would tell us that women in poor health at the time of abortion and women who undergo sterilization might well have higher complication rates, most investigators do not explore these factors. The JPSA data, however, examine complication rates of healthy women subject to the risks of abortion only, of women with preexisting complications only, of women with sterilizing operations only, and of women with preexisting complications and sterilizing operations. As might be expected, the differences are marked. The abortion only group, consisting mostly of early abortions by suction, had the lowest complication rates compared with all patients. And compared to all patients, complications "were twice as high for patients with preexisting complications only, three times as high for those with sterilizing operations only, and close to five times as high for women with both preexisting complications and sterilizing operations" (Tietze and Lewit, 1972:110).

Age, Class, Race, Number of Previous Pregnancies, Marital Status. Due to social factors such as, for example, no experience in recognizing pregnancy symptoms, inadequate resources, lack of emotional support, or negative attitudes about health care, certain groups of women tend to have later abortions and therefore take the higher risks associated with these abortions. In the JPSA study, late abortions occurred most frequently among women under eighteen, nonprivate patients, black women, and a small group of women with six or more children. Also women who were single, widowed, divorced, or separated tended to abort later than currently married women, and women with no previous pregnancies had comparatively high percentages of late abortions (Tietze and Lewit, 1972:102–3). Although the JPSA data indicate a trend toward an increasing proportion of early abortions, Joseph Rovinsky's (1971:339) comment regarding the first eight months with New York City's repeal law still holds true to a degree and will take time to change: "as a generalization, the young, unmarried, black girl having her first pregnancy is at greatest risk, being most likely to seek abortion late." The trend toward early abortions suggests that more women are aware of the lesser risk and lower cost of early abortion, and that hospitals have improved procedures so that waiting periods have been minimized (Tietze and Lewit, 1972:117–18).

LATE COMPLICATIONS

Although the evidence is far from conclusive, the attitude prevails that late complications from abortion represent a significant threat to a woman's health. The 1927 Russian conference placed special stress upon the danger of late complications, and some present-day investigators also place their emphasis upon late complications. A report from the Royal College of Obstetricians and Gynaecologists (1970:533) took the view that although Great Britain had no follow-up studies documenting the "long-term hazards," they did have reports from other countries which "show that late physical ill-effects are not uncommon." Also from Britain, Diggory et al. (1970:290) report 10 percent complications, "none of which was serious," out of 1,000 consecutive cases, but they especially note the need for information on the long-term complications.

Perhaps the threat of sterility subsequent to abortion is the most widely feared aftereffect. Ekblad (1955:219) reported that 1 percent of his sample were involuntarily sterile two to three years after the abortion, but he could not be sure if it was caused by the abortion. Kolstad (1957:57) found 3.4 percent sterile from four to seven years after abortion. In reviewing some of the literature from 1930 to the early 1950s, Kolstad found a range of from 0 to 5.4 percent sterility following abortion. He concludes that "sterility should be counted as a possible secondary complication subsequent to artificial abortion," but he also remarks that "sterility may equally be observed subsequent to a delivery" (Kolstad, 1957:58). More recently, Hirschler's (1970:131) evidence from Hungary suggested that abortion "is responsible for some cases of secondary sterility," while from a 1963 Japanese study, Muramatsu (1970:123) reported that "a statistically significant association" could not be established between abortion and sterility.

Russian authors especially have stressed the high incidence of menstrual disturbances associated with abortion. In Ekblad's

(1955:219) study, the 1 percent who were sterile also had menstrual disturbances. Kolstad's (1957:58–59) group had a 9 percent rate of menstrual disturbances, and he feels these results "point in the direction of a possibility that the patients may develop menstrual disorders as a consequence of induced abortion." From the Japanese data, Muramatsu (1970:123) reported that "menstruation is slightly delayed for two or three months immediately after the abortion, but soon reverts to the pattern established before the pregnancy." A serious problem with these and other figures on the percentage or rate of complications is the general lack of attention to the significance of the data. Without information on a control group, or some other type of baseline data to use as a comparison, the figures have little meaning. For example, a matched control group of women undergoing pregnancy and childbirth might show a 2 or a 20 percent rate of menstrual disturbances; unless we have that kind of information we are not sure whether to be dismayed or ecstatic about Kolstad's reported 9 percent rate.

The greatest body of evidence on late complications refers to connections between a history of abortion and problems in subsequent births. At the 1927 Kiev conference Szerdukov (quoted in Schlesinger, 1949:176–77) reviewed a study comparing one group of women having a history of abortion to a control group with no previous abortions. It was found that a rise in temperature during birth, the duration of birth, defects of the placenta, the percentage of stillborn embryos, and hormonal trauma occurred more frequently among the abortion group than the control group. Mehlan (1966:212) refers to two studies from Eastern Europe. One "stated that the risk of spontaneous abortion, premature birth, stillbirth, and various birth complications is doubled by repeated abortions." Another "found that one-half of the women with cervical insufficiency . . . had previously undergone legal abortion." Callahan (1970:39) refers to a report by Franc Novak which notes an increase in ectopic pregnancies in Rumania, Poland, and Yugoslavia which are suspected of being connected with previous abortions. Muramatsu (1970:123) summarized from the 1963 Japanese data that "the investigators reported an increased incidence of spontaneous abortions and premature birth, but could not establish a statistically significant association between a history of induced abortion and either ectopic pregnancy or secondary sterility. The course of delivery was unaffected." From Hungary, Hirschler (1970:130) observed that the incidence of spontaneous abortion, ectopic pregnancy, and defects of the placenta had not increased since the legalization of abortion. Although the incidence of prematurity increased since legalization, Hirschler remarks that "this may be attributed at least in part to greater urbanization, an increase in the number of working women, and the greater prevalence of smoking." The strongest current statement on the late complications of abortion comes from "four leading Israeli gynecologists," but the serious nature of these complications are perhaps influenced by the fact that many abortions in Israel are done illegally by physicians in their offices and that until 1970 the aspiration technique was rarely used in Israel.

> Research performed by us on the clinical material at our disposal has shown that induced abortion is an important cause and even a leading cause of different gynecological and obstetrical situations and complications, the more important of which are the following: chronic inflammation of the internal genital organs, secondary sterility, insufficiency of the os uteri, intrauterine adhesions, amenorrhea or hypomenorrhea, repeated miscarriages, premature births, disturbances of implantation of placenta, extrauterine pregnancy, and various types of neuro-vegetative disturbances. (quoted in Bachi, 1970:282)

Undoubtedly all of these ailments should be considered and investigated for their connection to abortion. But it is also necessary to compare the incidence of these complications before and after the legalization of abortion, to use control groups, and to consider other variables which might have an influence on the incidence of late complications. In the long run, knowledge regarding late complications may come to have a greater influence on a country's abortion policy than ideological attitudes. But at least in the short run, ideological positions are likely to twist the knowledge and to determine the policy.

CHAPTER SEVEN

FAMILY PLANNING AND ABORTION

When abortion and contraception are discussed, they are sometimes seen as competing ways to control births and sometimes as complementary. According to the former view, abortion is an antagonist of contraception. Liberalized abortion laws open the floodgates to induced abortion and encourage less dependence upon contraception. Widespread abortion then becomes the greatest obstacle to the spread of contraception. Seen as complementary methods, abortion "does not compete with contraception but serves as a backstop when the latter fails or when contraceptive devices or information are not available. As contraception becomes customary, the incidence of abortion recedes even without its being banned" (Davis, 1967:733). In spite of these disagreements about the place of abortion in family planning, few dispute the position that contraception, and not abortion, is the preferred approach to birth control.

THE STIGMA OF ABORTION

Many terms have been used to circumvent the stigma that was formerly attached to contraception and that is still attached to abortion. The bumper crop of terms has caused a good deal of confusion. In 1967 Kingsley Davis (1967:731) said: "As is well known, 'family planning' is a euphemism for contraception." In 1971 some family planners nevertheless worried that many women did *not* associate family planning with contraception and consequently failed to use existing family planning facilities. They recommended the terms "birth control" and "family planning" to identify facilities offering contraceptive counseling and service (Block et al., 1971:4). Birth control, as defined in a 1962 U.S. Department of Health, Education, and Welfare report, included contraception and abortion (cited in Hardin, 1971:6). In 1969 Pohlman and Pohlman (1969:9) invented the combination "birth planning" which "seems to be an improvement over 'birth control,' which indicates merely trying to prevent births from happening." Birth planning, the authors say, covers contraception, birth control, family planning, eugenics, planned parenthood, population planning, sterilization, abortion, infanticide, artificial insemination, and adoption.

Although abortion is now often associated with birth control and occasionally with family planning, it yet remains a somewhat shady companion. During the growth of the family planning and birth control movements, abortion was a topic to avoid. Hindell and Simms (1971:238) write of the British situation:

> The need for abortion law reform was first asserted in public in Britain in 1922. Stella Brown advocated it at the London Birth Control Conference, and was in consequence, as Janet Chance observed in her book the *Cost of English Morals* (1931) 'disavowed by many of the supporters of the Birth Control movement.' For years chilliness and embarrassment characterized the relation between birth-controllers and feminists on the one hand, and abortion law reformers on the other, despite their many common interests and sympathies. Perhaps inevitably so. It is enough to speak out boldly and courageously on one unpopular issue; to campaign for several is, in Britain at any rate, to be labelled a crank. The birth-control movement had enough problems of its own without attracting to itself the additional odium of abortion law reform.

And during a 1964 conference, Alan Guttmacher, President of the Planned Parenthood Federation, stated that he would have "a tough time in getting" the Executive Committee "to take a stand on a liberalization of abortion laws" (Guttmacher, 1965:175). By 1969, however, the Planned Parenthood Federation of America issued a statement supportive of abortion as a supplementary method of controlling family size. Abortion was beginning to lose some of its stigma, but it still had a considerable distance to travel.

The controversy surrounding the President's Commission on Population Growth and the American Future and the 1972 legislative fight in New York provide an excellent dramatization of the simultaneous acceptance-rejection of abortion and the total acceptance of contraception.

In July 1969 President Nixon appointed the Commission on Population Growth and the American Future, established "as a national goal the provision of adequate family planning services within the next five years to all those who want them but cannot afford them," and instructed "the Agency for International Development to give population and family planning high priority for attention, personnel, research, and funding among our several aid programs." The *New York Times* observed that this was "the first message on population problems ever sent by a President to Congress," and as far as "birth control [contraception], the President's message advocated more Federal support for family planning assistance rather than any fundamental change in the type of program the Government already underwrites." The *Times* also remarked that "the Roman Catholic church's opposition to artificial means of contraception once inhibited Federal efforts to restrain population growth. But Government involvement has become less controversial nowadays." * The President's message established that the United States was concerned about population problems and that family planning (contraceptive) programs were to have a large role in any action regarding population control. The speech also indicates how really acceptable, and even respectable, family planning has become. The first family planning stamp in the United States, issued by the Postal Service in 1972, confirms the re-

* See the *New York Times,* July 19, 1969, pp. 1, 8 for the text of the President's message and a report on it.

spectability of the family planning movement. And even though controversies lie beneath the surface of unanimity about family planning, Dorothy Millstone (1972:20) remarked that "the cause for which Margaret Sanger was jailed in 1916 has become as noncontroversial as Smokey the Bear."

In contrast to the policy on family planning (contraception), an April 1971 statement made clear the administration's position on abortion. In 1970 the military liberalized the rules on abortion at military hospitals, but since "historically, laws regulating abortion in the United States have been the province of states, not the Federal Government" and "that remains the situation today," President Nixon directed "that the policy on abortions at American military bases in the United States be made to correspond with the laws of the states where those bases are located." * Since legislators and courts were debating the abortion issue, President Nixon felt that "the country has a right to know my personal views."

> From personal and religious beliefs I consider abortions an unacceptable form of population control. Further, unrestricted abortion policies, or abortion on demand, I cannot square with my personal belief in the sanctity of human life—including the life of the yet unborn. For, surely, the unborn have rights also, recognized even in principles expounded by the United Nations.
>
> Ours is a nation with a Judeo-Christian heritage. It is also a nation with serious social problems—problems of malnutrition, of broken homes, of poverty and of delinquency. But none of these problems justifies such a solution.
>
> A good and generous people will not opt, in my view, for this kind of alternative to its social dilemmas. Rather, it will open its hearts and homes to the unwanted children of its own, as it has done for the unwanted millions of other lands.

In 1972 President Nixon had two chances to reiterate his views on abortion—when the New York legislature tried to repeal the repeal law and when the Commission on Population Growth and the American Future presented its recommendations. If Governor Rockefeller had not vetoed it, the 1972 New York bill would have restored the original New York statute. The President wrote a letter to Cardinal

* See the *New York Times*, April 4, 1971, p. 33 for the text of the President's statement on abortion.

Cooke, a leader of New York's anti-abortion forces, in which he stated that "I would personally like to associate myself with the convictions you deeply feel and eloquently express" (*New York Times,* May 7, 1972, p. 29). Allegedly the public disclosure of this letter represented "sloppy staff work" on the part of the White House since it was supposed to remain private correspondence (*New York Times,* May 11, 1972, p. 45). In fairly typical fashion, the New York anti-abortion advocates denied that these events, coming in an election year, had political significance, and the pro-abortion forces deplored President Nixon's interference in a state matter for political gain. An anti-abortion New York assemblyman was quoted as denying that the abortion bill was political, saying the issue transcended politics, and that "it is moral, it is a question of how we view life" (*New York Times,* May 10, 1972, p. 51). The pro-abortion assemblyman emphasized that "the issue was indeed political," and that "when you take your morality and put it on the floor of this Legislature, it's political" (*New York Times,* May 10, 1972, p. 51).

At the same time that President Nixon's disapproval of the 1970 New York legislation and support of the 1972 bill were publicized, his Commission on Population Growth and the American Future not only recommended that abortion laws be liberalized, but they held up the 1970 New York statute as the model legislation. The Commission's recommendations in full were:

> Therefore, with the admonition that abortion not be considered a primary means of fertility control, the Commission recommends that present state laws restricting abortion be liberalized along the lines of the New York State statute, such abortions to be performed on request by duly licensed physicians under conditions of medical safety.
>
> In carrying out this policy, the Commission recommends:
>
> That federal, state, and local governments make funds available to support abortion services in states with liberalized statutes.
>
> That abortion be specifically included in comprehensive health insurance benefits, both public and private. (Commission, 1972:178)

It should be pointed out that this represents the Commission's majority report since several Commissioners appended dissenting opinions. Moreover, the first phrase of the recommendation clearly eliminates abortion as a primary method of birth control. Referring to the President's reaction to the entire Commission report, a *New*

York Times editorial (May 11, 1972, p. 42) observed that "although he said the report would be 'of great value in assisting governments at all levels of public policy,' the President did not indicate what provisions he found valuable nor did he suggest any actions his Administration might take in order to carry out its suggestions." He was however specific on those Commission recommendations which were unacceptable—liberalized abortion and the unrestricted distribution of contraceptives to minors.

In spite of the anti-abortionists' claim that abortion debates in legislatures transcend politics, the administration's involvement in New York, the Commission's report, and the President's reaction to it made abortion in 1972, an election year, more of a political issue than ever before. Also by 1972, pro- and anti-abortionists made abortion a question of political survival for many legislators. Lists of candidates' positions on abortion were circulated and both sides vowed to defeat candidates who did not agree with them and to elect candidates who supported them.

Although the Commission report wants abortion to be considered a secondary method of fertility control, it still recommends that government funds be spent on abortion services. If implemented, the Commission's recommendations would have the effect of supporting abortion as a supplementary method of fertility control, as advocated by Planned Parenthood in 1969; it would also have the effect of allocating government funds for abortion services, just as President Nixon directed government monies to be used for family planning (contraception) in 1969. But even with our changing attitudes, the Commission's recommendations, and liberalized abortion laws in several states, abortion fares badly when compared to contraception, and President Nixon probably echoes the views of many that abortion is an unacceptable form of population control. Bernard Berelson (1969:11) rates family planning (contraception) generally high and abortion low as far as "ethical acceptability;" family planning rates "moderate to high" and abortion "moderate to low" with respect to "political viability." Berelson (1969:1) gives an excellent assessment of the reasons for the relative acceptability of family planning:

Why is family planning the first step taken on the road to population control? Probably because from a broad political standpoint it is the most acceptable one: since closely tied to maternal and child care it can be perceived as a health measure beyond dispute; and since voluntary, it can be justified as a contribution to the effective personal freedom of individual couples. On both scores, the practice ties into accepted values and thus achieves political viability. In some situations, it is an oblique approach, seen as the politically acceptable way to start toward "population control" on the national level by promoting fertility control and smaller family size among individual couples. Moreover, it is a gradual effort and an inexpensive one, both of which contribute to its political acceptability. Though the introduction of family planning as a response to a country's population problem may be calculated to minimize opposition, even that policy has been attacked in several countries by politicians who are unconvinced and/or see an electoral advantage in the issue.

In addition to promoting health and freedom, family planning is sometimes also seen as a way of helping families to escape from poverty. Abortion can also be seen as a method that aids in escaping from poverty or in providing freedom of choice about childrearing, but controversy surrounds the question of whether it contributes to health or is injurious to health. In the meantime, federal support for family planning services specifically excludes support for abortion services. The anti-abortion climate still exerts considerable pressure upon the views that are held about all aspects of abortion, including its impact upon health.

HEALTH HAZARDS

Some have tried unsuccessfully to fit abortion in as merely another method of birth control which involves no special health or moral questions. Garrett Hardin (1967:75) stated that "abortion is merely a special method of birth control, and its ethics must be analyzed as such. Every major religion of the world is now on record as favoring birth control [contraception]: the only doctrinal differences between them revolve around the methods permitted." Although Hardin tries to minimize ethical objections to abortion, in the end he argues for minimizing abortion, "for abortion, like alcohol and speed, is a danger, and we want to minimize it. Abortion is defensible as a form of birth control, but it is clearly the least desirable form, other things being equal" (Hardin, 1967:79). Glanville Williams also emphasizes the harmful consequences of abortion if it is used instead of contraception as a form of birth control. Referring to the first Soviet legalization in 1920, Williams (1957:220) says that "abortion appears to have been treated by the populace as a normal form of birth control, instead of being (as it should be) a last-ditch measure where the birth of a child is particularly undesirable. The result was that abortion had to be carried out on a scale that was patently injurious. This shows that, whether abortion is legalized or not, it is essential to reduce the scale of the problem by energetic education in contraception."

Very clearly, abortion is generally not considered as safe as contraception, even by those who discount the moral objections to abortion and see it as an integral part of any birth control program (Koya, 1954; Heer, 1965:83; Klinger, 1966:476). Yet Tietze (1969:8) has presented evidence that the mortality rate due to the use of oral contraceptives and to induced hospital abortions is approximately the same. He concludes that "in terms of the risk to life, the most rational procedure for regulating fertility is the use of a perfectly safe, although not 100 percent effective, method of contraception and the termination of pregnancies resulting from contraceptive failure under the best possible circumstances, i.e., in the operating room of a hospital."

The persisting high level of concern about the presumed danger of abortion relative to contraception again recalls the question of the role of ideology. Very little data are available on the effects of either the long-term use of oral contraceptives or induced abortion. Our ideological biases, however, have built a molehill out of the dangers stemming from oral contraceptives and a mountain out of the dangers stemming from abortion.

INEFFICIENCY

It is possible to believe that abortion compares favorably to contraception as far as ethical acceptability and health risks and still to prefer contraception on the grounds that it is more efficient. A reasonably effective contraceptive contributes significantly to the amount of time a woman can remain sexually active without becoming pregnant. In contrast, relying only upon induced abortion, the intervals between pregnancies can become very short. A woman who carries a pregnancy to term is not risking pregnancy again during gestation, and for some time after birth until her ovulation cycle has reestablished itself. But a woman who undergoes an induced abortion, and does not use contraceptives, risks pregnancy again much sooner. As Henry David (1970:253) summarizes Tietze's computations: abortion "increases the potential number of pregnancies in a given woman in the sense that a woman who aborts is capable of becoming pregnant again much earlier than a woman who carries her pregnancy to term." In consequence, a very high incidence of abortion is needed in order to limit family size; "induced abortion has much greater impact when used as a supplement to contraception than when relied upon alone" (Potter, 1963:165).

The most vivid illustration of the inefficiency of induced abortion for lowering the pregnancy rate is provided by abortion "repeaters." A Japanese survey, referred to by Potter (1963:163), found that those women having abortions during a one-year period averaged 1.1 abortions during the year. Klinger (1966:471) points out that "abortions occur at rather frequent intervals" in several Eastern European countries: in the Soviet Union for the period 1958–59, "16% of the aborting women had more than one induced abortion within a year"; "in Hungary the aborting women experiencing their third or higher order abortion increased from 25.5% in 1960 to 31.4% in 1964." The inefficiency of having to resort to frequent induced abortions and the concern about the impact of repeated abortions upon a woman's health has led some countries to restrict the number of abortions a woman may receive in a given time period. Several Eastern European countries require at least six months to elapse after an abortion before another one will be permitted, but the number of repeated abortions still remains high because of the limited availability of modern contraceptives and the almost total reliance upon abortion as the method of birth control by some women.

Other investigators have pointed out that abortion, in contrast to contraception, involves a greater use of physician time and hospital facilities and is therefore less efficient than contraception. With the widespread use of suction curretage and outpatient care the differences between abortion and contraception can be minimized to some extent, and the tendency in some countries to use skilled paraprofessionals to perform abortions can reduce the difference even further (Berelson, 1969:4).

AN ABORTION MENTALITY

Clashing attitudes and ideologies in the abortion controversy have produced some interesting phenomena; one of them is the idea of an "abortion mentality." A literal reading of what has been said about abortion might lead one to conclude that the abortion mentality is a dangerous communicable disease—one that spreads throughout a country once the abortion laws have been liberalized, and sometimes even before. Three symptoms of this disease can be recognized: a (dangerous) increase in the abortion rate; a (dangerous) decrease in the amount of guilt over abortions; and a (dangerous) growth of disrespect for life.

Concern is widespread over the hazards of criminal abortions, and pro-abortionists and anti-abortionists can sometimes agree on the need to do something about reducing criminal abortions. A few anti-abortionists will even go along with limited changes in the original laws, such as the reform law proposed in the American Law Institute's Model Penal Code, in order to make it possible for women who will otherwise seek out criminal abortions to have safer legal abortions instead. Unfortunately, a reform law does not meet the demand that exists for abortion, and either the number of criminal abortions continues unabated or those women who can afford it travel to other jurisdictions where they can have legal abortions.

A repeal law, on the other hand, does meet the need and reduces the harmful consequences of criminal abortions. If it did that alone and the total number of legal abortions equaled the total number of legal and illegal abortions previously, then the reluctant anti-abortionists would perhaps be pleased. Unfortunately, a repeal law changes the situation entirely, and not only do most women who formerly sought out criminal abortions take advantage of the law but so do many other women. Given a change in the legal climate, and perhaps an accompanying change in public attitudes toward abortion, we would certainly expect a rise, perhaps a dramatic rise, in the total abortion rate. Pro-abortionists as well as anti-abortionists are often alarmed by the increase, and they decry the "abortion mentality" that underlies it.

To many it appears that there is, in principle, some optimal quantity of legal abortions. Too few legal abortions drive women to criminal abortionists. Too many legal abortions signify the dreaded abortion mentality. But the optimal number or rate of legal abortions is elusive. Before any court decision on the District of Columbia's original abortion law, Connor and Aydinel (1970:137) expressed concern about "too many therapeutic abortions being done" in Washington, D.C. They estimated them at more than 1,000 per year and as probably more than were performed in Maryland, Colorado, or North Carolina which had reform laws. This meant that Washington, D.C., the nation's capital, was the "abortion center of the United States." According to Connor and Aydinel, no one benefits from abortion, and "contraception is the antidote for the ill requiring therapeutic abortion."

The attempt in Kansas in 1972 to return from a reform law to the original, restrictive statute suggests that the abortion mentality disease also appears in states with reform laws. The state senator who sponsored the bill contended that the reform law "had been abused" and that Kansas had become "the abortion center of the United States" (*Kansas City Star,* Feb. 1, 1972). His major concern was that 8,549 legal abortions took place during one year in Kansas, and that 5,305 of these were performed on women from other states. The senator is further quoted as saying that "people are using the abortion method as a birth control measure."

Statistics released by the Health Services Administration (HSA) of New York City (1972) showed that 278,122 abortions were performed during the first eighteen months of the new law, of which 109,372 occurred between July and December of 1971, and that a higher proportion were performed on nonresidents than residents. In addition the report showed that maternal mortality, infant mortality, out of wedlock births, and complication rates were down. Gordon Chase, HSA Administrator, said that these "figures show that abortion has become an accepted service in the City's hospitals and in special clinics," and that "we have helped to show the nation that elective abortion can be offered like any other medical procedure." An anti-abortion state senator said the abortion statistics proved his worst fears, although "he realized the statistics which horrified him were viewed as a sign of success by proponents" (*Rochester Democrat Chronicle,* Feb. 15, 1972).

Even health officials, who were generally pleased with the capacity of medical facilities to keep pace with the large demand and provide service with efficiency, safety, and dignity, were worried, among other things, "that abortion might become just another birth control method" (*Chicago Sun Times,* Feb. 15, 1972). Obviously, depending upon how one views abortion, it is possible to be alarmed about 1,000 or 8,549 legal abortions in one year or pleased with a city's capacity to handle 109,372 legal abortions in six months. But even pro-abortionists or those administering abortion services, such as the HSA in New York City, become concerned about the possibility that abortion will be used as the primary method of birth control. This would signal the beginning of an abortion mentality and an abuse of the law; even if the law permits it, women should not, and must not be permitted, to use abortion as their primary method of birth control.

It also appears from contemporary writings that some optimal level of guilt should be displayed after an abortion. If there is a great deal of guilt then induced abortion is obviously dangerous to the woman's psychological health and should be avoided. On the other hand, if there is little or no guilt about an abortion, then we are again faced with a symptom of abortion mentality, and the disease must be carefully watched for. Ottosson (1971:191) expressed concern about the possible existence of an abortion mentality in Sweden:

> It has been asked whether legislation encourages an abortion mentality, and, in one respect, it does. Swedish women have come to regard legal abortion as a civic right, something also sanctioned by the highest medical authority in the country. Between the application of the law and public opinion is a continuous reciprocity in which the toning down of the feelings of shame and guilt, which were previously attached to abortion operations, can be discerned. I do not believe that signs of a brutal attitude and lack of respect for life have appeared, which may possibly be connected with the fact that a woman does not regard a foetus as life until

she feels foetal movements. An abortion mentality in the sense that applications are made on weaker indications is possible, even probable, but in any case, in the part of the country where I have been working, the growing numbers of applications have about the same degree of urgency as previously.

This concern about an abortion mentality does not necessarily relate only to liberalized laws. Referring to the lack of penalties for women under some original U.S. laws, Thomas Barnard (1967:561) speculates that "while not exactly creating an 'abortion mentality,' as is said to be found in Scandinavia, perhaps this has already had a significant effect upon the women who may be considering whether or not to abort the fetus by convincing her of what she wants to believe: that it is not her wrongdoing but that of the abortionist."

For a woman trying to follow the threads of the controversy in order to insure her own access to legal abortion services, as well as her daughter's, the situation becomes rather confusing. If you have already displayed the appropriate amount of illness in order to qualify for an abortion in a state with a reform law, how much guilt are you then supposed to display after the abortion in order not to jeopardize the right to abortion of future generations? Too much is bad because it means that the psychological aftereffects of abortion are dangerous. Too little is bad because it means you have been smitten by the abortion mentality. This dual attitude of concern over high and low guilt is expressed clearly by Russell Shaw (1968:114): "It seems rather beside the point to argue, as one physician [Mandy, 1967:292] did, that there is no particular risk of guilt following abortion—because he had observed patients who admitted to as many as fifteen to twenty self-induced abortions without exhibiting any signs of guilt or depression. The mildest comment to be made about such a group of women is that they are atypical; the strongest is that one wonders what, if anything, they *would* feel guilty about."

On the one hand, Shaw tells us that women who do not feel guilty or depressed after abortions are atypical, for an alarming incidence of psychological aftereffects is inevitable. On the other hand, if women do not feel guilty about their abortions, that is equally alarming. Women should feel a certain amount of shame, guilt, depression, and a sense of wrongdoing or they will treat abortion as a "civic right," develop a casual attitude toward abortion, fail to use contraceptives, and society will risk losing its respect for life.

Each society develops its own attitudes about when abortion is appropriate and about the proper combination of contraception and abortion. More societies are recognizing that the prohibition of abortion serves no purpose and that abortion is essential as a backup method of birth control. Reliance upon abortion as the primary method of fertility control is, however, widely condemned. Even among those who would permit abortion in cases of contraceptive failure, the woman is often condemned. Contraceptive failure becomes the woman's flaw. Garrett Hardin (1967:79) mentions a symposium of physicians in which "one of the doctors spoke of the 'ignorance, inertia, or carelessness' that led to the need for abortion." Or the January 1972 issue of *Family Planning Digest* tells us about two surveys which found that although physicians "overwhelmingly favor the provision of family planning services" they have doubts about poor people's ability to use certain methods, and many physicians "favor punitive action—compulsory sterilization or withholding of support—in cases where welfare mothers have several illegitimate children." Edmund Overstreet (1971:24) observes that inadequate instruction by the prescribing physician accounts for contraceptive failures. He describes the trap a woman is caught in if physicians fail to perform an abortion for contraceptive failure: "They [women] argue quite reasonably: 'You were perfectly willing to give me medical care to help me prevent any further pregnancies; why won't you give me an abortion now that your own medical prescription has failed?' "

In short, those who find fault with the woman who seeks an abortion are, in William Ryan's (1971) terms, blaming the victim. Contraceptive failure may stem from defective contraceptives or defective instructions by a physician or a defective system for delivering health care, but it is easier for many to lay the blame at the feet of the victim.

By far the greatest alarm is created by, and the greatest opprobrium is attached to, the "repeaters." These are women who have more than one abortion, sometimes over a relatively short time period. Martin Ekblad (1955:97–98) gave one of the first descriptions of this group of women:

> The results of the examination thus constitute strong evidence that there is a large group of women who are now granted legal abortion but who would have given birth to the child if this possibility of legal abortion had not been open to them. These women are to be found chiefly among the married women living in a harmonious marriage. In these cases the indication has most frequently been that of asthenic insufficiency. Previously, and as a rule thanks to their personal disposition, these women had taken a new unwelcome pregnancy with resignation, submissively accepting it without protest. . . . As it is in this group that the highest frequency of recidivations is met with, i.e., the greatest number of new unintentional pregnancies, and as it is, moreover, by the same man, perhaps the legal abortion should be reserved chiefly for those amongst them who are so worn out that this constitutes an indication for simultaneous sterilization.

Or from New York City after eight months under the repeal law, Joseph Rovinsky (1971:339) reports that "recidivism is beginning to be troublesome." The abortion service at City Hospital Center offers extensive contraceptive education and service and tries to "motivate patients," but still "6% of abortions are performed on women previously aborted in our facility since July, 1970!" The causes of this troublesome problem "are under investigation by our psychiatric colleagues." "Recidivism" is a term usually applied to someone who repeats a criminal act. Clearly some people regard abortion repeaters as recidivists, despite the legality of abortion. And among the punishments to fit the crime, sterilization and psychiatric investigation are considered. Norms current in the United States inform us that contraception is the chief method of birth control, with abortion reserved only for occasional contraceptive failures or other special circumstances. The repeaters are therefore seen as deviants who abuse the abortion laws by using abortion as the major method of birth control. The abortion mentality again stands indicted.

ABORTION AND CONTRACEPTION

Using abortion as a major means of birth control, especially where contraceptives are available and accessible, may dismay the experts, but it may seem eminently sensible from the standpoint of the individual who wants to control reproduction. Henry David (1970:257) refers to an article by Emily Moore which speculates on "why some women prefer the 'risk' of abortion to regular contraceptive practice." Interestingly enough his summary of Moore's article answers the question and presents a fairly persuasive case for the use of abortion, but he still emphasizes the need to find out about the abortion repeaters.

> Except for sterilization and the intrauterine device, no other birth-prevention technique is a one-event operation. Abortion is coitus-independent, is 100 percent effective under the proper circumstances, and does not require the knowledge or consent of the sexual partner. It is not based on the probabilities of prevention, but on the certainty of a recognized pregnancy. It is the only method to avert a birth which may have been desired at the time of conception but which, for whatever reasons, may no longer be wanted. Compared with mechanical and chemical means of contraception, abortion is technically simple. It appears particularly important to initiate studies of repeated abortion-seeking behavior, especially in circumstances where modern methods of effective conception control are readily available and accessible. It would also be desirable to compare abortion knowledge with contraception knowledge, and how attitudes vary with level of knowledge.

Japan and Eastern Europe are usually singled out to support the fear that the widespread use of abortion replaces contraception. The rapid post World War II decline in the Japanese birth rate stands as "one of the amazing events in demographic history" (Koya, 1962:103), but the fact that abortion rather than contraception played the main role in this decline is interpreted as being highly alarming. The 1948 Eugenic Protection Law provided for abortion, contraception, and sterilization, and abortion became the preferred birth control method. At the time of this legalization of abortion, Japan was experiencing crushing overpopulation as a result of large-scale demobilization and repatriation (Muramatsu, 1965:67). Furthermore, it has been pointed out that not only was contraception not widely practiced in Japan but that abortion and infanticide were old traditions "practiced by peasants at times of economic difficulty" (Frederiksen and Brackett, 1968:1004; Muramatsu, 1965:71). Despite the lack of a strong contraceptive tradition, the presence of an abortion tradition, and urgent population problems apparent in daily life, Koya (1962:104) asks: "That the Japanese people are strongly motivated to limit the size of their families is self-evident from the low level of the birth rate, but why this is achieved largely through abortion instead of contraception is the pressing question."

This concern over the dominance of abortion led to campaigns to lower the abortion rate by promoting contraception since many were concerned with protecting women's health against the dangers of widespread abortion. In 1952 the government instituted family planning programs, and some of the pilot projects stand as classic examples that contraceptive use can reduce the number of abortions where abortion is the major method of birth control. During the early stages of these programs, the number of abortions increased until experience and skill in contraceptive use was acquired, but in the later stages the number of abortions declined. It was generally felt that education in the use of contraception could reduce the number of abortions but the prohibition of abortion would probably not reduce the number of abortions (Koya, 1962:109–10). Though underreported, abortions in Japan probably peaked around 1960, and the role of contraception is now greater than that of abortion in regulating fertility (H. David, personal communication).

The November 1969 issue of the *International Planned Parenthood News* is mainly devoted to a report on a conference held in September 1969 in Budapest which "aimed at arousing medical leadership toward effective contraceptive services in order to reverse the widespread practice of abortion." Franc Novak of Yugoslavia "declared that the strongest obstacle to substituting contraception was ignorance," and that "the absence of medical teaching on this topic can no longer be tolerated." At a 1963 conference Novak had said that "the greatest obstacle to the spread of contraception lies in liberal permission of artificial abortion" (quoted in Treffers, 1968:344). At the 1969 Budapest conference Thorsten Sjövall of Sweden "urged the introduction of more psychology and sexology into medical teaching. Many of the difficulties faced by the medical profession in adopting family planning as an integral part of their work arose from traditional resistance toward the idea of preventive as opposed to curative medicine." In a similar vein, David (1970:259–60) observes that "the impression prevails that the medical profession is the single most resistant group to implementing methods of family limitation," and that "while medical congresses have repeatedly passed resolutions endorsing the principle of family planning and contraception, individual practitioners have frequently resisted implementation, most likely for personal reasons." As a final general indicator of the lack of knowledge among the medical profession, Crist and Starnes (1972:61) remark concerning the McGill University *Birth Control Handbook* that "anyone who reads through the bibliography conscientiously is apt to end up better informed than many professionals (including physicians) in the field of family planning."

With respect to the kind of contraception practiced in Eastern Europe, Egon Szabady of Hungary was quoted as saying at the 1969 Budapest conference: "There are many signs pointing to the fact that insufficiently effective contraceptives and incomplete instructions for their use increase the number of abortions by giving a false sense of security." Reporting on contraceptive use, David (1970:258) stated that for Eastern Europe: "Coitus interruptus remains the most widely practiced method of conception limitation, with young couples favoring more modern contraceptive techniques." Compared to the United States, modern contraception is of recent origin and availability in Eastern Europe, and these countries have a long established tradition of socially acceptable abortion (David, 1972a:11). Henry David (1972a:11–12) speculates that the use of abortion and contraceptives to control reproduction is now growing more similar in the United States and Eastern Europe. With the availability of safe, legal abortion in the United States more women, especially younger women, are taking advantage of abortion while more women in Central and Eastern Europe "are becoming more contraception conscious and have better access to modern contraceptives." The publicity on side effects of the pill has also influenced some women to go off the pill, and undoubtedly some of these women rely upon abortion or a combination of abortion and a less effective contraceptive. Referring to the use of the pill in Eastern Europe, David (1970:258) observes that "wider use of the pill is encountering opposition from women concerned about possible side effects," and "public media are more ori-

ented to complications, especially in the face of lagging endorsements of contraception by medical practitioners."

FAMILY PLANNING IDEOLOGY

What is the family planning ideology as it pertains to contraception versus abortion? The major tenet is that contraception is preferable to abortion for reasons of morality, political feasibility, health, and efficiency. A second tenet, still held by some advocates of family planning, is that some women become lax in the use of contraceptives if widespread abortion is permitted and that numerous women will use abortion as the major method of birth control. The first tenet points to the preferability of contraception and the second tenet to a preference for abortion. As a result of this paradox, and of the growing public support for legalized abortion, the ideology of the family planning movement has now come to accept legal, voluntary abortion as a supplement to contraception. Contraception is fully accepted as the major method of birth control, and abortion tolerated in instances of contraceptive failure. It is still believed that the abortion mentality needs to be guarded against, but with improved medical training in family planning and sex education in the schools, it will be possible to educate the public to the preferred methods of contraceptive practice. Family planning and birth control can thereby work hand in glove with abortion control and keep the abortion mentality in check.

Many differences appear within the family planning movement in attitudes toward the place of abortion. Although the movement as a whole feared involvement with abortion reformers until the late 1960s, many individuals within the family planning movement were pioneers in bringing about liberalized abortion legislation. And for many years some family planning groups have supported liberal abortion laws and have referred clients to medical abortionists. But the family planning ideology still guides the thinking of many people and also guides research, planning, and policy. The time has surely come to pay less attention to the pathology of women (as contraceptors or aborters) and more attention to the pathology of our system of medical care. The family planning ideology needs to be critically examined rather than blindly followed. We also need to examine the

attitudes and practices of medical personnel toward contraception, the availability of contraceptives to various groups, the cost of contraceptives compared to abortion, and the safety of contraceptives. The burden of proof rests with those who want to promote contraception as the major method of birth control; the mantle of blame does not belong on the shoulders of the woman who attempts to control reproduction in the best way she can.

The demand to control reproduction is overwhelming. A woman will generally use the most effective, safest method that is available to her. A safe, effective, simple, low-cost contraceptive that is readily available and positively evaluated will be widely used, but abortion will still be necessary for those who do not plan ahead, for contraceptive failures, for changed circumstances, and a host of other reasons. Professionals certainly disagree regarding the safest and most effective approach to family planning, and one can therefore hardly expect all women to make the same choices. Nor can we expect that the same choices will be available to all women. Some women may rely upon an abortion rather than contraception until they are certain they are fertile. Faced with the possibility that the pill is less than safe, why should a woman take it for five, ten, or twenty years if she can use a less effective contraceptive—proven safe—and obtain an abortion in case of failure? Confronted with the unavailability of contraception or with embarrassment on the part of the woman and/or physician to discuss contraception, it is hardly surprising that some women will use abortion as their major method of birth control. Before we invest too many of our resources in studying the alleged deviance of women, let us concentrate our resources upon improving the family planning climate in which women find themselves.

CHAPTER EIGHT

SOCIAL AND CULTURAL ASPECTS OF ABORTION: CLASS AND RACE

The knowledge that individuals have about abortion and their attitudes and behavior are greatly influenced by the social and cultural context. If one wants to predict the circumstances under which a person regards abortion as moral or immoral, or whether a woman experiences relief or guilt after an abortion, the most important item of information would be the sociocultural interpretation of abortion. Social class, race, religion, place of residence, and marital status are among the social variables that influence a person's access to, use of, and attitudes toward abortion services and alternatives to abortion.

The rapid changes that have taken place in the United States in the past decade also underline time as an important variable.

SEXUAL BEHAVIOR, CONTRACEPTION, AND PREGNANCY

Abortion presumably terminates an unwanted pregnancy, but as Pohlman and Pohlman (1969:181–95) point out, defining "unwanted" and "wanted" can be a complex undertaking. Some people, for example, proceed as though pregnancy out of wedlock is usually unwanted (Meier, 1961:144–46) while others assume that it is usually wanted (Harrison, 1969:366–67). An "unwanted" pregnancy can be transformed into one that is "wanted": if the pregnancy is unwanted only because the woman is unmarried, she may marry; or the woman may adapt herself to the idea of continuing an unwanted pregnancy, eventually coming to want it. Because of changed circumstances, a wanted pregnancy can also become unwanted. An unwanted pregnancy may be carried to term, at which point the mother may keep the child or give the child up for adoption or foster care. Although it is often difficult to know what is meant by an unwanted or wanted pregnancy or whether an unwanted pregnancy has really become wanted, clearly there are several alternate ways of responding to an unwanted pregnancy. Within the United States the influence of social class and racial background upon various responses to an unwanted pregnancy has aroused a good deal of controversy.*

Many national and regional studies carried out in the last twenty years indicate that the poor, blacks, and the less educated want about the same number of children as others in society. Blacks, in fact, want as few or even fewer children than whites. Despite the desire for relatively small families within these groups, the studies also established that they wind up having larger families than they desire. The largest excess in fertility is to be found among the poor, nonwhites, and the less educated. Why do these groups have a greater

* See the following references for information on racial and social class differences with respect to sexual behavior, contraception, and pregnancy: Gebhard et al. (1958); Freedman et al. (1959); Rainwater (1960, 1965, 1970); Hill and Jaffe (1967); Whelpton et al. (1966); Bogue (1967, 1970, 1970a); Schulz (1969); Baird (1970); Cartwright (1970); Zelnik and Kantner (1970); Ladner (1971); Presser (1971); Ryan (1971); Ryder and Westoff (1971); Westoff and Westoff (1971); and Staples (1972).

proportion of excess fertility (children beyond the desired number)? In the first place, comparing blacks to whites, black women on the average engage in sexual relations earlier than white women and have their first child at a younger age than white women. The earlier birth of the first child for the black woman can have an important bearing upon her educational or occupational plans, and several investigators have suggested the limitations of using maternity wards as the major locations for providing contraceptive information. As Campbell (1968:238) has said, "it may be more important to delay the first child than to prevent the seventh." The responsibilities of caring for a first child, whether in or out of marriage, can effectively interfere with work and school plans and thus depress a woman's life chances. Beyond the early premarital years, little difference is found in the frequency of sexual intercourse, with whites possibly having a somewhat higher average frequency than blacks. For all married couples in the 1965 National Fertility Study, Westoff and Westoff (1971) report an average monthly frequency of sexual intercourse of 6.8 for whites and 6.3 for blacks.

Another important finding of the fertility studies suggests that the excess fertility among the poor, nonwhites, and the less educated stems from their less frequent and less effective use of contraceptives. Ryder and Westoff (1971:349–54), for example, report that although at each birth order a higher percentage of blacks do not want additional children, a lower percentage are actually using contraceptives. They also report much higher percentages of failure among blacks who use contraceptives than whites. Although they found little difference by educational level on the desire for children, those who did not complete high school show much lower percentages using contraceptives, and among those using them a consistently higher rate of failure. Some studies do not go beyond pointing out the different patterns of contraceptive use and effectiveness, but others have tried to explain the differences. The most convincing explanations have pointed out that the higher fertility groups have less knowledge of and less access to contraceptives, especially to the most effective methods (pills, IUDs). Once women make contact with a family planning clinic they tend to become effective contraceptive users. Several studies dealing with the experience of low-income women who have received contraceptives at clinics report very high percentages of women who use them successfully. Phyllis Champion's (1967:126) study led her to take an optimistic view of the potential for successful contraceptive use by low-income black couples. Her sample of low-income black women "showed no less perseverence, no 'weaker motivation' or no more evidence of 'improvidence' than Planned Parenthood has encountered elsewhere with its white patients from middle-class and suburban areas." Another recent study by Feldman et al. (1971) is also optimistic about the continued and successful use of contraceptives by low-income women. In this study, as in the Champion study, the women had voluntarily attended Planned Parenthood clinics and were taking the contraceptive pill.

To what extent would the equal and easy availability of the pill (or other effective contraceptives) to all racial and income groups reduce the racial and social class discrepancies in unwanted pregnancies for the population at large? It is only since 1967, when the federal government included family planning in its anti-poverty program, that there has been any substantial movement toward providing the poor with equal access to family planning services. Jaffe (1972) has suggested that these family planning services have contributed toward the substantial decline in fertility that has been observed in recent years among the poor. Jaffe warns that much still needs to be done since a large demand for family planning services exists not only among the poor, but also among the near-poor who cannot afford private medical care yet who do not qualify for subsidized care. The extension of family planning services to all who want them but who now find them inaccessible is likely to further decrease the higher fertility rate of the poor. No group lacks motivation to practice birth control. As Dorothy Millstone (1972:23) so vividly expressed it: "The coalition Mrs. Sanger was fighting for now exists. The fact is everyone wants protection against unwanted childbirth: the AFDC mother, the middle- and upper-class matron, the corporate executive, the high school cheerleader, the college man and woman, the hippie —everybody. They don't have to be bribed or coerced to accept it."

Obviously, less use of contraceptives and higher rates of contraceptive failure result in larger percentages of unwanted pregnancies. A woman can carry the child to term, keep the child or place the child for adoption or foster care, or she can abort. Public concern has focused on the unmarried woman who keeps her child—that is, the infamous illegitimate births—and especially upon the higher proportion of illegitimate births among the poor and blacks than among the middle class and whites. As several investigators have pointed out, far more white women than black women opt for a "shotgun" marriage which converts an illegitimate pregnancy into a legitimate birth (Gebhard et al., 1958; Coombs et al., 1970; Rains, 1971; Ryan, 1971). With respect to adoption, Rains (1971) observes that illegitimately pregnant white women are more likely to receive help. More cynically Ryan (1971:102) assesses the adoption prospects for black and white babies: "Black babies and babies of mixed racial parentage, who are classified as black, are a less readily marketed product in the adoption exchange; they are lumped together with those having genuine defects. In the adoption market, the best-seller is the infant who is fair, structurally intact, and mechanically sound."

At all points of choice the middle-class white woman usually has more alternatives than the lower-class black woman. The white woman has greater access to contraception, abortion, forced marriage, and adoption. Some evidence suggests that blacks prefer illegitimate childbirth to abortion (Rodman et al., 1969:319), but this evidence has too often been extended to mean that lower-class and black women "are accepting and philosophical about bearing out-of-wedlock babies because welfare provides such a simple and practical economic solution to the problem. Thus, there is supposed to be a direct relation between the prevalence of bastards and the expanding rolls of Aid to Families with Dependent Children" (Ryan, 1971:92). In the first place Ryan (1971:103, 106) finds that "only a minority of unmarried mothers depend on public assistance," and "to suggest that anyone—or at least more than a tiny handful of erratic or disturbed persons—would choose the bitter existence of AFDC as a way of life except as a last resort, is to demonstrate ignorance either of the basic nature of humanity, or of what life is like on AFDC." The lower-class woman has fewer alternatives to an unwanted pregnancy and has therefore "stretched" her values in order to grant greater acceptability to the behavior patterns, such as illegitimacy, to which she is often led by force of circumstances (Rodman,

1963). In contrast, the middle-class woman is able to maintain a highly negative attitude toward illegitimacy because she can rely almost completely upon abortion, adoption, or a forced marriage to conceal premarital pregnancies.

Changes in adoption practices, in access to services, and in attitudes are going to alter this situation. The adoption picture is changing: adoption agencies urge people to adopt older children, previously excluded groups (singles and older couples) adopt, more women have abortions, and more unmarried white women than previously keep their illegitimate children. This all adds up to fewer children to be adopted by more people, and some observers have expressed concern over a "shortage" of children to adopt. For a long time the unwed mother and her child have been singled out as major "social problems" while other possible targets in the arena—unequal access to resources or services, arbitrary restrictions of adoption agencies, or forced marriages and their associated marital difficulties—have largely escaped public rebuke. As Prudence Rains (1971:175–76) says,

> the definition of illegitimacy as a social problem, a social problem with sources usually traced to sexual behavior, is something of a political act. For it is a definition which not only tends to deflect attention from social inequalities in access to other solutions to the problem of pregnancy—primarily abortion—but also supplies support for the questionable view that having and keeping an illegitimate child is the least acceptable solution to the problem of pregnancy.

If abortion becomes available to all women, it can be a widely used alternative to illegitimacy. But Rains (1971:177) also expresses the view of many when she says that "it is difficult to sustain the position that abortion is ethically or socially preferable to illegitimacy as a solution to the problem of illegitimate pregnancy." In the end she pleads for social policies "which will address the problems of unwed mothers" (Rains, 1971:178). It is, however, politically dangerous to endorse either expanded services to unwed mothers or liberalized abortion laws and greater access to abortion.

RACE, CLASS, AND ABORTION

If we use excess fertility as a criterion, then the poor, blacks, and other minority groups are the largest potential users of abortion. Two major lines of evidence in the literature during the 1950s and 1960s reveal that these groups do not have equal access to abortion facilities. First, higher rates of abortions were reported for private patients than for public or general service patients. Second is the higher rate of abortions reported for white patients than for nonwhites or other minority groups. Table 6 summarizes a selection of this evidence from four different studies.

TABLE 6: LEGAL ABORTIONS PER 1,000 LIVE BIRTHS

Time Period	*Population*	*White*	*Nonwhite*	*Private Service*	*General Service*
1951–53	New York City	4.1	1.4	3.6	1.9
1954–56	New York City	2.9	0.7	2.9	1.0
1957–59	New York City	2.8	0.6	2.4	0.6
1960–62	New York City	2.6	0.5	2.4	0.7
1960–61[a]	U.S. sample			3.17	.87
1963–65	U.S. sample	2.0	1.1		
1968	Georgia: married	0.8	0.1		
1968	Georgia: single	11.8	0.1		
1969	Georgia: married	1.2	0.4		
1969	Georgia: single	36.3	1.6		
1970 (*Jan.–June*)	Georgia: married	3.0	1.2		
1970 (*Jan.–June*)	Georgia: single	96.0	4.0		

Sources: Gold et al. (1965) for New York City; Hall (1965) and Tietze (1968) for U.S. samples; and Rochat et al. (1971) for Georgia. For details consult the original sources.

[a] These are the mean years for which data are reported from sixty major hospitals. The range of years over which data were reported is from 1951 to 1963. The rates per 1,000 live births were computed from the figures provided by Hall (1965:524–5).

It is clear from Table 6 that the rate of legal abortions per 1,000 live births is considerably higher for whites than for nonwhites (principally blacks). These differences are consistent throughout, for New York City, for the state of Georgia, and for the United States samples. The rate of legal abortions for Puerto Ricans in New York City, during the same time period, is even lower than the rate for blacks (Gold et al., 1965:966). With respect to the abortion rates for voluntary hospitals in New York City, Table 6 shows that the rate for private service patients is consistently higher than the rate for general service patients. The difference is even more pronounced, for each of the reported time periods, if we compare the abortion rate at private hospitals with the rate at municipal hospitals. For example, in the years that show the largest discrepancy, 1960–62, the rate at the former was 3.9 and at the latter 0.1, or a rate that is thirty-nine times greater at the private hospitals. As stated by Theodore Irwin (1970:23): "Several surveys have shown that four out of five therapeutic abortions are done on private patients—the affluent, white, and married." The affluent, white, and unmarried now also need to be included. In Table 6, we can see that the highest rates in Georgia are reported for single white women, and the largest white-black discrepancies appear for single women. In 1970, that rate was twenty-four times greater for whites than for blacks.

One possible consequence of the discrimination against the poor and against blacks in access to legal hospital abortions would be a greater turning by these groups to illegal nonhospital abortions. Although available figures on illegal abortions are understandably skimpy, the evidence that does exist suggests that the white and the affluent have also had preferential access to illegal abortions, particularly to those carried out by physicians. Lawrence Lader (1970:25–28), speaking from extensive personal knowledge of nonhospital abortions, feels that the costs and the communication networks effectively deny abortions by skilled surgeons to the poor. He notes "that far too many people are going to local midwives and hacks. Harlem Hospital receives about 400 botched abortions a year; another on the fringe of Harlem gets 250 to 300. Many never appear in abortion statistics, since staffs are humane enough to keep them from police reports if possible." Referring to Great Britain, Alice Jenkins (1961:35–36) states that their pre-reform law "presses most cruelly" on the poor who could not afford the medical care available to "the woman with knowledge, influence and financial resources." And Guttmacher (1967a:8–9) points out that "in the United States abortion is largely carried out clandestinely by physicians, particularly for the well-to-do. The poor are more likely to attempt to abort themselves or to resort to nonmedical amateurs."

One consequence of the greater reliance by the poor and blacks upon illegal abortions performed by unskilled abortionists is the higher rate of maternal mortality due to abortion. Harriet Pilpel (1967:101), discussing the situation in New York during the early

1960s, reports that 93 percent of the therapeutic abortions were performed on white private patients. She also notes that 42 percent of the pregnancy-related deaths resulted from illegal abortions and that 50 percent of these women were black, 44 percent Puerto Rican, and only 6 percent white. Her conclusion: "Even the denial of equal protection represented by segregated schools appears less heinous than this class and economic discrimination." The Gold et al. (1965:965) study of New York City from 1951 to 1962 shows that the black maternal mortality rate was about four times greater than the white rate, while the black maternal mortality rate due to abortions was about nine times the white rate, and the Puerto Rican rate was between the black and white rate. The report by Rochat et al. (1971:544) for Georgia, from 1950 to 1969, indicates a total maternal mortality rate, and an abortion-related maternal mortality rate, that are about four times higher for blacks than for whites. During the years 1965 to 1969, however, the black maternal death rate due to abortion is fourteen times the white rate. Based on national data from the National Center for Health Statistics, the black rate for abortion-related maternal mortality is 2.4 times the white rate for the years 1939–1941, 4.4 times the white rate for 1949–51, and 5.5 times the white rate for 1959–61 (Shapiro et al., 1968:148); it was 6 times the white rate in 1968 (Monthly Vital Statistics Report, 1971:7).

Gebhard and colleagues also provide information on the incidence of abortion by race and social class. They found that the percentage of pregnancies that terminate in abortion is generally higher among women at the higher educational levels, and this is especially the case among unmarried women, black and white (Gebhard et al., 1958:61, 78, 160–61). Among the married the differences between educational levels are much smaller; in fact, in the white group, the percentage of pregnancies that end in an induced abortion are somewhat higher at the lowest educational level (Gebhard et al., 1958:139, 165). In a comparison of blacks and whites, both for premarital and marital conceptions, we find that whites have higher percentages ending in induced abortions at the lower educational levels, while at the higher educational levels there is little or no difference between blacks and whites. This study, based on data that derive from interviews with women, confirms the findings of other studies reporting statistics derived from hospital records. Ignoring some variations, the data point to the greater reliance upon abortion on the part of whites over blacks, and on the part of the more affluent or more educated over the less affluent and less educated.

CHANGES IN ACCESS TO ABORTION FACILITIES

The large majority of the studies reporting differential abortion rates by social class or race are based upon experiences during the 1950s and the 1960s. During these years, medical indications for therapeutic abortions (to save the mother's life) were declining in importance because of medical advances, and hospital committees were being formed to make decisions about requests for abortion. These developments made it more difficult to get an abortion, and abortion rates dropped throughout most parts of the United States. During these same years, however, especially during the 1960s, the movement to incorporate social and psychological factors into the definition of health was growing, and an upsurge of interest in abortions occurred. As a result, most of the liberalized abortion laws passed between 1967 and 1970 included mental health factors as an indication for therapeutic abortions, and this led to a great deal of pressure upon psychiatrists to provide legal justification for requested abortions. The information needed to locate the most liberal hospitals and psychiatrists, the money for psychiatric consultation as well as for the abortion, and the experience needed to deal with a large array of largely white and often hostile medical personnel in order to get approval for an abortion were generally less available to black women and poor women; consequently, the abortion rate differentials between whites and blacks and between private patients and ward patients increased during the 1950s and 1960s.

During the 1950s and 1960s the abortion laws in the United States were restrictive, there was the potential of a public outcry against those who broke the laws, and enforcement was sporadic. As a result, public hospitals stuck much more closely to the letter of the abortion laws than did private hospitals. As Overstreet (1971:18) points out, abortions are desired for a great many social and economic reasons, and these "can only be approved by the subterfuge of threat to the mother's mental health." For the most part, the physician is prepared only to accommodate his own private patient, or someone that he knows on a personal basis. Typically, only private patients were likely to find physicians sufficiently interested in their welfare to bear the small risk involved in making a liberal interpretation of the abortion laws (Bell, 1971:127; Guttmacher, 1967a:10–12) or in otherwise circumventing the law. Callahan (1970:139) refers to a 1967 survey by Johan Eliot reporting that more private than public hospitals accept German measles as an indication for abortion. Hall (1965:522), reporting on the years 1950 through 1960, points out that "abortions were more common among the private patients at Sloan Hospital for virtually all of the more debatable indications, such as arthritis, inactive tuberculosis, and rubella." And Kenneth R. Whittemore (1970:24) points to the substantial discrepancies between private and service patients in the number of pregnancies "accidentally" terminated as a result of a hospital D. and C. on women not listed as pregnant. In the general hospital he studied, service patients accounted for approximately half of all patients but for only about 5 percent of the lab results reporting "evidence of fetus" from D. and C.'s ostensibly performed for reasons other than terminating a pregnancy.

In brief, the evidence is rather clear that during the 1950s and 1960s the abortion rates have been higher for whites and for private patients, and that their discrepancy with rates for minority groups and public patients has increased. What about the distribution of rates by race and by social class before 1950 and after 1970? One report notes that the discrepancy was not present in Buffalo hospitals during the 1940s:

> In the 1940's, when the majority of abortions were done for medical reasons, the incidences on the ward and private services were about the same. In the 1950's, when medical reasons accounted for fewer abortions, the incidence on the private service rose to twice that of the ward service. In the 1960's, when the number of abortions for psychiatric or fetal reasons rose dramatically, the incidence on the private service soared to better than twenty times greater than that of the clinic service. (Niswander, 1967:53)

The changes in the rates that have taken place since the reform laws of 1967, and more especially since repeal laws went into effect in

1970, are of special interest. Although the statistics are still fragmentary, they are perhaps a harbinger of changes to come. Russell and Jackson (1969) report on the first full year's experience with the liberalized abortion law in California. During that year, 1968, the therapeutic abortion rate per 1,000 deliveries was 7 for Medicaid patients and 14 for non-Medicaid patients; further, county hospitals approved 71 percent of their abortion applications in contrast to 90 percent for non-county hospitals. These figures, along with those reported in Table 6 for Georgia since the liberalization of the law there, indicate that the reform laws have not eliminated the differential rates but perhaps have modified them. The figures for Georgia show a slight lessening of the differential from 1968 to 1970. And Overstreet (1971:22) feels that California has improved: "This situation is no longer quite as discriminatory as it was before, because under the new law hospitals involved in the care of indigent patients are doing a fair job of carrying their share of the indicated abortions. But economic discrimination does hit the lower middle class American woman who is just above the level of welfare eligibility." Theodore Irwin (1970), referring to the liberalized law in Maryland, also feels that it has increased access of the poor to abortions. He reports that Johns Hopkins Hospital started 1968 with about 85 percent of its therapeutic abortions for private patients and ended the year with a 50–50 distribution. But the most dramatic changes have taken place in those states where repeal laws have been passed. Although pre-repeal data are not provided, Hawaii's early experience under a repeal law indicates that proportionately more lower income women are having abortions than women of other income levels (Smith et al., 1971; Steinhoff et al., 1971).

In New York, based on the experience of one hospital, Strausz and Schulman (1971) noted a large increase in the percentage of blacks and Puerto Ricans receiving abortions from the first three months after the law was changed to the subsequent two months. Pakter and Nelson (1971:6–7) give abortion rate estimates for New York City residents which are comparable to those presented in Table 6 and cover the nine months subsequent to the repeal of New York's abortion laws: 422.4 for whites and 594.0 for blacks; 384.7 for private service and 525.9 for general service patients. These rates for legal abortions per 1,000 live births far exceed any of the other figures reported in Table 6 and testify to the very high demand for abortion services. The figures also indicate that the repeal law in New York has reversed the prior pattern, and now shows higher abortion rates for those groups that have higher rates of excess fertility.

The high abortion rates in New York are typical of the rates found in many other countries that have passed similar abortion laws, such as Bulgaria, Czechoslovakia, Japan, and Yugoslavia. They are also typical of the rates in several European and Latin American countries with strict abortion laws but widespread evasion. France, for example, is estimated to have as many illegal abortions as live births (Callahan, 1970:286, 289), and one survey has shown an inverse relationship between social class and abortion rates (Texier, 1969; cf. Safilios-Rothschild, 1969). It therefore appears that when abortions are readily available, either because of highly liberal legislation or widespread evasion of restrictive laws, the groups that are lower in the scale of social stratification, and presumably less successful in controlling births through contraception, are the groups that make greatest use of abortion facilities.

ATTITUDES TOWARD ABORTION

Most societies, including the United States, have followed pro-natalist population policies that "repress birth limitation and reward reproduction" (Blake, 1971:540). The anti-abortion climate has been part of that pro-natalist approach, and attitudes throughout the society have generally been quite unfavorable toward abortion.

During the 1960s at least eight national surveys conducted in the United States collected information on attitudes toward abortion. The questions asked have not been the same in all eight surveys, but they were identical in five of the surveys that were carried out between 1962 and 1969 by the Gallup organization. The results for these five polls are summarized in Table 7. The following questions were asked about abortion (part d was not asked in the 1962 and 1965 surveys):

Do you think abortion operations should or should not be legal in the following cases:

a. Where the health of the mother is in danger?
b. Where the child may be born deformed?

c. Where the family does not have enough money to support another child?
d. Where the parents simply have all the children they want although there would be no major health or financial poblems involved in having another child? (Blake, 1971:541)

It is clear that throughout the 1960s there was very substantial approval of abortion for medical reasons—cases of danger to the mother's health or possible fetal deformity—and also a very substantial disapproval of abortion for nonmedical reasons. The percentages changed little and indicate that people became only slightly more favorable toward abortion during the decade.

TABLE 7: PERCENTAGE OF PEOPLE IN THE U.S. DISAPPROVING OF ABORTION FOR VARIOUS REASONS

	1962	*1965*	*1968a*	*1968b*	*1969*
Mother's health	16	15	10	10	13
Fetal deformity	29	31	25	22	25
Cannot afford child	74	74	72	68	68
No more children wanted			85	81	79

Source: Blake (1971).
Note: The percentages are all based on national samples done by the Gallup organization and apply to white men and women.

Some of the findings in these surveys, however, are masked by presenting percentages only for the total sample as in Table 7. Men are more favorable toward abortion than women; non-Catholics are more favorable than Catholics; non-Southerners are more favorable than Southerners; those with more education are more favorable than those with less. The educational differences are especially marked. Among white non-Catholics in 1969, for example, 5 percent of the college-educated men and 22 percent of the grade-school-educated men disapproved of abortion for reasons of preserving the mother's health; 4 percent of college-educated women and 28 percent of grade-school-educated women disapproved. The following percentages disapproved of abortion if the child might be born deformed: 14 percent of college men and 28 percent of grade school men; 9 percent of college women and 42 percent of grade school women. If the parents could not afford another child, the following percentages disapproved: 50 percent of college men and 66 percent of grade school men; 61 percent of college women and 76 percent of grade school women. If no further children are desired, the following percentages disapproved: 63 percent of college men and 79 percent of grade school men; 70 percent of college women and 86 percent of grade school women (Blake, 1971:542–44).

These figures from the 1969 survey roughly indicate the nature of some public attitudes toward abortion, but one important trend from 1962 to 1969 should be noted. Among those with less education, very little change occurred throughout the decade, and insofar as any change did take place it has usually been in the direction of a more negative attitude toward abortion. In contrast, among the college-educated, attitudes changed through the years in the direction of more favorable attitudes toward abortion for all reasons. To illustrate with one of the most pronounced changes, white, non-Catholic, college-educated men shifted from 70 percent who disapproved of abortion in 1962—if the parents could not afford another child—to 50 percent who disapproved in 1969. Blake (1971) contends that, despite the limited changes made throughout the 1960s by the population as a whole, the possibility of liberalized legislation was considerably improved during the 1960s because of the substantial changes in public opinion among the most influential segments of the United States population.

Liberalized legislation did come about in many states during the late 1960s and especially in 1970, and since 1970 there also appears to be a dramatic change in public attitudes toward abortion. A 1971 national survey carried out for the President's Commission on Population Growth and the American Future asked the following question: "Do you think abortions should or should not be permitted where the parents already have all the children they want?" Forty-nine percent replied that it should be permitted, 42 percent that it should not be permitted, and 9 percent had no opinion (Lipson and Wolman, 1972:40). The only question comparable to those asked in the five Gallup polls reported above, it shows 42 percent disapproving compared to between 79 and 85 percent disapproving in 1968 and 1969.

It can be assumed that part of the difference is due to the wording of the questions. The Gallup polls, by deliberately stating that there were "no major health or financial problems involved in having another child" undoubtedly served to increase the percentage disapproving. But it is likely that at least part of the difference is due to a real swing in public opinion. The replies to another question asked in 1971 also suggest a liberalization of attitudes. "Do you think that the decision to have an abortion in the early months of pregnancy should be made solely by the couple and their doctor, or do you think that such abortions should be permitted only under certain circumstances?" Fifty percent thought the couple and doctor alone should decide, 41 percent thought it should be permitted only under certain circumstances, 6 percent stated that it should never be permitted, and 3 percent had no opinion (Lipson and Wolman, 1972:40). Another Gallup poll, conducted in January 1972, "showed that 57 percent of Americans agreed with the statement, 'The decision to have an abortion should be made solely by a woman and her physician.' For the first time in any such national survey a majority of Catholics—54 percent—indicated support of this position" (quoted in Lipson and Wolman, 1972:39).

One current sign of the more favorable attitudes toward abortion is that more psychiatrists are calling them therapeutic and fewer are calling them harmful. Professionals and lay people have also become more open about abortion. Hardin (1971:2) has said: "Our greatest advance in the last decade has been in removing the taboo from the word 'abortion.' Five years ago many people thought it was courageous of me to discuss the subject in public. They were wrong, of course; but since this was a flattering error, I did not correct them. Now, no one flatters me in this way; everybody talks about abortion."

Although physicians have often been charged with obstructing changes toward more liberal abortion laws and practices, their attitudes toward abortion have been more favorable than those of the general public. In 1965, responses from more than 5,000 U.S. psychiatrists showed that 90 percent were favorable toward abortion "when there is significant risk that the child would be born mentally or physically defective" (Crowley and Laidlaw, 1967:559–60) compared to 69 percent of a national sample who approved of abortion in cases of fetal deformity, as shown in Table 7. In 1968, responses from 425 staff physicians at two hospitals in Seattle, Washington showed that 73 percent were in favor of abortion for economic or social reasons (Brown et al., 1970:78). Also in 1968, 87 percent of Michigan physicians favored some form of change in the abortion law which forbade abortion except to save the woman's life (Serena et al., n.d.). In 1969, when 79 percent of a national sample disapproved of an abortion when the parents did not want another child and 68 percent disapproved if parents could not afford another child (Table 7), a *Modern Medicine* (Nov. 3, 1969) poll showed that 63 percent of all physicians replying answered yes (51 percent answered with an unqualified yes) to the question: "Should abortion be available to any woman capable of giving legal consent upon her own request to a competent physician?" Because of differences in the physician populations surveyed, in the rates of return and associated bias, and in the questions asked, it is impossible to make any conclusions about changes through time. Pfeiffer (1970:405) nevertheless does make the following remarks about a trend:

> With regard to the question of performing abortions on request, medical as well as general opinion is already undergoing change. A 1967 study of the views of 5,289 members of the American Psychiatric Association indicated that only 23.5% favored abortion on request.
>
> In November 1969 *Modern Medicine* published a poll indicating that of the roughly 13% of physicians in the United Sates participating in the poll, 51% favored "abortion on request." A total of 2,041 psychiatrists participated in this poll and of these 72% favored abortion on request, without qualification. While both of the polls of psychiatrists include only a minority of the specialty, the trend in the direction of honoring a woman's request for an abortion seems unmistakable.

The major problem with Pfeiffer's conclusion stems from the apparently similar, but actually very different questions that were asked. In the 1967 study (Crowley and Laidlaw, 1967:559) the question was: "Do you believe a pregnancy should be interrupted whenever the woman requests it?" In the 1969 study (*Modern Medicine,* Nov. 3, 1969) the question was: "Should abortion be available to any woman capable of giving legal consent upon her own request to a competent physician?" The 1967 question makes the woman's request sound casual and the physician's response to it precipitous. The 1969 question adds stature to the woman's request, introduces a "competent" physician, and makes the response to the woman's request sound more deliberate by using the term "available." Despite the uncertainty about changes through time, it does appear that the attitudes of physicians are more favorable than the attitudes expressed by the general public, and since most of the physicians are white, college-educated males their more favorable attitudes are in line with the findings of the public opinion surveys.

The data on the United States also show that blacks generally hold less favorable attitudes toward abortion than whites, but these data also leave many questions unanswered. A national sample of 5,600 married women, interviewed in 1965, was asked whether they thought it would be all right for a woman to have a pregnancy "interrupted" under six different circumstances—danger to the woman's health, rape, fetal deformity, woman unmarried, the couple could not afford more children, and the couple did not want any more children. The greatest differences between blacks and whites appear when we look at those who approved of abortion when the woman's health was endangered but rejected all other reasons—21 percent of the whites and 34 percent of the blacks fall into this category. The second greatest difference shows up when we look at those who accepted only danger to the woman's health, rape, and fetal deformity—27 percent of the whites and 17 percent of the blacks fall into this category. The differences are much less in other cases. For instance 9 percent of the white women and 12 percent of the black women opposed abortion for all of the reasons, and 8 percent of the whites and 7 percent of the blacks approved abortion for all of the reasons (Westoff et al., 1969:14).

In the 1971 survey done for the Commission on Population Growth and the American Future (Lipson and Wolman, 1972:40–41), the greatest difference between black and white attitudes appeared in response to the question: "Are there circumstances other than preserving the mother's life under which you think abortion should be legal?" Among whites 62 percent replied yes (32 percent no, 6 percent no opinion) in contrast to 43 percent of the blacks (41 percent no, 16 percent no opinion). Similar differences occurred on the question: "Do you think that the decision to have an abortion in the early months of pregnancy should be made solely by the couple and their doctor, or do you think that such abortions should be permitted only under certain circumstances?" Fifty-one percent of the whites compared to 33 percent of the blacks thought the decision should be made by the couple and their doctor, 41 percent of the whites and 43 percent of the blacks thought abortion should be permitted only under certain circumstances, 5 percent of the whites and 14 percent of the blacks thought abortion should never be permitted, and 3 percent of the whites and 10 percent of the blacks gave no opinion. But the differences shrink on the question: "Do you think abortions should or should not be permitted where the parents already have all the children they want?" Among whites, 50 percent thought it should be permitted (42 percent not permitted, 8 percent no opinion); among blacks, 44 percent thought it should be permitted (42 percent not permitted, 14 percent no opinion). The differences disappear on the question: "Do you think the government should or should not help make abortion available to all women who want it?" For whites, 66 percent answered that it should be made available (23 percent no, 11 percent no opinion); among blacks, 67 percent thought it should be made available (16 percent no, 17 percent no opinion). In discussion groups on birth control with black women in four U.S. cities Kantner and Zelnik (1969:11) report that abortion was hardly ever mentioned spontaneously, and they speculate that "the attitudes toward abortion are so negative that the word is 'blocked' from normal discourse." In a North Carolina sample of black women, Vincent et al. (1970) report very high percentages opposed to abortion in response to an open-ended question. But Harter and Beasley (1967) found no statistically significant differences between whites and blacks on most questions asked of a sample of women in the New Orleans metropolitan area, and black physicians responding to a Michigan survey had more favorable attitudes toward abortion than white physicians (Serena et al., n.d.).

If one takes this evidence as demonstrating that black attitudes are generally less favorable toward abortion than white attitudes, several explanations can be offered for the differences. One explanation would be the larger proportion of blacks at the lower educational levels; since those with less education are more negative, blacks would therefore be more negative. But Westoff et al. (1969:16) controlled for educational level, and the black-white differences persisted. Another possible explanation is that proportionately more blacks than whites have a Southern background and belong to fundamentalist Protestant religions, and these characteristics are associated with less favorable attitudes toward abortion (Blake, 1971:547; Ryder and Westoff, 1971:278, 281).

Blacks have also had different experiences regarding abortion than whites. They have had less access to hospital abortions or to skillfully done illegal abortions and have had to rely to a greater extent upon self-induced abortions or illegal abortions by unskilled practitioners. This has probably contributed to knowledge about the dangers of abortion and influenced attitudes negatively. From her work with illegitimately pregnant black girls, Prudence Rains (1971:37) found that "whenever abortion was mentioned spontaneously or in answer to a question of mine, girls spoke only in terms of self-induced abortions and the dangers involved."

What actually happens when access to legal, safe abortions becomes available to black women? Do their presumably unfavorable attitudes keep them away from such services? Does a presumed preference for illegitimate childbirth over abortion prevent blacks from using newly accessible abortion services? In the area of abortion, like the area of contraceptive practice, blacks and the poor *are* taking advantage of newly available services. Serena et al. (n.d.) pointed out that a very high percentage of the women seeking abortions in Michigan, even under a restrictive law, were black. Gabrielson et al. (1971:736) suggest that although black women had less favorable attitudes toward abortion than white women, they were apparently seeking out abortions to a greater extent: "The cliche that abortion is a therapy accepted by whites but categorically rejected by blacks is not supported by this study." But most convincing are the abortion rates for blacks (per 1,000 live births) in the states with the most liberal abortion laws and practices. These rates have gone up dramatically, and in some instances they have moved very quickly from being much lower than the white rates to being higher than the white rates. This suggests that the attitude differences may have been exaggerated and that in any case a demand for long-denied abortion services exists despite less favorable attitudes. The danger is that policymakers will use attitude differences between blacks and whites or the poor and nonpoor as a justification for denying "unwanted" services. As a poor, black woman remarked on TV when abortion services in municipal hospitals in New York City were in danger of being closed down except for cases involving danger to the woman's life: "I don't know what we'll do or where we'll go if they shut down here."

CHAPTER NINE

BLACK GENOCIDE

Is the movement to liberalize abortion laws, as well as the entire birth control movement, a form of black genocide? Racial oppression is an integral part of world and American history, and birth control programs in Third World countries and in United States ghettos are often regarded as the work of white colonials engaged in black genocide. The basic charge is that blacks become the major target of birth control services designed to reduce their birth rate. The basic defense is that the goal of the birth control movement is to provide equality of access to services, and the special efforts in Third World countries and ghetto areas are meant to compensate for the lack of service that has historically been the lot of these groups. The equally marked zeal of adherents to the birth control movement and to the black liberation movement render the charges and countercharges highly emotional and political.

Black militants are quick to point out the genocidal implications of making sterilization a precondition for an abortion or making population control programs a precondition for financial aid to Third World countries. White population controllers are just as quick to point out the special economic advantages that birth control has for poor families and poor nations. Ehrlich and Ehrlich (1970:301) state that research studies raise serious questions about "the desirability of aid programs not coupled with population control programs. They might provide temporary increases in the standard of living, but these are soon eaten up by population expansion." Charles Simmons, in sharp contrast, states: "Behind the smokescreen of a world population explosion, the US is playing first string in a racist con game by offering the poor peoples of the world dollars for development on one condition—that they must also take contraceptives" (*Muhammad Speaks,* May 8, 1970).

Several concerned social scientists and activists recently addressed themselves to the general question: "Is black genocide possible in America?" They are pessimistic about white reactions to legitimate black demands. Using such examples as white extermination of American Indians, white internment of Japanese Americans, and white enslavement of Afro-Americans, these commentators believe that black genocide is possible (Willhelm, 1971; Yette, 1971; Valentine, 1972).

THE POPULATION CONTROLLERS

Brash advocates of population control contemplate a variety of coercive measures that raise the hackles of suspicion of many blacks. Because of a rapidly expanding world population and the difficulty of maintaining adequate supplies of food and other resources, a great deal of attention is given to ways of controlling population growth. Family planning advocates emphasize the right to voluntary parenthood and strive to make it possible for families to have the number of children they want through voluntary methods. Population controllers stress the need to go beyond family planning, on the grounds that people want too many children. As Garrett Hardin (1970:427) says in a *Science* editorial, "if parenthood is a right, population control is impossible." Considering that family planners, pushing voluntary contraception, and more recently voluntary abortion and sterilization, are sometimes seen as promoters of black genocide, it is little wonder that population controllers, with their coercive proposals, are often seen in that light.

Population controllers view themselves as facing an uphill battle in a noble cause. Pro-natalist policies are widespread, and efforts to limit population size, where they exist, are almost entirely dominated by gentle family planners. Since family planning alone is considered ineffective for population control, the embattled population controllers must strive all the harder to get a hearing for their important ideas. At times, their single-minded devotion to combatting the world's population explosion runs afoul of other movements. Hardin (1968:1246–47) attacks "freedom to breed" and explains the necessity of limiting family size through "mutual coercion, mutually agreed upon by the majority of the people affected." Kingsley Davis (1967:738) documents the timidity and ineffectiveness of the family planning movement throughout the world and entertains several proposals to limit reproduction, including "a requirement that illegitimate pregnancies be aborted." But coercion agreed upon by a majority or compulsory abortion of illegitimate pregnancies, although offered with good intentions in behalf of a worthy cause, appear to be aimed at minority groups generally and blacks in particular. The Black Muslim newspaper, *Muhammad Speaks,* keeps up a constant attack upon the advocates of population control and equates population control with black genocide. In one issue, Diogenes X said: "In New York thousands of fruitful wombs of Black mothers have been converted into dark and cold graves for their babies" (*Muhammad Speaks,* Sept. 3, 1971, p. 3). Or as D. Schulder and F. Kennedy (1971:158) put it: "Some of the people active in population control . . . have a bad stench of racism." The diverging perspectives of population controllers and blacks who see themselves as the prime targets of control create an atmosphere of constant controversy.

In the spirit of thinking the unthinkable, population controllers come up with many proposals that go beyond the family planning approach. Some of these proposals, from Bernard Berelson's (1969) review, are: temporary sterilization administered through the water supply, through staple foods, or through the implantation of contraceptive capsules; government licenses to have children; government payments for the effective practice of contraception; tax or welfare penalties for those who bear more than a limited number of children. One of the difficulties of many of the population controllers' proposals is that they bear down more heavily against the poor than the nonpoor and against blacks than whites. The population controllers are sincere in trying to head off a population catastrophe, dogmatic in their approach, and yet sensitive to the values of society that give their proposals a harsh reception (McCracken, 1972:45, 49). As Ehrlich and Ehrlich (1970:256) put it, "compulsory control of family size is an unpalatable idea to many, but the alternatives may be much more horrifying." The horrors of the population crisis, however, are considered by some to be exaggerated. Barry Commoner (1971:211–14, 232–44) has strongly criticized those who believe overpopulation to be the major cause and population control the major cure of the world's environmental crisis. According to Commoner, a production technology that is blind to its environmental consequences is the major problem. He is especially harsh with those who advocate coercive population control measures for "immoral, misleading, and politically regressive reasons." He identifies Paul Ehrlich with these coercive measures and this has led to a stormy personal and ideological feud between Commoner and Ehrlich (Holden, 1972).

Family planning advocates have confidence that their approach, without coercive measures, will work to control population size. And Harriet Pilpel, speaking for civil libertarians, expresses a similar viewpoint: "Unless and until it is clear that voluntary measures, legally and factually available (which they never have been), won't and can't eliminate the threat of overpopulation, government coercion and compulsion are contra-indicated" (*Civil Liberties,* Nov. 1971, p. 6). Others are confident that our burgeoning technology will provide adequate food and resources to avoid a population catastrophe. In consequence, the population controllers are unpopular, most of their advice is unheeded, and they add fuel to the fire of black genocide charges.

COMPULSORY STERILIZATION

Although most of the proposals of the population controllers are remote, compulsory sterilization has been practiced on a small scale by many hospitals for several decades. We are not referring to the compulsory sterilization of Nazi Germany or the eugenic compulsory sterilization laws in many states of the United States aimed against "mental defectives" (Polsky, 1971:37). The latter were most actively enforced during the 1930s and are now much less frequently used, although they are still part of many states' statutes (Paul, 1968:77–78; Kittrie, 1971:298–99). We are referring, rather, to a form of compulsory sterilization still practiced in hospitals in the United States, Britain, Canada, and other countries throughout the world. How does this form of compulsory sterilization work? When the law places the abortion decision in the hands of physicians and hospitals, they sometimes agree to perform an abortion only if the woman also accepts sterilization. This compulsory sterilization blatantly exhibits the arbitrary power exercised by physicians and hospitals. The rationale for requiring sterilization is that it is in the patient's best interest. For example, if abortion is justified because pregnancy would be dangerous to the woman's health, then sterilization insures that the woman will not be endangered by further pregnancies. This rationale, however, has several flaws. In the first place, women often exaggerate their illness to justify the abortion for health reasons. Second, recovery is possible in many situations where physicians require sterilization. Third, if the pregnancy does endanger a woman's health, she clearly is entitled to an abortion without any arbitrary preconditions. Fourth, assuming sterilization is medically indicated, it should be recommended to the woman and left to her decision, with no trace of coercion. But some physicians feel threatened when women take over these decisions; they are mere technicians, they "are being employed solely as mechanics" carrying out the instructions of others (W.C.W. Nixon, 1957:326). In consequence, some physicians and hospitals maintain their rationalizations for coercive measures and clothe compulsory sterilization in a humanitarian cloak.

Compulsory sterilization cannot be shrugged off as an isolated practice in a few hospitals. It is, rather, a procedure occasionally followed by a great many hospitals. In a large-scale survey of teaching hospitals throughout the United States and Canada, Johan W. Eliot et al. (1970:93) report: "Some women desiring an abortion were required to have a simultaneous sterilization operation as a condition of approval of the abortion in from one-third to two-thirds of these teaching hospitals in different regions of the country. This practice was most common in the Mountain States, the Far West, and Canada, and lowest in the New England and Plains States. In all, 53.6 percent of teaching hospitals made this requirement for some of their patients."

Considering the illegality of the requirement, it is likely that an even higher percentage of hospitals sometimes insist upon sterilization as a condition of abortion. Moreover, physicians have a great deal of leeway in encouraging a woman to accept sterilization in order to enhance her chances of obtaining a favorable decision on abortion. The large number of hospitals acknowledging that they sometimes practice this form of compulsory sterilization indicates that it is not uncommon and that it has been thoroughly rationalized within the medical profession.

The procedure has become sufficiently well established to be called "the package deal." Rosen (1958:131) points out that some women who had therapeutic abortions for psychiatric indications "had been sales-talked" into, or "had been forced to agree" to, sterilization "as a condition for being aborted." He says, "so far as I could judge, no indication whatsoever existed for such sterilization," and he considers several patients "fortunate to have been illegally rather than therapeutically aborted, and thus spared sterilization."

During a Women's Teach-In at Wayne State University on October 22, 1970, the following exchange took place between a black woman student in the audience and a white woman gynecologist on the panel:

BLACK STUDENT: The real reason that many low-income women and minority group women are refusing to have abortions or other operations is that they are afraid of what will happen to them. I know one woman who died needing an appendix operation, and she was afraid to go for the operation. Women are afraid they will come out sterilized or with parts of their body missing.

WHITE GYNECOLOGIST: We call that superstition.

A heated exchange continued in which the physician denied any basis for fear while the student said she knew of women who were sterilized against their wishes. Mutual respect and understanding were absent in the fiery exchange, which revealed a wide gap between the student and the physician. It also illustrated the concern about compulsory sterilization among blacks. Brenda Hyson expresses a similar black reaction to abortion and sterilization: "The abortion law hides behind the guise of helping women, when in reality it will attempt to destroy our people. How long do you think it will take for voluntary abortion to turn into involuntary abortion, into compulsory sterilization? Black people are aware that laws made supposedly to ensure our well-being are often put into practice in such a way that they insure our deaths" (quoted in Schulder and Kennedy, 1971:156).

Mr. Muhammad says: "Sterilization operations are being performed on [black women] in the North and the South. Some have confessed that they did not know this was happening to them until it was all over" (*Muhammad Speaks,* July 23, 1965). And the *Birth Control Handbook* (1970:43) states: "Poor women, especially black women, suffer the worst humiliation at the hands of male doctors and their hospital boards. These women are commonly 'offered' abortion —with the stipulation that they must accept sterilization as well. The rationale that such measures are necessary to alleviate the population crisis is merely a cover for racist genocide."

The level of suspicion about compulsory sterilization is high within some segments of the black community, and it feeds on anecdotal information. We have not found any figures on compulsory sterilization by racial category. But to dismiss black suspicion as superstition is clearly unwarranted in the face of evidence that the package deal is not uncommon. The evidence that it is aimed at the poor and at blacks more than at the wealthy and at whites is not available, but in view of known discrimination in other areas, a woman's fear of involuntary sterilization seems to be perfectly rational. The serious debates in several state legislatures to extend eugenic compulsory sterilization laws to unwed mothers was aimed at blacks (Morrison, 1965), and though such laws were not passed, the debates were hardly calculated to inspire black trust in white institutions.

A woman's fear about missing body parts also seems rational in the face of at least one hospital's remarkable practice of using hysterectomy instead of tubal ligation as the procedure of choice for indigent women requesting sterilization for socioeconomic reasons. From the University of Kentucky Medical Center, Van Nagell and Roddick (1971:703) note that usually vaginal hysterectomy is performed "not to prevent conception but to correct some form of pelvic pathology," but "vaginal hysterectomy may well be the procedure of choice when surgical sterilization is desired by the indigent multiparous patient who is *most* susceptible to the *future* development of benign and malignant uterine disease and who *probably* will not return for adequate postoperative follow-up" (emphasis added).

Although some would still insist upon sterilization as a condition for abortion (Connor and Aydinel, 1970:134), recognition is increasingly being given to the inadvisability of the package deal, and most references to compulsory sterilization refer critically to the practice. Terms such as "punitive," "coercive," "vindictive," and "unconstitutional" have been directed at the practice (W.C.W. Nixon, 1957:326; Hill and Jaffe, 1965:207; Schur, 1965:22; Peel and Potts, 1970:167; Pilpel, 1970:111). Many have come to feel that the physician, in the guise of trying to aid the woman, metes out punishment for the woman's transgressions. At any rate, it appears clear that in too many instances the woman is not permitted to make her own decision about sterilization. Marder et al. (1970:658) have emphasized the need to maintain the sterilization decision as an issue entirely separate from the abortion decision in order to avoid even the appearance of any pressure upon the woman to undergo sterilization. Several studies reported in the February 1972 issue of the *IPPF Medical Bulletin* suggest that the aftereffects of sterilization are most favorable for those women who make the decision themselves and take the initiative in obtaining the operation. Patt et al. (1969:412), reporting on women who had therapeutic abortions for psychiatric indications, say: "Rarely did patients wish to have the child-bearing function closed them permanently, despite the rejection of pregnancy implicit in abortion." But medical practices sometimes seem to thwart the woman's desires. On the one hand she may be coerced into being sterilized when she does not want the operation in order to obtain an abortion. On the other hand she may find it difficult or impossible to be sterilized when she wants the operation:

enemies. Nations could successfully survive economic catastrophe; but decline in fertility struck at the very marrow of their being." She quotes Hans Hertel to the effect that "the fight with arms yields merely temporary decisions. The birth rate decides the fate of nations for a long time ahead." The same concern about relative population size and birth rates also applies to different sections within the same nation. The birth rate in predominantly nonwhite countries has been higher than the birth rate in predominantly white countries, and the birth rate of blacks in the United States has been higher than the birth rate of whites. This has touched some sensitive political nerves, and the controversy about black genocide revolves partly around the question of numbers.

When more developed and predominantly white countries offer family planning assistance to less developed and predominantly nonwhite countries, the charge of genocide is bound to arise. When predominantly white professionals offer family planning services in predominantly black neighborhoods, the charge of black genocide is also bound to arise. Although the intentions of family planners may be entirely honorable, they are sometimes confused with racist concerns about numbers. Wade Greene (1972:44) reports a visceral comment from a white man: "You're telling the white people not to have any more kids, and the niggers are screwing like crazy, and they're going to have three hundred million people, and we're going to wind up the minority." William Shockley (1972:303) expressed his "fears that contemporary United States population trends are such that we are disproportionately multiplying the least foresighted elements of our population," and he urges us to reverse those trends. In consequence, efforts to influence population trends are viewed with suspicion. The *Birth Control Handbook* (1970:2) comments on the use of "subtle birth control methods to control the population of nonwhite people." *Muhammad Speaks* (Feb. 15, 1965) makes the following assessment:

> Behind the massive "birth control" campaigns and the synthetic "population explosion" crisis lies, according to some African and Asian leaders, a ruthless drive to eliminate the stupendous population dominance of nonwhite nations.
>
> Already a number of high-ranking African and Asian leaders are equating the "birth-curb" drive, stimulated and whipped up particularly

> One 21-year-old woman with four children reque
> New York hospital and was told she had to have se
> that her life would be endangered by another pregn
> ation could be performed.
>
> Another 21-year-old mother of two children was
> by a doctor who offered to perform a vasectomy on
> Both women returned to Puerto Rico for the operatior
>
> A 29-year-old woman with five children was refus
> New York City hospital. After she pleaded extensiv
> arguing that her husband was a disabled veteran unab
> pital performed the surgery. (Scrimshaw and Pasquarie

Some evidence (Hall, 1965:527) suggests that volu like legal abortion, is less available to ward patier patients. Assuming that the poor and the black m ward services, we are left with a situation in whicl access to voluntary abortion and sterilization and are more fearful that these services are being exten coercive manner.

A number of recent developments have contribut ing to the fore the charge of compulsory sterilizatio cide. Welfare costs have become a favorite target of various coercive proposals have been offered to rec have been introduced in several state legislatures mothers of illegitimate children undergo sterilization welfare benefits or a prison term (Paul, 1968). In a rized in the January 1972 issue of *Family Planning D* percentages of physicians favored compulsory sterili coercive measures for welfare mothers with three ill dren. While the extent of compulsory sterilization is package deal is common enough and public attitude enough to lend some credence to those who cry black ge

POWER IN NUMBERS

Nations have long been preoccupied with populatior power lay in numbers. Birth rates have therefore beer intense interest to nationalists, and pro-natalist policie lished in most countries. As Jessie Bernard (1970:169) important that no nation permit itself to be outbred by by Britain and America, with genocide, inasmuch as it is applied basically to nonwhites.

Some black leaders within the United States express similar suspicions. Dick Gregory (1971:66) says: "My answer to genocide, quite simply, is eight black kids—and another baby on the way."

The black community, of course, is divided about the virtues of birth control programs and abortion reform and about the accuracy of the charges of black genocide. Richard Austin, Michigan's secretary of state, discounts the charge of black genocide—"Some people say black power would suffer if abortions were available to all women. But power is not contingent upon sheer numbers. It lies, rather, in effective political action, in economic influence, in upgrading of skills and education" (*Detroit News,* Dec. 6, 1971).

Perhaps the conflict weighs most heavily upon the black woman, because she faces decisions about birth control under strongly divergent pressures. She is attracted to the white woman's liberation struggle to win equal pay and equal freedom for women and to win the right to make birth control and childbearing decisions without state interference; she is repelled by the thought of pursuing a struggle that would pit her against black men while a larger struggle for black freedom needs to be waged. She is also attracted to the black man's militant ideology which insists that the organization of birth control programs, along with other white actions, is a genocidal plot directed against blacks; at the same time she is repelled by the idea of becoming a breeder for the black revolution. Many black women have tried to resolve the conflicting pressures by repudiating both women's liberation and birth control as genocide (Morrison, 1971). Patricia Robinson et al. (1968) declared: "Black women are being asked by militant black brothers not to practice birth control because it is a form of whitey committing genocide on black people. . . . For us, birth control is freedom to fight genocide of black women and children." Mary Treadwell (1972:4), Executive Director of Pride, Inc., in Washington, D.C., also addressed herself to the numbers question:

> . . . a few members of my community will tell me that legalized abortion is simply another white man's trick to foster racial genocide. They will say that we need to reproduce as many black children as possible—which

only adds numbers. There is no magic in a home where someone has reproduced five or more black babies and cannot manage economically, educationally, spiritually, nor socially to see that these five black babies become five highly trained black minds.

And finally, Shirley Chisholm testifies before a U.S. Senate subcommittee:

I know that in my own Bedford-Stuyvesant community, black women are glad to get direction in the area of family planning. I know that thousands of black women have been maimed by botched abortions because they couldn't get the family planning help that white women could get. I have heard some repercussions that family planning is a form of genocide. But the people this would effect—in Harlem and Bedford-Stuyvesant—think otherwise. I have had hundreds of black women come to me over the past 10 years because they wanted family planning. (quoted in Lincoln, 1970:12)

WILL BIRTH CONTROL ELIMINATE POVERTY?

The pill has enough magic in it to prevent conception, but it is not sufficiently magical to eliminate poverty. Yet the question of whether birth control can eliminate poverty, or at least provide an escape from poverty for many families, constantly recurs. And related questions, on whether birth control will reduce crime or the welfare load or illness, also crop up.

The universal availability of birth control is recognized as one basic approach toward reducing poverty. "Escape from poverty" is one of the three objectives of the family planning program supported by the U.S. federal government (*Need for Subsidized Family Planning Services*:3). Family planning is, in fact, considered to be "one of the surest and least costly ways of breaking the poverty cycle" (Contis:vii). Although the United States effort is directed toward family planning narrowly defined as contraception, other programs include abortion and sterilization as part of the attack upon poverty. Family planning enthusiasts recognize that contraception, abortion, and sterilization will not solve the poverty problem, and other approaches are needed to cope with current poverty and the related needs for adequate food, housing, jobs, income, and health care. Advocates of family planning then ask: "Since family planning will not, by itself, solve major national social and economic problems, is it then worthwhile to keep pressing single-mindedly for its universal availability." Their answer, of course, is a resounding yes (Millstone, 1972:21).

The decision to proceed full speed ahead with programs for voluntary contraception, abortion, and sterilization is condemned in some quarters. A principal reason is that these birth control efforts detract attention from, and prevent an assault upon, other and larger problems. What about hunger, poor health, unemployment, income inequality? These problems are easier to ignore in the wake of an active birth control program that seeks to reduce the same problems. As Samuel Yette (1971:243) suggests, "given priority in cost and availability over the care and feeding of the poor already born, birth control, as practiced by OEO and advocated by others, does become suspect in the context of health brutality against the Blackpoor." Yette's (1971:109–10) account of the White House Conference on Food and Nutrition, December 2–4, 1969, provides a vivid example of the ideological influence upon perceptions and priorities:

> The White House conference . . . was worse than a farce. Not only did it dash the hopes of the hungry in a way almost unprecedented, it also succeeded in advancing—against strong sentiments of the poor at the conference—the administration's own program of imposing birth control on the Blackpoor. . . .
>
> In his December 2 speech opening the conference, President Nixon dashed the hopes of many by not proposing any specific measures for immediate relief of hunger. His primary concern obviously was toward reducing the number of the *hungry*—not hunger itself—for it was on how to reduce the hungry that he had specific recommendations and specific action.
>
> The most emphatic of his three recommendations to the conference urged that the conferees support his birth control proposals to Congress. This had to be a strange emphasis at a conference which ostensibly had been called to deal with those hungry.

Yette (1971:110–13) points out how only vigorous action by Fannie Lou Hamer prevented one of the panels on "Pregnant and Nursing Women and Infants" from offering proposals for compulsory abortion and compulsory sterilization for certain categories of unmarried women.

Several writers have noted that few blacks are active in the struggle for abortion reform because of the priority they place upon other problems. Schulder and Kennedy (1971:157) suggest that "abortion is a relatively rare crisis as contrasted to such problems as unemployment, racism, poverty, bad housing, police rioting, and war." A Black Caucus formed at the National Congress on Optimum Population and Environment, held in Chicago in 1970, stated that "birth control was not a solution to everyday realities which Black people must face" (*Muhammad Speaks,* July 3, 1970, p. 30). Jesse Jackson said that "the issue is not population control, but to provide properly planned and controlled distribution of resources and raw materials" (*Muhammad Speaks,* July 9, 1971, p. 9).

Moral issues are very much part of the black genocide charge, and one of the moral controversies revolves about the birth control objective to reduce infant mortality or other suffering that is related to poverty. The moral argument for abortion is particularly weak insofar as "depriving a fetus of life is justified . . . on grounds that had he lived, he might have died anyway, or that he might have been regarded as a social problem" (*Wall Street Journal,* Apr. 7, 1972, p. 8). As Christy Ashe (1970:7) commented, "I don't count birth control by abortion an affirmative answer to the question of suffering."

Richard Neuhaus and Norman Podhoretz have also expressed their disagreement with the moral arguments of the population controllers that justify coercion in people's reproductive lives as a means of alleviating hunger or suffering. As Neuhaus (1971:209) puts it, "given the choice between the coercive and brutal proposals for diminishing the number of guests, on the one hand, and multiplying the bread, on the other, multiplying the bread is infinitely preferable." He continues:

> There is an elitist arrogance in the assumption that life on a breadline is not worth living, that surely anyone on the line would prefer death to his present existence. A distinguished medical proponent of abortion on demand once assured me that no one should be forced to be born who was not guaranteed "the minimal requirements for a decent existence." Among the minimal requirements he included a stable family life, loving parents, quality education, and the economic security to have an equal start in competition for the best that American life has to offer. When I pointed out that, by his criteria, most of the people I work with in Brooklyn should have been aborted in the womb, he responded with utmost sincerity, "but surely many, if not most, of the people who live in

our horrible slums would, if they could be objective about it, agree with me that it would have been better for them not to be born." (Neuhaus, 1971:210–11)

Podhoretz (1972:6, 8) recounts a similar experience which takes us beyond the question of black genocide to genocide against the physically or mentally handicapped. At a conference in Washington, D.C., he was surprised to find eminent scientists prepared to question a mongoloid's right to life:

> One very distinguished scientist . . . told me he saw no reason why anyone who accepted abortion should balk at infanticide, particularly when the infant in question was known to be defective whereas the fetus to be aborted might be normal and sound. . . . I replied that in my judgment anyone who sees no difference between a fetus and a newborn baby ought to be condemning abortion as murder and not applauding infanticide as enlightened. Certainly, I said, mongoloids are defective, but so are many other kinds of people. Some are blind, some are deaf, . . . and some have missing limbs; some are given to madness and some are the prey of disease. If mongoloids can be put to death, why not these, and if these, why not anyone who fails of absolute perfection? Not overly bothered by any of this, he shrugged—and went on to tell me about a colleague of his, a molecular biologist of the greatest renown, who believes that no newborn infant should be declared human until it has passed certain tests regarding its genetic endowment; if it fails these tests, it forfeits the right to live.

Perhaps it is a long step backwards from "failing" school tests or IQ tests during adolescence to "failing" genetic tests at birth, but the same questions come to the fore. Who is constructing the tests, whose standards are being used, whose biases are creeping into life-and-death decisions?

The question of black genocide thus brings us back full circle to the host of moral, legal, and medical conflicts that swirl about the abortion controversy. If we vest eugenic power in the hands of a few, can we trust the judgments they make to improve the quality of life? Under legally coercive policies to control population and to improve the nation's health, the reproductive rights of some people may be trampled upon—perhaps mongoloids, perhaps those on public welfare, perhaps all individuals to some extent. It is therefore ethically preferable to select a voluntary approach to population control (Callahan, 1972) and to opt for voluntary abortion. But under circumstances where the laws permit voluntary abortion, who will be coerced by poverty or by benign hospital or public policies to undergo abortion? Clearly we need to go beyond laws that permit voluntary abortion; we need to pursue social changes that will promote a more humane distribution of income and medical services and that will make decisions about abortion, about other birth control procedures, and about other actions that are important to the health and welfare of a people, truly voluntary.

BIBLIOGRAPHY

Aarons, Z. Alexander. Dec. 1967. "Therapeutic Abortion and the Psychiatrist," *American Journal of Psychiatry,* 124:745–54.

American Law Institute. July 30, 1962. *Model Penal Code*. Changes and Editorial Corrections in May 4, 1962 *Proposed Official Draft*. Philadelphia: American Law Institute.

Anderson, E. W. May–June 1966. "Psychiatric Indications for the Termination of Pregnancy," *World Medical Journal,* 13:81–83.

Ashe, Christy. Aug. 1970. "Abortion . . . or Genocide?" *Liberator,* pp. 4–9.

Augenstein, Leroy. 1969. *Come, Let Us Play God*. New York: Harper & Row.

Babbitz v. McCann, 310 F. Supp. 293 (E.D. Wis. 1970).

Bachi, Roberto. 1970. "Abortion in Israel," in Robert Hall, editor, *Abortion in a Changing World,* I, 274–83.

Baird, Sir Dugald. Apr. 1970. "The Obstetrician and Society," *American Journal of Public Health,* 60:628–40.

Ball, Donald W. Winter 1967. "An Abortion Clinic Ethnography," *Social Problems,* 14:293–301.

Barnard, Thomas H., Jr. Jan. 1967. "An Analysis and Criticism of the Model

Penal Code Provisions on the Law of Abortion," *Western Reserve Law Review*. 18:540–64.

Barnes, Allan C. 1969. In Keith Russell and Edwin Jackson, "Therapeutic Abortion in California."

Bates, Jerome E. and Edward S. Zawadzki. 1964. *Criminal Abortion*. Springfield, Ill.: Charles C. Thomas.

Beauvoir, Simone de. 1944. *The Second Sex*. Translated and edited by H. M. Parshley. New York: Bantam.

Beck, Mildred B. 1971. "Abortion: The Mental Health Consequences of Unwantedness," in R. Bruce Sloane, editor, *Abortion*, pp. 53–64.

Bell, Robert R. 1971. *Social Deviance: A Substantive Analysis*. Homewood, Ill.: Dorsey.

Berelson, Bernard. Feb. 1969. "Beyond Family Planning," *Studies in Family Planning*, 38:1–16.

Berelson, Bernard, Richmond K. Anderson, Oscar Harkavy, John Maier, W. Parker Mauldin, and Sheldon J. Segal, editors. 1966. *Family Planning and Population Programs*. Proceedings of the International Conference on Family Planning Programs, Geneva, August, 1965. Chicago: University of Chicago Press.

Bergström, S., E. Diczfalusy, U. Borell, S. Karim, B. Samuelsson, B. Uvnas, N. Wiqvist, and M. Bygdeman. Mar. 17, 1972. "Prostaglandins in Fertility Control," *Science*, 175:1280 *et passim*.

Bernard, Jessie S. 1970. In Elliot Liebow, "Attitudes Toward Marriage."

Birth Control Handbook. 1970. Montreal, Que: McGill Students' Society.

Blake, Judith. Feb. 12, 1971. "Abortion and Public Opinion: The 1960–1970 Decade," *Science*, 171:540–49.

Block, Eric, W. Godfrey Cobliner, Irwin H. Kaiser, Mamdouh Moukhtar, Seymour L. Romney, Harold Schulman, Joseph J. Smith, and Ivan K. Strausz. July 1971. "'Birth Control' and/or 'Family Planning,'" *Family Planning Perspectives*, 3:4.

Bogue, Donald J., editor. 1967. *Sociological Contributions to Family Planning Research*. Chicago: University of Chicago, Community and Family Study Center.

——. 1970. *Further Sociological Contributions to Family Planning Research*. Chicago: University of Chicago, Community and Family Study Center.

Bogue, Donald J. Apr. 1970a, Part 2. "Family Planning in the Negro Ghettos of Chicago," *Milbank Memorial Fund Quarterly*, 48:283–307.

Bolter, Sidney. Oct. 1962. "The Psychiatrist's Role in Therapeutic Abortion: The Unwitting Accomplice," *American Journal of Psychiatry*, 119:312–16.

Boulas, S. H., R. W. Preucel, and J. H. Moore. Feb. 1962. "Therapeutic Abortion," *Obstetrics and Gynecology*, 19:222–27.

Brekke, Bard. 1958. In Mary Steichen Calderone, editor, *Abortion in the United States*.

Brody, Harry, Stewart Meikle, and Richard Gerritse. Feb. 1, 1971. "Therapeutic Abortion: A Prospective Study. I," *American Journal of Obstetrics and Gynecology*, 109:347–53.

Brown, Norman K., Roger J. Bulger, E. Harold Laws, and Donovan J.

Thompson. Jan. 5, 1970. "The Preservation of Life," *Journal of the American Medical Association,* 211:76–82.

Calderone, Mary Steichen, editor. 1958. *Abortion in the United States.* Proceedings of a Conference sponsored by the Planned Parenthood Federation of America, Inc. at Arden House and The New York Academy of Medicine. New York: Hoeber-Harper.

Callahan, Daniel. 1970. *Abortion: Law, Choice and Morality.* New York: Macmillan.

——. Feb. 4, 1972. "Ethics and Population Limitation," *Science,* 175:487–94.

Campbell, Arthur A. May 1968. "The Role of Family Planning in the Reduction of Poverty," *Journal of Marriage and the Family,* 30:236–45.

Carroll, Charles. Spring 1968. " 'Liberalized' Abortion—A Critique," *Child and Family,* 7:157–65.

Cartwright, Ann. 1970. *Parents and Family Planning Services.* New York: Atherton.

Champion, Phyllis. 1967. "A Pilot Study of the Success or Failure of Low Income Negro Families in the Use of Birth Control," in Donald Bogue, editor, *Sociological Contributions to Family Planning Research,* pp. 112–28.

Charles, Alan and Susan Alexander. Nov. 1971. "Abortions for Poor and Nonwhite Women: A Denial of Equal Protection?" *Hastings Law Journal,* 23:147–69.

Christakos, Arthur C. Feb. 1971. "Genetics in Therapeutic Abortion," *Southern Medical Journal,* 64:105–8.

Christian, C. Donald. n.d. "Medical Indications," in Jaroslav Hulka, editor, *Therapeutic Abortion,* pp. 54–59.

Cisler, Lucinda. Aug. 1970. "Abortion Reform: The New Tokenism," *Ramparts,* 9:19–21.

Commission on Population Growth and the American Future. 1972. *Population and the American Future.* New York: New American.

Commoner, Barry. 1971. *The Closing Circle.* New York: Knopf.

Connor, Edward J. and Orhan H. Aydinel. Mar. 1970. "Therapeutic Abortion —Washington, D.C.," *Medical Annals of the District of Columbia,* 39:133–37.

Contis, George. "Timetable for Action," in *Need for Subsidized Family Planning Services,* p. vii.

Cooke, Robert E., Andre E. Hellegers, Robert G. Hoyt, and Herbert W. Richardson, editors. 1968. *The Terrible Choice: The Abortion Dilemma.* Based on the Proceedings of the International Conference on Abortion sponsored by the Harvard Divinity School and the Joseph P. Kennedy, Jr. Foundation. New York: Bantam.

Coombs, Lolagene C., Ronald Freedman, Judith Friedman, and William F. Pratt. Mar. 1970. "Premarital Pregnancy and Status Before and After Marriage," *American Journal of Sociology,* 75:800–20.

Crist, Takey and Lana Starnes. Jan. 1972. "Student Printing Presses Bring Birth Control Story to Colleges," *Family Planning Perspectives,* 4:60–61.

Crowley, Ralph M. and Robert W. Laidlaw. Oct. 1967. "Psychiatric Opinion Regarding Abortions: Preliminary Report of a Survey," *American Journal of Psychiatry,* 124:559–62.

Curran, William J. Mar. 1971. "The Legal Authority of Health Departments to Regulate Abortion Practice," *American Journal of Public Health*, 61:621–26.

Cutler, Donald R., editor. 1969. *Updating Life and Death: Essays in Ethics and Medicine*. Boston: Beacon.

Daily, Edwin F. July 1971. "A Clearing House for Abortion Appointments," *Family Planning Perspectives*, 3:12–14.

Dauber, Bonnie, Marianne Zalar, and Phillip J. Goldstein. Apr. 1972. "Abortion Counseling and Behavioral Change," *Family Planning Perspectives*, 4:23–27.

David, Henry P. 1970. *Family Planning and Abortion in the Socialist Countries of Central and Eastern Europe*. New York: The Population Council.

——. Jan. 1972. "Abortion in Psychological Perspective," *American Journal of Orthopsychiatry*, 42:61–68.

——. 1972a. "Abortion Trends in European Socialist Countries and in the United States," prepared for presentation at the Annual Meeting of the American Orthopsychiatric Association, Detroit, Michigan, April 1972.

Davis, Kingsley. Nov. 10, 1967. "Population Policy: Will Current Programs Succeed?" *Science*, 158:730–39.

Devereux, George. 1967. "A Typological Study of Abortion in 350 Primitive, Ancient, and Pre-Industrial Societies," in Harold Rosen, editor, *Abortion in America*, pp. 97–152.

Dietz, Margaret. 1970. "Psychiatric Sequelae of Abortion: When and Why." Detroit, Merrill-Palmer Institute, unpublished paper.

Diggory, Peter, John Peel, and Malcolm Potts. Feb. 7, 1970. "Preliminary Assessment of the 1967 Abortion Act in Practice," *Lancet*, 1:287–91.

Doe v. Bolton, 319 F. Supp. 1048 (N.D. Ga. 1970).

Dr. X as told to Lucy Freeman. 1962. *The Abortionist*. Garden City, N.Y.: Doubleday.

Drinan, Robert F. Apr. 1970. "Should There Be Laws Against Abortion?" *U.S. Catholic*, pp. 15–19.

Droegemueller, William, Stewart E. Taylor, and Vera E. Drose. Mar. 1, 1969. "The First Year of Experience in Colorado with the New Abortion Law," *American Journal of Obstetrics and Gynecology*, 103:694–702.

Dunbar, Flanders. 1967. "A Psychosomatic Approach to Abortion and the Abortion Habit," in Harold Rosen, editor, *Abortion in America*, pp. 22–31.

Ebon, Martin, editor. 1971. *Everywoman's Guide to Abortion*. New York: Universe Books.

Ehrlich, Paul R. and Anne H. Ehrlich. 1970. *Population/Resources/Environment*. San Francisco: W. H. Freeman.

Ekblad, Martin. 1955. "Induced Abortion on Psychiatric Grounds: A Follow-up Study of 479 Women," *Acta Psychiatrica et Neurologica Scandinavica*, Supplementum 99.

Eliot, Johan W., Robert E. Hall, J. Robert Willson, and Carolyn Houser. 1970. "The Obstetrician's View," in Robert Hall, editor, *Abortion in a Changing World*, I, 85–95.

Engström, Lars E. 1970. "Experience With the M-Pill," in Robert Hall, editor, *Abortion in a Changing World*, I, 61–66.

Feldman, Joseph G., Swtantarta Ogra, Jack Lippes, and Harry A. Sultz. June 1971. "Patterns and Purposes of Oral Contraceptive Use by Economic Status," *American Journal of Public Health,* 61:1089–95.

Felton, Gerald and Roy Smith. Jan. 1972. "Administrative Guidelines for an Abortion Service," *American Journal of Nursing,* 72:108–9.

Field, Mark G. Aug. 30, 1956. "The Re-legalization of Abortion in Soviet Russia," *New England Journal of Medicine,* 255:421–27.

Finkbine, Sherri. 1967. "The Lesser of Two Evils," in Alan Guttmacher, editor, *The Case for Legalized Abortion Now,* pp. 15–25.

Fisher, Mrs. Marc Hughes. 1970. In Robert Hall, editor, *Abortion in a Changing World,* Vol. II.

Fleck, Stephen. July 1970. "Some Psychiatric Aspects of Abortion," *Journal of Nervous and Mental Disease,* 151:42–50.

Fletcher, Joseph F. 1970. "A Protestant Minister's View," in Robert Hall, editor, *Abortion in a Changing World,* I, 25–29.

Frederiksen, Harold and James W. Brackett. Dec. 1968. "Demographic Effects of Abortion," *Public Health Reports,* 83:999–1010.

Freedman, Ronald, P. K. Whelpton, and Arthur A. Campbell. 1959. *Family Planning, Sterility and Population Growth.* New York: McGraw-Hill.

Friedman, Jacob H. Apr. 1962. "The Vagarity of Psychiatric Indications for Therapeutic Abortion," *American Journal of Psychotherapy,* 16:251–54.

Gabrielson, Ira W., Sadja Goldsmith, Leah Potts, Vicki Mathews, and Mary O. Gabrielson. Apr. 1971. "Adolescent Attitudes Toward Abortion: Effects on Contraceptive Practice," *American Journal of Public Health,* 61:730–37.

Galdston, Iago. 1958. In Mary Steichen Calderone, editor, *Abortion in the United States.*

Gebhard, Paul H., Wardell B. Pomeroy, Clyde E. Martin, and Cornelia V. Christenson. 1958. *Pregnancy, Birth and Abortion.* New York: Harper.

Geijerstam, Gunnar af. 1970. "Abortion in Scandinavia," in Robert Hall, editor, *Abortion in a Changing World,* I, 315–24.

——. 1970a. In Robert Hall, editor, *Abortion in a Changing World,* Vol. II.

George, B. James, Jr. 1967. "Current Abortion Laws: Proposals and Movements for Reform," in David Smith, editor, *Abortion and the Law,* pp. 1–36.

——. Summer 1972. "The Evolving Law of Abortion," *Western Reserve Law Review,* 23:708–55.

Gold, Edwin M., Carl L. Erhart, Harold Jacobziner, and Frieda G. Nelson. July 1965. "Therapeutic Abortions in New York City: A 20-Year Review," *American Journal of Public Health,* 55:964–72.

Goodman, Harold. n.d. "Fetal Indications," in Jaroslav Hulka, editor, *Therapeutic Abortion,* pp. 45–53.

Green, Wade. Mar. 11, 1972. "The Militant Malthusians," *Saturday Review,* pp. 40–49.

Greenhouse, Linda J. Jan. 25, 1970. "Constitutional Question: Is There a Right to Abortion?" *New York Times Magazine,* pp. 30 *et passim.*

——. June 28, 1970a. "After July 1, an Abortion Should Be as Simple to have as a Tonsillectomy, but—," *New York Times Magazine,* pp. 7 *et passim.*

Gregory, Dick. Oct. 1971. "My Answer to Genocide," *Ebony,* pp. 66–72.

Grisez, Germain G. 1970. *Abortion: The Myths, the Realities, and the Arguments.* New York: Corpus Books.

Griswold v. Connecticut, 381 U.S. 479 (1965).

Group for the Advancement of Psychiatry. Oct. 1969. "The Right to Abortion: A Psychiatric View," *GAP Publication No. 75,* 7:197–230.

Guttmacher, Alan F. 1958. In Mary Steichen Calderone, editor, *Abortion in the United States.*

——. 1965. In Minoru Muramatsu and Paul Harper, editors, *Population Dynamics.*

——. 1967. "The Shrinking Non-psychiatric Indications for Therapeutic Abortion," in Harold Rosen, editor, *Abortion in America,* pp. 12–21.

Guttmacher, Alan F., editor. 1967a. *The Case for Legalized Abortion Now.* Berkeley, Calif.: Diablo Press.

Guttmacher, Alan F. 1969. *Birth Control and Love.* New York: Macmillan.

——. 1970. In Robert Hall, editor, *Abortion in a Changing World,* Vol. II.

Guttmacher, M. S. 1967. "The Legal Status of Therapeutic Abortions," in Harold Rosen, editor, *Abortion in America,* pp. 175–86.

Hall, Robert. Feb. 15, 1965. "Therapeutic Abortion, Sterilization, and Contraception," *American Journal of Obstetrics and Gynecology,* 91:518–32.

——. Dec. 15, 1965a. "New York Abortion Law Survey," *American Journal of Obstetrics and Gynecology,* 93:1182–83.

——. Mar. 1967. "Present Abortion Practices in Hospitals of New York State," *New York Medicine,* 23:124–26.

——. Nov. 1967a. "Abortion in American Hospitals," *American Journal of Public Health,* 57:1933–36.

Hall, Robert, editor. 1970. *Abortion in a Changing World,* 2 vols. Proceedings of an International Conference Convened in Hot Springs, Virginia, November 17–20, 1968, by the Association for the Study of Abortion. New York: Columbia University Press.

Hall, Robert. Mar. 1971. "Abortion: Physician and Hospital Attitudes," *American Journal of Public Health,* 61:517–19.

Hammond, Howard. June 1, 1964. "Therapeutic Abortion: Ten Years' Experience with Hospital Committee Control," *American Journal of Obstetrics and Gynecology,* 89:349–55.

Hardin, Garrett. 1967. "Abortion and Human Dignity," in Alan Guttmacher, editor, *The Case for Legalized Abortion Now,* pp. 69–86.

——. Dec. 13, 1968. "The Tragedy of the Commons," *Science,* 162:1243–48.

——. July 31, 1970. "Parenthood: Right or Privilege?" *Science,* 169:427.

——. 1971. "We Need Abortion for the Children's Sake," in Carl Reiterman, editor, *Abortion and the Unwanted Child,* pp. 1–6.

Harper, Fowler. 1958. In Mary Steichen Calderone, editor, *Abortion in the United States.*

Harrison, Colin P. May 1969. "Teenage Pregnancy—Is Abortion the Answer?" *Pediatric Clinics of North America,* 16:363–69.

Harter, Carl L. and Joseph D. Beasley. Nov. 1967. "A Survey Concerning Induced Abortions in New Orleans," *American Journal of Public Health,* 57:1937–47.

Harting, Donald and Helen J. Hunter. Oct. 1971. "Abortion Techniques and Services: A Review and Critique," *American Journal of Public Health,* 61:2085–2105.

Haselkorn, Florence, editor. 1971. *Family Planning: A Source Book and Case Material for Social Work Education.* New York: Council on Social Work Education.

Hayman, Charles R., Robert R. Caldwell, Charlene Lanza, Essex C. Noel, Donald S. Smith, William J. Washington, Jr., and Wallace Weiss. Feb. 1972. "Rape and Its Consequences," *Human Sexuality,* 6:13 *et passim.*

Health Services Administration of New York City. Feb. 20, 1972. Press release.

Heer, David M. July 1965. "Abortion, Contraception, and Population Policy in the Soviet Union," *Soviet Studies,* 17:76–83.

Hellman, Louis M. 1958. In Mary Steichen Calderone, editor, *Abortion in the United States.*

Hendin, David. 1971. *Everything You Need to Know About Abortion.* New York: Pinnacle Books.

Hill, Adelaide C. and Frederick S. Jaffe. 1967. "Negro Fertility and Family Size Preferences: Implications for Programming of Health and Social Services," in Talcott Parsons and Kenneth B. Clark, editors, *The Negro American,* pp. 205–24.

Hindell, Keith and Madeleine Simms. July–Sept. 1968. "How the Abortion Lobby Worked," *Political Quarterly,* 39:269–82.

——. 1971. *Abortion Law Reformed.* London: Peter Owen.

Hirschler, Imre. 1970. Presented by Christopher Tietze in Robert Hall, editor, *Abortion in a Changing World,* Vol. II.

Holden, Constance. July 21, 1972. "Ehrlich versus Commoner: An Environmental Fallout," *Science,* 177:245–47.

Hong, Sung-Bong. 1970. In Robert Hall, editor, *Abortion in a Changing World,* Vol. II.

Hulka, Jaroslav F., editor. n.d. *Therapeutic Abortion: A Chapel Hill Symposium.* Sponsored by the Department of Obstetrics and Gynecology and the Carolina Population Center, University of North Carolina, Chapel Hill.

Ingraham, Hollis S. and Robert J. Longood. Feb. 1971. "Abortion in New York State Since July 1970," *Modern Treatment,* 8:7–26.

Irwin, Theodore. Mar. 1970. "The New Abortion Laws: How Are They Working?" *Today's Health,* 48:21 *et passim.*

Jaffe, Frederick S. Jan. 1972. "Low-Income Families: Fertility Changes in the 1960s," *Family Planning Perspectives,* 4:43–47.

Jenkins, Alice. 1961. *Law for the Rich.* London: Victor Gollancz.

Kahn, James B., Judith P. Bourne, John D. Asher, and Carl W. Tyler. May 1971. "Surveillance of Abortions in Hospitals in the United States, 1970," *HSMHA Health Reports,* 86:423–30.

Kantner, John F. and Melvin Zelnik. Nov. 1969. "United States: Exploratory Studies of Negro Family Formation—Common Conceptions About Birth Control," *Studies in Family Planning,* 47:10–13.

Kantner, John F., Stephen Armstrong, and John D. Allingham. May 1968.

"American Attitudes on Population Policy: Recent Trends," *Studies in Family Planning,* 30:1–7.

Kibel, Howard D. Jan. 1972. "Staff Reactions to Abortion," *Obstetrics and Gynecology,* 39:128–33.

Kiser, Clyde V., editor. 1962. *Research in Family Planning.* Princeton: Princeton University Press.

Kittrie, Nicholas N. 1971. *The Right to Be Different.* Baltimore: Johns Hopkins Press.

Kleegman, Sophia. 1958. In Mary Steichen Calderone, editor, *Abortion in the United States.*

Klinger, Andras. 1966. "Abortion Programs," in Bernard Berelson et al., editors, *Family Planning and Population Programs,* pp. 465–76.

Kolstad, Per. 1957. "Therapeutic Abortion: A Clinical Study Based upon 968 Cases from a Norwegian Hospital, 1940–53," *Acta Obstetricia et Gynecologica Scandinavica,* 36:Supplement 6.

Koya, Yoshio. July 1954. "A Study of Induced Abortion in Japan and Its Significance," *Milbank Memorial Fund Quarterly,* 32:282–91.

——. 1962. "Why Induced Abortions in Japan Remain High," in Clyde Kiser, editor, *Research in Family Planning,* pp. 103–10.

——. 1966. "The Harmful Effects of Induced Abortion," *World Medical Journal,* 13:170–71.

Kummer, Jerome M. Sept. 1955. "The Prevention of Psychiatric Complications of Pregnancy and the Puerperium," *American Practitioner and Digest of Treatment,* 6:1315–20.

——. Apr. 1963. "Post-abortion Psychiatric Illness—A Myth?" *American Journal of Psychiatry,* 119:980–83.

Labby, Daniel H., editor. 1968. *Life or Death: Ethics and Options.* Seattle: University of Washington Press.

Lader, Lawrence. 1966. *Abortion.* Boston: Beacon.

——. 1970. In Robert Hall, editor, *Abortion in a Changing World,* Vol. II.

Ladner, Joyce A. 1971. *Tomorrow's Tomorrow: The Black Woman.* Garden City, N.Y.: Doubleday.

Laidlaw, Robert. 1958. In Mary Steichen Calderone, editor, *Abortion in the United States.*

Lear, Martha Weinman. Jan. 30, 1972. "Q. If You Rape a Woman and Steal Her TV, What Can They Get You for in New York? A. Stealing Her TV," *New York Times Magazine,* pp. 11 *et passim.*

Lee, Nancy Howell. 1969. *The Search for an Abortionist.* Chicago: University of Chicago Press.

Levene, Howard I. and Francis J. Rigney. July 1970. "Law, Preventive Psychiatry, and Therapeutic Abortion," *Journal of Nervous and Mental Disease,* 151:51–59.

Lidz, Theodore. 1958. In Mary Steichen Calderone, editor, *Abortion in the United States.*

——. 1967. "Reflections of a Psychiatrist," in Harold Rosen, editor, *Abortion in America,* pp. 276–83.

Lieberman, Jethro K. 1970. *The Tyranny of the Experts.* New York: Walker.

Liebow, Elliot. Apr. 1970, Part 2. "Attitudes Toward Marriage and Family

Among Black Males in Tally's Corner," *Milbank Memorial Fund Quarterly*, 48:151–80.

Lincoln, Richard. Jan. 1970. "S.2108: Capital Hill Debates the Future of Population and Family Planning," *Family Planning Perspectives*, 2:6–12.

Lipson, Gerald and Dianne Wolman. Jan. 1972. "Polling Americans on Birth Control and Population," *Family Planning Perspectives*, 4:39–42.

Louisell, David W. and John T. Noonan, Jr. 1970. "Constitutional Balance," in John Noonan, editor, *The Morality of Abortion*, pp. 220–60.

Lucas, Roy. June 1968. "Federal Constitutional Limitations on the Enforcement and Administration of State Abortion Statutes," *North Carolina Law Review*, 46:730–78.

Mabbutt, Fred R. July/Aug. 1972. "What of Private Rights in a Scientific Age?" *Current*, pp. 16–24.

McCracken, Samuel. May 1972. "The Population Controllers," *Commentary*, 53:45–52.

McDermott, John F., Jr. and Walter F. Char. July 1971. "Abortion Repeal in Hawaii: An Unexpected Crisis in Patient Care," *American Journal of Orthopsychiatry*, 41:620–26.

Mandy, Arthur J. 1967. "Reflections of a Gynecologist," in Harold Rosen, editor, *Abortion in America*, pp. 284–96.

Marder, Leon. Mar. 1970. "Psychiatric Experience with a Liberalized Therapeutic Abortion Law," *American Journal of Psychiatry*, 126:1230–36.

Marder, Leon, Charles A. Ballard, and Helen Franse. June 1970. "Psychosocial Aspects of Therapeutic Abortion," *Southern Medical Journal*, 63:657–61.

Margolis, Alan J. and Edmund W. Overstreet. Sept. 1970. "Legal Abortion Without Hospitalization," *Obstetrics and Gynecology*, 36:479–81.

Means, Cyril C., Jr. Fall 1968. "The Law of New York Concerning Abortion and the Status of the Foetus, 1664–1968: A Case of Cessation of Constitutionality," *New York Law Forum*, 14:411–515.

——. 1971. "The Phoenix of Abortional Freedom: Is a Penumbral or Ninth-Amendment Right About to Arise From the Nineteenth-Century Legislative Ashes of a Fourteenth-Century Common-Law Liberty?" *New York Law Forum*, 17:335–410.

Mehlan, K. H. 1966. "The Socialist Countries of Europe," in Bernard Berelson et al., editors, *Family Planning and Population Programs*, pp. 207–26.

Meier, Gitta. Sept. 1961. "The Effect of Unwanted Pregnancies on a Relief Load: An Exploratory Study," *Eugenics Quarterly*, 8:142–53.

Meyerowitz, Sanford and John Romano. July 14, 1969. "Who May Not Have an Abortion," *Journal of the American Medical Association*, 209:260–61.

Millstone, Dorothy L. Jan. 1972. "Family Planning, Yes! . . . but . . . ," *Family Planning Perspectives*, 4:20–23.

Monthly Vital Statistics Report. Mar. 29, 1971. "Advance Report Final Mortality Statistics, 1968."

Moore, J. G. and J. H. Randall. Jan. 1952. "Trends in Therapeutic Abortion: A Review of 137 Cases," *American Journal of Obstetrics and Gynecology*, 63:28–30.

Morris, Marian Gennaria. Jan./Feb. 1966. "Psychological Miscarriage: An End to Mother Love," *Trans-action,* 3:8–13.

Morrison, Joseph L. Mar. 1965. "Illegitimacy, Sterilization, and Racism: A North Carolina Case History," *Social Service Review,* 39:1–10.

Morrison, Toni. Aug. 22, 1971. "What the Black Woman Thinks About Women's Lib," *New York Times Magazine,* pp. 14 *et passim.*

Müller, Carl. May–June 1966. "The Dangers of Abortion," *World Medical Journal,* 13:78–80.

Muller, Charlotte F. Oct. 1970. "Health Insurance for Abortion Costs: A Survey," *Family Planning Perspectives,* 2:12–20.

Muller, Charlotte F. and Frederick S. Jaffe. Jan. 1972. "Financing Fertility-Related Health Services in the United States, 1972–1978: A Preliminary Projection," *Family Planning Perspectives,* 4:6–19.

Muramatsu, Minoru. 1965. "Action Programs of Family Planning in Japan," in Minoru Muramatsu and Paul Harper, editors, *Population Dynamics,* pp. 67–75.

——. 1970. In Robert Hall, editor, *Abortion in a Changing World,* Vol. II.

Muramatsu, Minoru and Paul A. Harper, editors. 1965. *Population Dynamics: International Action and Training Programs.* Proceedings of the International Conference on Population, May, 1964, the Johns Hopkins School of Hygiene and Public Health. Baltimore: Johns Hopkins Press.

Murdock, Harry M. 1967. "Experiences in a Psychiatric Hospital," in Harold Rosen, editor, *Abortion in America,* pp. 198–206.

Nadler, Henry L. 1971. "Fetal 'Indications' for Termination of Pregnancy," in R. Bruce Sloane, editor, *Abortion,* pp. 92–98.

Need for Subsidized Family Planning Services: United States, Each State and County, 1968. A Report Produced by Center for Family Planning Program Development, the Technical Assistance Division of Planned Parenthood-World Population for the Family Planning Program, Office of Health Affairs, Office of Economic Opportunity, Executive Office of the President.

Neuhaus, Richard. 1971. *In Defense of People.* New York: Macmillan.

Niswander, Kenneth R. 1967. "Medical Abortion Practices in the United States," in David Smith, editor, *Abortion and the Law,* pp. 37–59.

Niswander, Kenneth R. and Robert J. Patterson. May 1967. "Psychologic Reaction to Therapeutic Abortion, 1. Subjective Patient Response," *Obstetrics and Gynecology,* 29:702–6.

Nixon, W. C. W. 1957. *Proceedings of the Royal Society of Medicine,* 50:326–27.

Noonan, John T., Jr., editor. 1970. *The Morality of Abortion: Legal and Historical Perspectives.* Cambridge: Harvard University Press.

Novak, Franc. 1970. "Experience with Suction Curettage," in Robert Hall, editor, *Abortion in a Changing World,* I, 74–79.

O'Donnell, Thomas J. 1970. "A Traditional Catholic's View," in Robert Hall, editor, *Abortion in a Changing World,* I, 34–38.

Oettinger, Katherine B. Oct. 1971. "Pregnancy Detection: A Critical Service Link," *Family Planning Perspectives,* 3:15–18.

Osofsky, Joy D. and Howard J. Osofsky. Jan. 1972. "The Psychological Reaction of Patients to Legalized Abortion," *American Journal of Orthopsychiatry,* 42:48–60.

Ottosson, Jan-Otto. Apr. 1971. "Legal Abortion in Sweden: Thirty Years' Experience," *Journal of Biosocial Science,* 3:173–92.

Overstreet, Edmund W. 1971. "California's Abortion Law—A Second Look," in Carl Reiterman, editor, *Abortion and the Unwanted Child,* pp. 15–26.

——. Mar. 1971a. "Logistic Problems of Legal Abortion," *American Journal of Public Health,* 61:496–99.

Overstreet, E. W. and H. F. Traut. Jan. 1951. "Indications for Therapeutic Abortion," *Postgraduate Medicine,* 9:16–25.

Packer, Herbert L. and Ralph J. Gampbell. May 1959. "Therapeutic Abortion: A Problem in Law and Medicine," *Stanford Law Review,* 11:417–55.

Pakter, Jean and Frieda Nelson. July 1971. "Abortion in New York City: The First Nine Months," *Family Planning Perspectives,* 3:5–12.

Pakter, Jean, David Harris, and Frieda Nelson. Feb. 1971. "Surveillance of the Abortion Program in New York City: Preliminary Report," *Modern Treatment,* 8:169–201.

Pare, C. M. B. and Hermione Raven. Mar. 28, 1970. "Follow-up of Patients Referred for Termination of Pregnancy," *Lancet,* 1:635–38.

Paris, Erna. Sept. 1971. "Nice Girls Don't Get Raped Do They?" *Chatelaine,* 44:31 *et passim.*

Parsons, Talcott and Kenneth B. Clark, editors. 1967. *The Negro American.* Boston: Beacon. (Originally published in *Daedalus,* Fall 1965 and Winter 1966.)

Patt, Stephen L., Richard G. Rappaport, and Peter Barglow. Apr. 1969. "Follow-up of Therapeutic Abortion," *Archives of General Psychiatry,* 20:408–14.

Paul, Julius. Aug. 1968. "The Return of Punitive Sterilization Proposals: Current Attacks on Illegitimacy and the AFDC Program," *Law and Society Review,* 3:77–106.

Peck, Arthur. Dec. 1968. "Therapeutic Abortion: Patients, Doctors, and Society," *American Journal of Psychiatry,* 125:797–804.

Peck, Arthur and Harold Marcus. Nov. 1966. "Psychiatric Sequelae of Therapeutic Interruption of Pregnancy," *Journal of Nervous and Mental Disease,* 143:417–25.

Peel, John and Malcolm Potts. 1970. *Textbook of Contraceptive Practice.* Cambridge: Cambridge University Press.

People v. Belous, 71 Cal. 2d 954, 458 P. 2d 194, 80 Cal. Rptr. 354 (1969).

Pfeiffer, Eric. Nov. 1970. "Psychiatric Indications or Psychiatric Justification of Therapeutic Abortion?" *Archives of General Psychiatry,* 23:402–7.

Phelan, Lana Clarke and Patricia Therese Maginnis. 1969. *The Abortion Handbook for Responsible Women.* Canoga Park, Calif.: Weiss, Day & Lord.

Phillips. Donald F. Aug. 16, 1970. "Abortion, the Hospital and the Law," *Hospitals,* 44:59–62.

Pike, Catherine Cline. Oct. 1969. "Therapeutic Abortion and Mental Health," *California Medicine,* 111:318–20.

Pilpel, Harriet F. 1967. "The Abortion Crisis," in Alan Guttmacher, editor, *The Case for Legalized Abortion Now,* pp. 97–113.

——. 1970. In Robert Hall, editor, *Abortion in a Changing World,* Vol. I.

Plagenz, Lorry. July 1969. "States Legislate Abortion Reform, But Hospitals Are Reluctant to Comply," *Modern Hospital,* 113:82–85.

Plant, Barbara. 1971. "A Survey of the U.S. Abortion Literature, 1890–1970." M.A. thesis, University of Windsor, Windsor, Ontario.

Podhoretz, Norman. May 1972. "Beyond ZPG," *Commentary,* 53:6, 8.

Pohlman, Edward. 1971. "Abortion Dogmas Needing Research Scrutiny," in R. Bruce Sloane, editor, *Abortion,* pp. 10–20.

Pohlman, Edward and Julia Mae Pohlman. 1969. *The Psychology of Birth Planning.* Cambridge, Mass.: Schenkman.

Polsky, Samuel. 1971. "Legal Aspects of Abortion," in R. Bruce Sloane, editor, *Abortion,* pp. 36–47.

Potter, Ralph B., Jr. 1969. "The Abortion Debate," in Donald Cutler, editor, *Updating Life and Death,* pp. 85–134.

Potter, Robert G., Jr. 1963. "Birth Intervals: Structure and Change," *Population Studies,* 17:155–66.

Presser, Harriet B. July 1971, Part 1. "The Timing of the First Birth, Female Roles and Black Fertility," *Milbank Memorial Fund Quarterly,* 49:329–61.

Rains, Prudence Mors. 1971. *Becoming an Unwed Mother: A Sociological Account.* Chicago: Aldine, Atherton.

Rainwater, Lee. 1960. *And the Poor Get Children: Sex, Contraception, and Family Planning in the Working Class.* Chicago: Quadrangle Books.

——. 1965. *Family Design: Marital Sexuality, Family Size, and Contraception.* Chicago: Aldine.

——. 1970. *Behind Ghetto Walls: Black Families in a Federal Slum.* Chicago: Aldine.

Ramsey, Paul. 1968. "The Morality of Abortion," in Daniel Labby, editor, *Life or Death,* pp. 60–93.

Rapoport, Lydia and Leah Potts. 1971. "Abortion of Unwanted Pregnancy as a Potential Life Crisis," in Florence Haselkorn, editor, *Family Planning,* pp. 249–66.

Reiterman, Carl, editor. 1971. *Abortion and the Unwanted Child.* New York: Springer.

Resnik, H. L. P. and Byron J. Wittlin. Jan. 1971. "Abortion and Suicidal Behaviors: Observations on the Concept of 'Endangering the Mental Health of the Mother,' " *Mental Hygiene,* 55:10–20.

Rice, Charles E. 1969. *The Vanishing Right to Live.* New York: Doubleday.

Robinson, Patricia, Patricia Haden, Sue Rudolph, Joyce Hoyt, Rita Van Lew, and Catherine Hoyt. Sept. 11, 1968. "The Sisters Reply," in *Poor Black Women.* Boston: New England Free Press.

Rochat, Roger W., Carl W. Tyler, and Albert K. Schoenbucher. Mar. 1971. "An Epidemiological Analysis of Abortion in Georgia," *American Journal of Public Health,* 61:543–52.

Rodman, Hyman. Dec. 1963. "The Lower-Class Value Stretch," *Social Forces,* 42:205–15.

Rodman, Hyman, F. R. Nichols, and Patricia Voydanoff. May 1969. "Lower-

Class Attitudes Toward 'Deviant' Family Patterns: A Cross-Cultural Study," *Journal of Marriage and the Family,* 31:315–21.

Roe v. Wade, 314 F. Supp. 1217 (N.D. Texas 1970).

Roemer, Ruth. Nov. 1967. "Abortion Laws: The Approaches of Different Nations," *American Journal of Public Health,* 57:1906–22.

——. Mar. 1971. "Abortion Law Reform and Repeal: Legislative and Judicial Developments," *American Journal of Public Health,* 61:500–9.

Rosen v. Louisiana State Board of Medical Examiners, 318 F. Supp. 1217 (E.D. La. 1970).

Rosen, Harold. 1958. In Mary Steichen Calderone, editor, *Abortion in the United States.*

——. 1967. "Psychiatric Implications of Abortion: A Case Study in Social Hypocrisy," in David Smith, editor, *Abortion and the Law,* pp. 72–106.

Rosen, Harold, editor. 1967a. *Abortion in America.* Boston: Beacon. (Originally published under the title *Therapeutic Abortion* by Julian Press, 1954.)

Rossi, Alice S. Sept./Oct. 1966. "Abortion Laws and Their Victims," *Transaction,* 3:7–12.

Rovinsky, Joseph J. Sept. 1971. "Abortion in New York City: Preliminary Experience with a Permissive Abortion Statute," *Obstetrics and Gynecology,* 38:333–42.

Royal College of Obstetricians and Gynaecologists. May 30, 1970. "The Abortion Act (1970): Findings of an Inquiry into the First Year's Working of the Act conducted by the Royal College of Obstetricians and Gynaecologists," *British Medical Journal,* 2:529–35.

Russell, Keith P. Aug. 1951. "Therapeutic Abortion in a General Hospital," *American Journal of Obstetrics and Gynecology,* 62:434–38.

——. Oct. 1952. "Therapeutic Abortion in California in 1950," *Western Journal of Surgery,* 60:497.

——. Jan. 10, 1953. "Changing Indications for Therapeutic Abortion," *Journal of the American Medical Association,* 151:108–11.

——. 1964. In Howard Hammond, "Therapeutic Abortion."

Russell, Keith P. and Edwin W. Jackson. Nov. 1, 1969. "Therapeutic Abortions in California: First Year's Experience Under New Legislation," *American Journal of Obstetrics and Gynecology,* 105:757–65.

Ryan, Kenneth J. 1967. "Humane Abortion Laws and the Health Needs of Society," in David Smith, editor, *Abortion and the Law,* pp. 60–71.

Ryan, William. 1971. *Blaming the Victim.* New York: Pantheon Books.

Ryder, Norman B. and Charles F. Westoff. 1971. *Reproduction in the United States 1965.* Princeton: Princeton University Press.

Safilios-Rothschild, Constantina. Aug. 1969. "Sociopsychological Factors Affecting Fertility in Urban Greece: A Preliminary Report," *Journal of Marriage and the Family,* 31:595–606.

St. John-Stevas, Norman. 1964. *The Right to Life.* New York: Holt, Rinehart and Winston.

Schaupp, Karl, Jr. 1964. In Howard Hammond, "Therapeutic Abortion."

Scheff, Thomas J. Summer 1968. "Negotiating Reality: Notes on Power in the Assessment of Responsibility," *Social Problems,* 16:3–17.

Schlesinger, Rudolf, editor. 1949. *Changing Attitudes in Soviet Russia:* Vol. I, *The Family in the U.S.S.R.* London: Routledge & Kegan Paul.

Schulder, Diane and Florynce Kennedy. 1971. *Abortion Rap*. New York: McGraw-Hill.

Schulz, David A. 1969. *Coming Up Black: Patterns of Ghetto Socialization*. Englewood Cliffs, N.J.: Prentice-Hall.

Schur, Edwin M. 1965. *Crimes Without Victims: Deviant Behavior and Public Policy*. Englewood Cliffs, N.J.: Prentice-Hall.

——. Mar. 1968. "Abortion," *The Annals,* 376:136–47.

Scrimshaw, Susan C. and Bernard Pasquariella. Oct. 1970. "Obstacles to Sterilization in One Community," *Family Planning Perspectives,* 2:40–42.

Segal, Sheldon J. 1970. "Experience with Other Antizygotic Agents," in Robert Hall, editor, *Abortion in a Changing World,* I, 67–73.

Senay, Edward C. Nov. 1970. "Therapeutic Abortion," *Archives of General Psychiatry,* 23:408–15.

Senior, Clarence. 1958. In Mary Steichen Calderone, editor, *Abortion in the United States.*

Serena, Barbara, Patricia Sullivan, Jack Stack, Roy Smith, and Johan Eliot. n.d. "Attitudes Toward Michigan's Abortion Law and Experience with Requests for Abortion of Michigan Physicians," the Michigan Council for the Study of Abortion in collaboration with the University of Michigan Center for Population Planning.

Shainess, Natalie. May 1970. "Abortion Is No Man's Business," *Psychology Today,* 3:18 *et passim.*

Shapiro, Fred C. Aug. 20, 1972. " 'Right to Life' has a Message for New York State Legislators," *New York Times Magazine,* pp. 10 *et passim.*

Shapiro, Sam, Edward R. Schlesinger, and Robert E. L. Nesbitt, Jr. 1968. *Infant, Perinatal, Maternal, and Childhood Mortality in the United States.* Cambridge: Harvard University Press.

Shaw, Russell. 1968. *Abortion on Trial.* Dayton, Ohio: Pflaum Press.

Shockley, William. Jan. 1972. "Dysgenics, Geneticity, Raceology: A Challenge to the Intellectual Responsibility of Educators," *Phi Delta Kappan,* pp. 297–307.

Sim, Myre. July 20, 1963. "Abortion and the Psychiatrist," *British Medical Journal,* 2:145–48.

——. 1969. *Guide to Psychiatry,* 2d ed. London: E. & S. Livingstone.

Simon, Nathan M. 1971. "Psychological and Emotional Indications for Therapeutic Abortion," in R. Bruce Sloane, editor, *Abortion,* pp. 73–91.

Simon, Nathan M. and Audrey G. Senturia. Oct. 1966. "Psychiatric Sequelae of Abortion: Review of the Literature, 1935–1964," *Archives of General Psychiatry,* 15:378–89.

Simon, Nathan M., Audrey G. Senturia, and David Rothman. July 1967. "Psychiatric Illness Following Therapeutic Abortion," *American Journal of Psychiatry,* 124:59–65.

Sloane, R. Bruce. May 29, 1969. "The Unwanted Pregnancy," *New England Journal of Medicine,* 280:1206–13.

Sloane, R. Bruce, editor. 1971. *Abortion: Changing Views and Practices.* New

York: Grune & Stratton. (Originally published in *Seminars in Psychiatry,* Aug. 1970.)

Smith, David T., editor. 1967. *Abortion and the Law*. Cleveland: Press of Case Western Reserve University.

Smith, Kenneth D. and Harris S. Wineberg. 1969–70. "A Survey of Therapeutic Abortion Committees," *Criminal Law Quarterly,* 12:279–306.

Smith, Roy G., Patricia G. Steinhoff, Milton Diamond, and Norma Brown. Mar. 1971. "Abortion in Hawaii: The First 124 Days," *American Journal of Public Health,* 61:530–42.

Speidel, J. Joseph and R. T. Ravenholt. Aug. 1971. "Present Status of Prostaglandins," *IPPF Medical Bulletin,* 5:3–4.

Spivak, Manuel M. Feb 1, 1967. "Therapeutic Abortion: A 12-Year Review at the Toronto General Hospital, 1954–1965," *American Journal of Obstetrics and Gynecology,* 97:316–23.

Staples, Robert. June 1972. "The Sexuality of Black Women," *Sexual Behavior,* 2:4–15.

Steinhoff, Patricia G., Roy G. Smith, and Milton Diamond. 1971. "The Characteristics and Motivations of Women Receiving Abortions," Presented at the American Sociological Association Meeting, Denver, Colorado, August 30–Sept. 2, 1971.

Stephenson, H. A. Nov. 1954. "Therapeutic Abortion," *Obstetrics and Gynecology,* 4:578–80.

Stewart, Gary K. and Phillip J. Goldstein. Apr. 1971. "Therapeutic Abortion in California: Effects on Septic Abortion and Maternal Mortality," *Obstetrics and Gynecology,* 37:510–14.

Stone, Abraham. 1958. In Mary Steichen Calderone, editor, *Abortion in the United States.*

Stone, Alan A. Feb. 1970. "The Psychiatric Dilemma," *Human Sexuality,* 4:29, 32.

Strausz, Ivan K. and Harold Schulman. Aug. 1971. "500 Outpatient Abortions Performed Under Local Anesthesia," *Obstetrics and Gynecology,* 38:199–205.

Szasz, Thomas S. Fall 1962. "Bootlegging Humanistic Values Through Psychiatry," *Antioch Review,* 22:341–49.

Taussig, Frederick J. 1936. *Abortion Spontaneous and Induced: Medical and Social Aspects*. St. Louis: Mosby.

Taussig, Helen B. Aug. 1962. "The Thalidomide Syndrome," *Scientific American,* 207:29–36.

Taylor, Howard C. and Lawrence C. Kolb. 1958. In Mary Steichen Calderone, editor, *Abortion in the United States.*

Texier, Geneviève. 1969. "A Sociologic Approach to Abortion," (in French), *Gynécologie pratique,* 20:363–73.

Tietze, Christopher. July 15, 1968. "Therapeutic Abortions in the United States," *American Journal of Obstetrics and Gynecology,* 101:784–87.

——. Sept. 1969. "Mortality with Contraception and Induced Abortion," *Studies in Family Planning,* 45:6–8.

——. Mar. 1970. "Abortion Laws and Abortion Practices in Europe," *Advances in Planned Parenthood,* 5:194–212.

Tietze, Christopher and Sarah Lewit. Oct. 1971. "Legal Abortions: Early Medical Complications, An Interim Report of the Joint Program for the Study of Abortion," *Family Planning Perspectives,* 3:6–14.

——. June 1972. "Joint Program for the Study of Abortion (JPSA): Early Medical Complications of Legal Abortion," *Studies in Family Planning,* 3:97–122.

Trainer, Joseph B. 1965. *Physiologic Foundations for Marriage Counseling.* St. Louis: Mosby.

Treadwell, Mary. Jan. 1972. "Is Abortion Black Genocide?" *Family Planning Perspectives,* 4:4–5.

Tredgold, R. F. Dec. 12, 1964. "Psychiatric Indications for Termination of Pregnancy," *Lancet,* 2:1251–54.

Treffers, P. E. May 1968. "Family Size, Contraception, and Birth Rate Before and After the Introduction of a New Method of Family Planning," *Journal of Marriage and the Family,* 30:338–45.

United States v. Vuitch, 305 F. Supp. 1032 (D.D.C. 1969) and 91 S. Ct. 1294 (1971).

Valentine, Charles A. 1972. "Black Studies and Anthropology: Scholarly and Political Interests in Afro-American Culture," Addison-Wesley Modular Publications, Module 15.

Van Nagell, J. R., Jr. and J. W. Roddick, Jr. Nov. 1, 1971. "Vaginal Hysterectomy as a Sterilization Procedure," *American Journal of Obstetrics and Gynecology,* 111:703–7.

Vincent, Clark E., C. Allen Haney, and Carl M. Cochrane. Aug. 1970. "Abortion Attitudes of Poverty-Level Blacks," *Seminars in Psychiatry,* 2:309–17.

Walker, W. B. and J. F. Hulka. Apr. 1971. "Attitudes and Practices of North Carolina Obstetricians—The Impact of the North Carolina Abortion Act of 1967," *Southern Medical Journal,* 64:441–45.

Walter, George S. Sept. 1970. "Psychologic and Emotional Consequences of Elective Abortion," *Obstetrics and Gynecology,* 36:482–91.

Wertheimer, Roger. Fall 1971. "Understanding the Abortion Argument," *Philosophy and Public Affairs,* 1:67–95.

Westoff, Leslie Aldridge and Charles F. Westoff. 1971. *From Now to Zero.* Boston: Little, Brown.

Westoff, Charles F., Emily C. Moore, and Norman B. Ryder. Jan. 1969, Part 1. "The Structure of Attitudes Toward Abortion," *Milbank Memorial Fund Quarterly,* 47:11–37.

Whelpton, Pascal K., Arthur A. Campbell, and John E. Patterson. 1966. *Fertility and Family Planning in the United States.* Princeton: Princeton University Press.

White, Robert B. Winter 1966. "Induced Abortions: A Survey of Their Psychiatric Implications, Complications, and Indications," *Texas Reports of Biology and Medicine,* 24:531–58.

Whittemore, Kenneth R. 1970. In Robert Hall, editor, *Abortion in a Changing World,* Vol. II.

Whittington, H. G. Mar. 1970. "Evaluation of Therapeutic Abortion as an Element of Preventive Psychiatry," *American Journal of Psychiatry,* 126:1224–29.

Willhelm, Sidney. 1971. *Who Needs the Negro?* Garden City, N.Y.: Anchor.

Williams, Elizabeth M. Apr./May 1972. "Things Your Husband Never Told You About Sex," *New Woman,* 1:18 *et passim.*

Williams, Glanville. 1957. *The Sanctity of Life and the Criminal Law.* New York: Knopf.

Wilson, David C. 1967. "The Abortion Problem in the General Hospital," in Harold Rosen, editor, *Abortion in America,* pp. 189–97.

Yette, Samuel F. 1971. *The Choice: The Issue of Black Survival in America.* New York: Putnam.

Yow, Martha. 1970. "A Pediatrician's View," in Robert Hall, editor, *Abortion in a Changing World,* I, 106–10.

Zelnik, Melvin and John F. Kantner. Dec. 1970. "United States: Exploratory Studies of Negro Family Formation—Factors Relating to Illegitimacy," *Studies in Family Planning,* 60:5–9.

INDEX